DEFEATING
BIG
GOVERNMENT
SOCIALISM

ALSO BY NEWT GINGRICH FROM CENTER STREET

BEYOND BIDEN
Rebuilding the America We Love

TRUMP AND THE AMERICAN FUTURE
Solving the Great Problems of Our Time

AMERICA'S GREATEST CHALLENGE
Confronting the Chinese Communist Party

TRUMP'S AMERICA
The Truth about Our Nation's Great Comeback

UNDERSTANDING TRUMP

DUPLICITY: A Novel
(Book 1 of the Major Brooke Grant series)

TREASON*: A Novel*
(Book 2 of the Major Brooke Grant series)

VENGEANCE*: A Novel*
(Book 3 of the Major Brooke Grant series)

REDISCOVERING GOD IN AMERICA
Reflections on the Role of Faith in Our Nation's History and Future

DEFEATING
BIG
GOVERNMENT
SOCIALISM

Saving America's Future

NEWT
GINGRICH

CENTER
STREET®

NASHVILLE   NEW YORK

Center Street
Hachette Book Group
1290 Avenue of the Americas, New York, NY 10104
centerstreet.com
twitter.com/centerstreet

First Edition: July 2022

Center Street is a division of Hachette Book Group, Inc. The Center Street name and logo are trademarks of Hachette Book Group, Inc.

The publisher is not responsible for websites (or their content) that are not owned by the publisher.

The Hachette Speakers Bureau provides a wide range of authors for speaking events. To find out more, go to www.HachetteSpeakersBureau.com or call (866) 376-6591.

Print book interior design by Timothy Shaner, NightAndDayDesign.biz

Library of Congress Cataloging-in-Publication Data has been applied for.

ISBNs: 978-1-5460-0319-9 (hardcover), 978-1-5460-0332-8 (large print), 978-1-5460-0322-9 (ebook)

Printed in the United States of America

LSC-H

Printing 1, 2022

This book is dedicated to the courageous people of Ukraine. In risking their lives for freedom, they join the three hundred Spartans at Thermopylae, the farmers at Concord and Trenton, and all those who understand that freedom requires bravery. Their example has changed history, as courage often does.

CONTENTS

INTRODUCTION 1

1   BIG GOVERNMENT SOCIALISM
    ISN'T WORKING—AND IT CAN'T 15

2   DANGER AND OPPORTUNITY 37

3   WHAT WORKS: HISTORY,
    STABILITY, AND STRENGTH 63

4   THE ROT AT THE TOP 81

5   HUMAN NATURE, GOVERNMENT,
    AND THE RULE OF LAW 107

6   POVERTY AND DESPAIR 125

7   OPPORTUNITY AND HOPE 145

8   CRISIS AND CHAOS 163

9   PRAGMATISM AND PROSPERITY 183

10 INHERENT HUBRIS 203

11 CIVILITY AND GRACE 221

    CONCLUSION: THE PATRIOTISM
    OF PERSISTENCE 241

    ACKNOWLEDGMENTS 251

    NOTES 255

DEFEATING
BIG
GOVERNMENT
SOCIALISM

INTRODUCTION

This book is about the rise of Big Government Socialism in America and is a guide to winning the arguments around elections—upcoming and beyond. It comes from Prime Minister Margaret Thatcher's rule that "first you win the argument, then you win the vote."

The 2022 and 2024 elections are among the most vital in American history. Down one road is continued decay and decline under Big Government Socialism and obsolete, unionized, gigantic bureaucracies. Down the other road is a revitalization of the American system of patriotism, hard work, free enterprise, and continuous problem solving.

I wrote this book because I believe that the United States is in deep trouble. If we are complacent, we will cease to be a free nation. We face both domestic and foreign threats to our survival.

This book is designed to enable you, the citizens, to win the argument with your friends, neighbors, relatives, and coworkers. The goal is to help encourage Americans to save their own country by understanding what is threatening us and what we must do to survive as a free, prosperous, and safe nation.

The threats at home and abroad are real.

The core tenets of Big Government Socialism—wealth redistribution, woke thought-policing, and dictatorial government control—have become the core tenets of the American Democratic Party. The few moderates who are left are either being coerced to fall in line or pushed out of office by the radical wing, which has taken over. As I detail in this book, the rise of the Big Government Socialists is only going to create more problems, divisions, and conflicts in America.

The rise of Communist China is an existential threat. Many of our elites refuse to even recognize the threat from Beijing. (For many, it is because they make so much money from China and put profit above patriotism.) Our bureaucracies refuse to modernize at a rate necessary to compete with China. Our news media is too filled with trivia, gossip, and childish stories to truly educate the country and host a debate about how to succeed in the competition with the Chinese Communist dictatorship.

On a more immediate and conventional note, Vladimir Putin's ability to focus Russian resources on military power has been increased dramatically by the Biden administration's effort to cut American oil and gas production. This is increasing the value and profit of Russian production—and the leverage they get through Western European dependence on Russian natural gas. As we saw with Russia's invasion of Ukraine in February 2022, the Biden administration strategy for coping with Russian adventurism is insufficient. At the time of this writing in early March, the Ukrainians are heroically defending themselves against Putin's aggression.

Between the Iranian dictatorship's focus on acquiring nuclear weapons, the North Korean focus on matching nuclear weapons with delivery systems capable of reaching the United States, and the steadily growing worldwide threat of Islamist radical terrorism, the dangers of a cataclysmic, America-crippling event compound. As the foreign clouds continue to darken and grow, the threats to freedom here at home are also expanding.

As a member of Congress and Speaker of the House, I swore to defend the United States against all enemies foreign and domestic. Today there are enemies of freedom abroad seeking our defeat. Tragically, there are also those who would destroy freedom here at home (some deliberately and some out of ignorance).

The decay of freedom here at home was impressed upon me during a visit to Capitol Hill in the fall of 2021.

I was there to speak to the Republican Study Committee at its weekly lunch. The Study Committee is the largest organization of conservative Republicans in the House. They had more than sixty members at lunch, including the number two House Republican, Steve Scalise, who chaired the Study Committee before winning election as Whip.

After I spoke and took questions, Scalise and Representative Jim Banks (the leader of the Study Committee and a rising star in House Republican activities) both asked me to join them and walk on the House floor. I was both flattered and intrigued. I had not been on the House floor since I left the Congress in 1999. My wife, Callista, and I were in the visitors' gallery when Pope Francis spoke in 2015, but I felt as a former Speaker that I should not get too close to the daily business of the House. That was the job of the currently elected members and the leadership.

Scalise and Banks explained that they thought it would shake up the Democrats to see me back on the floor working on the Republican victory in 2022. It sounded like fun, and I agreed to join them in venturing into the heart of Nancy Pelosi Land. The journey from the room in the visitors' center to the floor was a lot more revealing and sobering than I would have expected.

The difference in atmosphere between the Senate's wing of the Capitol and the House's wing was stunning. It was the opposite of what I would have expected from my twenty-year experience as a House member. Traditionally, the one-hundred-member Senate is the more austere and dignified body. After all, its members serve six-year terms, and only one-third of them seek reelection each election cycle. The House is much larger, and each one of its 435 members must run for reelection every two years. It is traditionally more casual, more open, and generally friendlier.

I often tell audiences that the best way to imagine the two cultures is that the Senate is a country club, and the House is a truck stop (and I mean that with the utmost affection). However, under the Pelosi dictatorship, the House has become a hostile center of paranoia and negativity. The Senate survived COVID-19 and the riot of January 6, 2021, with a resilience that helped it remain the institution it had become over the previous generations. Senators in both parties still talk with each other despite partisan differences. On secondary and smaller issues, Democrats and Republicans work together and often produce bipartisan solutions that pass by unanimous consent or with sizable bipartisan majorities.

As I walked through the corridors of the three Senate office buildings, members and staff from the Democratic side greeted me, and there was a feeling that we were all in this business of self-government together—even if we disagreed philosophically and in partisan identity. The militant hostility of the left-wing House Democrats has not permeated the Senate, even though members such as Senators Bernie Sanders and Elizabeth Warren were clearly advocates for a more radical—indeed socialist—America.

I felt that I could walk freely through Senate office buildings and even in the Senate side of the Capitol. However, as I crossed the great Rotunda at the center of the Capitol Building, I immediately knew I was entering a vastly different environment. On the House side, there was a profound feeling of paranoia, control, harsh partisanship, and rigidity.

I had first experienced this new more closed, more policed House a few months earlier when I went to the Cannon House Office Building for a meeting with the staff of the Conservative Opportunity Society (COS). This was an activist group of conservative members that I had helped organize thirty-nine years ago. COS had been the weekly action planning meeting for a dozen or more House Republicans starting in 1983. Its goal was to create a more activist, militant House Republican Party that was willing to fight to be in the majority. (At that time, we had been in the minority for twenty-nine years.) It was this activist cadre of energetic members who created the issue base and floor debating capability that would grow eleven years later into the first House Republican majority in forty years.

I was shocked when I arrived at the Cannon Building and was forced to produce my driver's license to prove who I was. (I don't mean this out of conceit or self-importance. As a former Speaker, I have never had to ask permission or clearance to enter congressional buildings since I left Congress.) The congressional staffer who had volunteered to come get me had to sign me in, indicate what meeting I was going to and where, and get a visitor's badge, which I had to return upon leaving. I learned that all meetings held with whistleblowers now had to occur off the Hill, because no whistleblower wanted Pelosi's police and staff to know with whom and where they were meeting.

When I eventually met with the COS staff, my sense that things had dramatically changed was confirmed. Several veteran Republican staff members told me they had never seen the level of vicious partisanship that currently exists in the House. Even younger staff members said they were regularly treated as "enemies of the state" by Democratic members and staff. This was my first personal experience of the dictatorial, paranoid, ruthless control system Pelosi has imposed.

When I arrived at the floor of the House with Representatives Banks and Scalise weeks later, I had a similar, but even more controlled, experience. Even though we had already been screened to get into the Capitol Building, there was an additional layer of security that controlled the House floor. The entrances to the floor had metal detectors exactly like the ones used by the Transportation Security Administration at airports.

A certain amount of security would have been understandable after the January 6, 2021, attacks, but this was beyond reason. Pelosi and the Democrats were acting as though Republican members themselves were a threat. Duly elected members of Congress, who had been selected by their fellow citizens to lead the country, had to obey the petty rules or pay fines—or even be physically blocked from entering the House Chamber. It was clear the staff was dominant, and the members were subordinate.

All these control elements distanced the members from the citizens they were supposed to represent. In the nineteenth century, folks would drop in and hang out in the galleries, drinking and watching the entertainment of House debate. On occasion, libations would be sent to the floor to enable long-talking members to refresh themselves. The atmosphere was collegial, and members were simply elected citizens who did not see themselves as separate from the voters who sent them there.

When I arrived in 1979, the House was still an amazingly open place, as were the Capitol grounds. The idea of building fences, calling out the National Guard, having a huge police force, imposing mask mandates on members, and restricting or eliminating public access would have struck us as a violation of the nature of the American system of freedom and representative self-government. For the twenty years I served in the House, interns could take large groups of visitors from back home through the Capitol with a sense of freedom, because it was the People's House. We treasured it, and we defended its openness and its sense of equality between members and citizens. We felt we were representatives, and we owed familiarity to those we represented. This was true for Republicans and Democrats alike. We all understood that while we disagreed on matters of policy, we were all still there to do the People's work—with their consent. The House floor I was visiting under Pelosi was a starkly different place. It is clear she runs a dictatorship based on fear and ruthlessness that we have not seen in any other Speakership in American history. She has turned the People's House into Pelosi's House.

The Speaker of the House is the second most powerful elected official in Washington after the president of the United States. Technically, a Speaker who has a one-vote majority (218–217) could do virtually anything as long as he or she can keep that one vote. Senate majority leaders have much less direct, raw power—and must work with their ninety-nine colleagues. Under Senate rules, any single member can wreak havoc on the system and cause virtually everything to grind to a halt (the careers of Senators Jesse Helms and Bob Byrd were built in part on this ability to bring everything to a halt until they got what they wanted). Few senators exercise these rights to the fullest because their colleagues could then retaliate by doing the same thing to them and blocking everything they tried to get done. Nonetheless, the power of individual senators within the rules of the Senate are vastly greater than the power of individual members of the House.

What has limited Speakers in the past from using their potential power to the fullest has been a series of constitutional and House rules—and precedents that protect both the individual member and the two political parties. I had grown up surrounded by this sense of the rights of free people and the important, almost romantic, responsibilities and roles of their elected leaders.

I was born in Harrisburg, Pennsylvania, to an extremely patriotic family (many of my relatives had fought in World War II). I was surrounded by the history of a free people. To the east was Philadelphia, with the Liberty Bell and Independence Hall. When my relatives would take me there to see where George Washington, Benjamin Franklin, Thomas Jefferson, and other patriots first declared our independence and then developed the U.S. Constitution to preserve our freedoms, I became enthralled with the sense of historic achievement—and the notion that we stood on their shoulders. Their courage, endurance, sacrifice, and brilliance had enabled us to be free—to be Americans.

To the south was Gettysburg. It is the battlefield of the largest clash of the Civil War. Gettysburg was three days of bloodletting that ended General Robert E. Lee's deepest penetration of the

North and saved the Union. It was also the site of President Abraham Lincoln's address that helped dedicate the first national military cemetery. His brief speech, possibly the best short statement of freedom ever delivered, was something we had to memorize in school. For me, it became a living statement of our faith in God's gift of freedom to all people—and especially to Americans. Gettysburg had additional meaning because my father went to Gettysburg College before rejoining the Army (he had served in World War II and reenlisted to fight in Korea).

As an Army brat, I grew up surrounded by men and women who dedicated their lives to defending America against all enemies foreign and domestic. Domestic enemies mattered as much as foreign enemies. In my childhood, there really were Soviet agents operating in the United States (as many as five hundred, according to some studies).

At the heart of our unique freedom were the rule of law and the Constitution. The Constitution converted the great promise of the Declaration of Independence, that we are "endowed by our Creator with certain unalienable rights among which were life, liberty and the pursuit of happiness," into a practical mechanism for securing those rights. It was clear that the Founding Fathers in Philadelphia in 1787 wanted a government strong enough to protect us from foreign powers—and a Constitution that protected us from our own government.

As I studied history, earned a PhD, and went on to teach and write it, I was increasingly impressed with the role of a free, elected legislature in the protection and implementation of freedom. The magic of the Magna Carta (Great Charter) in 1215, which brought the king under the law and began to establish the principle of no taxation without the consent of the taxed (admittedly in the early days applying only to the nobles), was the base from which our rights increasingly grew and were codified.

The truth is, I deeply admired those who were called the Whig historians. These nineteenth-century British scholars and writers saw the previous six hundred years as progress toward orderly freedom and liberty for everyone. Lord Acton's dictum that "power tends to corrupt, absolute power corrupts absolutely" struck me as a key to understanding the dangers of unlimited power. The extraordinary lifelong effort of William Wilberforce to abolish the slave trade and use the power of the Royal Navy to destroy slave trading was a great example of the power of religious impulse turned into civic achievement. William Pitt's Britain standing alone against Napoleon's dictatorship was an amazing foreshadowing of Winston Churchill's Britain standing alone against Adolf Hitler's evil regime.

The lessons of history drove home to me why the last line of the first stanza of our national anthem is "the land of the free, and the home of the brave." Those earlier generations understood that if you were not brave, you could not remain free. Indeed, the wars they fought proved their willingness to do what it took to create and preserve genuine freedom. For me, history was filled with the lessons of proud, free people risking everything for their rights and the future of their children, grandchildren, and country.

When I came to Congress after losing twice (in 1974 during Watergate and in 1976 with Jimmy Carter of Georgia at the head of the Democratic ticket), I felt that I was part of the long line of people who had defended freedom and expanded the concept of liberty. This concept of the United States House as a center of freedom was really driven home for me by a visit late in the Soviet era. Under Mikhail Gorbachev's opening of the Soviet Union (known as *perestroika* and *glasnost*), a group of Soviet reporters and editors were allowed to visit Washington. As the Republican Whip (the second-ranking leader when in opposition), I was asked to host the Soviet journalists.

We met in my office just off the House floor, and since we were not in session, I decided to take them on the floor of the House (which in this pre-Pelosi era was open to anyone as long as a member accompanied them). As we talked about how the House worked and its history, it occurred to me that since we were out of session, I could give a couple of the Soviet reporters and editors a unique opportunity. I picked one to stand where the president stands when he gives the State of the Union address and one to sit where the Speaker sits. I explained that the Speaker and the president of the Senate (the vice president of the executive branch) sat above the president, because he was there as their guest, and in their building, they were in charge. I explained the division of powers as a central design of the Founding Fathers to spread power out to avoid dictatorship. This seemed like an especially useful lesson for people just coming out from under the Soviet dictatorship, which of course had centralized all power in the Kremlin.

When we started to leave the chamber, the man who had been sitting in the Speaker's chair came down, and he was trembling. I asked him if he was okay. He surprised and humbled me with his answer. He explained he was from Latvia, saying, "We Latvians were conquered by the Soviets in 1940, but we never identified with the Russians or the Soviet dictatorship. We were taught over and over that America was the enemy, but we had relatives living in America, and we never believed these lies. Now you have allowed me to sit in the center of freedom on the planet. It is an honor I will treasure all my life."

I have never forgotten the intensity of his emotions and the principle that made him so emotional. Presidents are essentially elected kings. Out of necessity for national security and practical administration of bureaucracies, the White House centralizes power. So, it is the legislative branch that is the defender of freedom. Each of its members wields a little power, but none can be all-powerful. The Congress represents the bulwark of freedom.

This division of roles between the central leader and the elective system reflects hundreds of years of development in Great Britain. There are lessons from the English Civil War and the subsequent dictatorship of Oliver Cromwell that deeply impressed our Founding Fathers more than a century later. Our Founders were determined to protect us from our own government by distributing power.

It was against this background that I was deeply sobered by venturing into the Pelosi system of centralized control, police ordering elected members around, and members being treated as potential terrorists. Forcing members of Congress to feel subordinated to a central authority in this way is a complete break with the American tradition of freedom and ordered liberty under the Constitution and the rule of law.

Speaker Pelosi's arrogance was captured back in 2010 during the fight over Obamacare when she told a gathering of state and local officials, "We have to pass the bill so you can find out what's in it." This style of insisting on a "yes" vote from members who are ignorant of what they are voting on has become the hallmark of the Pelosi system. Bills with thousands of pages of detail—and trillions of dollars in spending—are brought forth without hearings or time for anyone to really understand what is in them. The result is profoundly bad legislation that contains many "poison pill" items that the public deeply oppose. The Democrat members loyally vote "yes" because they are told to—not because they know what they are supporting.

Under the Pelosi Speakership, the House schedule for meetings is kept purposefully limited, so members do not have the time to get together and organize resistance. As I sat on the floor of this new Speaker-defined House, it struck me that our freedoms were being eroded, and the institution the Founding Fathers had designed to be the closest to the people was now isolated by a willful leader who had contempt for the people and their representatives. She wants her will to be done, not the will of the American people.

This visit to the House floor made clear to me how vital it was to renew the American system of self-government. We need strong citizens and limited bureaucracies. Achieving this means defeating the Pelosi dictatorship and the Big Government Socialism it is attempting to impose on all Americans. At the same time, I hope this book will launch a generation of modernization, renewal, and revitalization that will enable us to extend freedom to every American while outstripping all foreign threats.

Our nation must be a free, safe, prosperous, self-governing America that operates under the rule of law and the Constitution. I hope you will find this book helpful in winning this argument and building a better future for all Americans.

CHAPTER ONE

BIG GOVERNMENT
SOCIALISM ISN'T
WORKING—AND IT CAN'T

W e must win a set of arguments to defeat Big Government
Socialism.

By Big Government Socialism, I mean the fanatical belief on
the American left that claims a better, fairer future can be created
if a gigantically powerful government controls or owns production and is guided by massive bureaucracies of professionals who
focus on process rather than achievement. This is not the idyllic,
pseudo-utopian, (and fictional) Scandinavian-style socialism to
which American progressives like to allude. It is a big, formida-
ble, technologically enhanced version of socialism—which has
roots in the system that was developed by Friedrich Engels and
Karl Marx and brutally imposed on people by Vladimir Lenin,
Joseph Stalin, Mao Zedong, and other ruthless tyrants.

First, we must win the argument that Big Government
Socialism is not working. This should be the easy one. For the last
year and a half, we have had vivid proof of this. Big bureaucratic

15

government has proven it can't control the border, reduce crime, withdraw effectively from Afghanistan, modernize fast enough to compete with China, get schools to educate effectively, cope with the challenges of a pandemic, or perform a litany of other duties vital to our survival. Again and again, we are witnesses to systems not working.

The degree to which Big Government Socialism's bureaucratic structures get out of touch with reality was vividly illustrated in early 2022, when Vice President Kamala Harris tweeted: "Because of the Bipartisan Infrastructure Law, America is moving again. That's what infrastructure is all about: getting people moving."[1] Unfortunately for her, that tweet went out as hundreds of people were stranded for up to twenty-four hours on Interstate 95 south of Washington, D.C., in dangerous icy conditions.[2] It just reinforced the sense that big government doesn't know what is going on.

The entire experience of public health systems breaking down during the COVID-19 pandemic is a clear example of how much Big Government Socialism simply can't deliver the speed and quality that people expect. Any serious analysis of the last two and a half years since the emergence of the novel coronavirus in Wuhan, China, would illustrate the confusion, lack of information, changing analyses, conflicting advice, and unrealistic rules. Hundreds of thousands of Americans could still be alive today if the public health system were not an obsolete collection of widely differing local organizations and an increasingly bureaucratic, incompetent, and self-protecting federal bureaucracy at the Centers for Disease Control and Prevention, the Food and Drug Administration, the Department of Health and Human Services, and the National Institutes of Health.

Compare the difference in death rates from COVID-19 in well-organized countries such as Singapore, Japan, and South Korea with the American tragedy. According to data compiled by Statista,[3] as of February 10, 2022, Singapore has seen a COVID-19 death rate of 154.36 people per million. Japan's rate was 156.62 per million, and South Korea's is 134.66. By contrast, U.S. deaths per million people were reported at a tragically astonishing 2,765.79. The gap in death rates was more than just an East Asian phenomenon. Canada (934.15), Denmark (673.88), Finland (385.12), and Australia (174.34) all had better outcomes and saved more lives than the United States. India, which has a larger, more dense population than the United States, saw a per-million death rate of 370.69. America's underperformance of public health was profound. Ineffective, Washington-based Big Government Socialist COVID-19 policies affected every state in the country.

Our government school system has fallen further behind Chinese and Indian schools in preparing young people to succeed in a competitive world. In some cities, the collapse of government-run schools is startling. In Baltimore, for example, in 2017 there were six schools in which not a single student had been able to pass the state exams.[4] In thirteen other Baltimore schools the same year, no students were proficient in math.[5] In 2019, only 10.7 percent of sixth to eighth graders in Baltimore were proficient in math, and only 9.2 percent of high schoolers were proficient in Algebra I. Yet the answer to this stunning failure (which hits minorities and the poor especially hard) has been for teachers' unions to demand more power. They are placing students last while protecting incompetent, nonperforming teachers—and the entire system of failure. The process of "dumbing down" American education has been astonishingly fast and deeply destructive for students and national security. Faced with obvious failure, the teachers' unions and their allies have moved to eliminate grades, minimize mathematics, eliminate advanced classes, and seek to hide failures in a sea of mediocrity.

Faced with overwhelming evidence that virtual teaching has been a failure—and especially a failure for minority and poor students—the teachers' unions have been militant about not returning to school—and in many cities they have led strikes. In effect, the public has been required to pay billions for employees who refuse to come to work but insist on being paid. The problem has become so bad that some Democratic mayors, even though the teachers' unions were their biggest supporters, have begun to warn that teachers who fail to show up will simply not be paid.

Parallel to the teachers' unions' refusal to be accountable has been a system of measuring attendance that ignores absentee students to maximize payments. In some big-city schools (including Baltimore) many students simply do not show up. Nevertheless, these so-called "ghost students" are listed as attending, so the school can get more money from the taxpayers.[6] The system is so blatant that some systems have "pizza day" for the two or three days a year when attendance is strictly counted for payment information. The result is an amazing surge of missing students who show up to eat, but not to learn.

As I previously mentioned, the national security system has become so bureaucratic and riddled with incompetence that it couldn't win after twenty years in Afghanistan and eighteen years in Iraq. It has demonstrated that it can't plan a withdrawal from Afghanistan effectively, and it can't modernize fast enough to keep up with the Chinese Communists in innovation or strategic agility. America runs a real risk of losing a major war with

China because the Big Government Socialism at the heart of our national security system is simply incompetent, self-serving, and run on cronyism and dishonesty.

If the military is this riddled with senior-level corruption and dishonesty, imagine what the civilian bureaucracies and their political and business allies are like. And if the news media must operate in this swamp of dishonesty, guess how corroded and accepting of dishonesty it becomes. Furthermore, the propaganda media, the senior bureaucracies, and the highest levels of big corporations, big foundations, and big trade associations are all dominated by a "woke culture" that follows Humpty Dumpty's rule in *Through the Looking-Glass and What Alice Found There*:

> "When I use a word," Humpty Dumpty said, in rather a scornful tone, "it means just what I choose it to mean— neither more nor less."
>
> "The question is," said Alice, "whether you can make words mean so many different things."
>
> "The question is," said Humpty Dumpty, "which is to be master—that's all."

Woke culture depends on the elites' ability to redefine words, invent new ones, and insist on everyone adopting the new lexicon. In a real sense, the heart of woke culture is Humpty Dumptyism.

Consider the following:

- Despite centuries of regionally naming epidemics, there could be no Chinese virus—or even a Wuhan virus— because it would offend the Chinese Communist Party.

- To argue that there are only two pronouns, or two sexes, is to be assaulted as a homophobic, transphobic, binary genderist, etc.
- To suggest that the content of your character is more important than the color of your skin is merely defending white privilege (even when the phrase comes from Rev. Martin Luther King Jr.).
- To suggest that males have an unfair advantage in competing with females in most sports (just the use of the terms *male* and *female* is, of course, anti–Humpty Dumpty) is to be transphobic.
- Defending requirements that voters show identification is racist.
- Arguing for grades based on merit is racist.

The list goes on and on. Wokeism is a quasi-religious movement that brings passion and intolerance together to reshape the world. In its determination to impose its new words—and, indeed, a new world—upon those around it, the woke movement is in the tradition of the French Revolution, the Russian Revolution, and Chinese Cultural Revolution. In each case, the ideas and language of the past had to be rejected and replaced by a new model with new words and no tolerance for dissent.

The leaders of the French Revolution decided they had to get rid of the Gregorian calendar, because it had too many Christian associations. They invented a new calendar with new months, weeks, and days. In the new utopian calendar, Messidor (harvest) became the month from June 19 to July 18. There were thirty days in each month, with three weeks of ten days each. Since they could no longer use the names of the seven-day week, they invented new day names to go with their new month names. The first day of the ten-day week was primitive. To match the actual 365-day cycle, they added five days at the end of the year for festivals and vacations. The new revolutionary calendar was adopted in 1792 and lasted seventeen years, until Napoleon abolished it as of January 1, 1806, and reverted to the Gregorian calendar. Wokesters might take note of how rapidly the nuttiest parts of the French Revolution were repudiated once the initial wave of fanaticism faded away.

However, at the present time there is an alliance between the Big Government Socialists and the woke fanatics that has support for gigantic bureaucracies. In return the bureaucracies support new words and principles—and the imposition of woke values and language on Americans who refuse to voluntarily accept them. The problem with this alliance of the Big Government Socialists and the wokesters is that they seek to impose policies on the people (which the people do not want and often resist).

In a country in which elections still count, it is virtually impossible for Big Government Socialists to be candid about what they are doing. President Joe Biden cannot openly admit that thousands of people are crossing our border illegally every day without law enforcement or medical scrutiny. Furthermore, he cannot admit that his administration is secretly shipping these noncitizens all over the country and not telling anyone. That kind of honest admission would destroy his presidency (if indeed it is not already destroyed).

Similarly, the Biden administration can't acknowledge that the prices of beef and pork are going up—or that its policies raised the cost of petroleum products that go into fertilizer (making farming and raising livestock extra expensive). It can't verbally accept that it has increased inflation, which raises prices on everything. It can't admit that it has adopted policies that encourage people to stay home rather than work (which also raises the cost of labor to farms, meatpackers, distributors, and others). The natural economic consequence of these policies is, of course, that essential food prices rise. Publicly acknowledging this would focus the public anger directly on Democrats, which Biden will never do.

Instead of accepting the truth that ideologically driven government policies are needlessly raising the cost of food, gasoline, heating oil, and medical care—and crippling logistics supply chains in the process—it is essential for Big Government Socialists to find scapegoats upon which to heap blame. The Biden administration's attempt to blame the four major meat processors and distributors for the rise in the cost of meat would be laughable if it were not so dangerous.[7] Biden's anti-market, pro-government control approach will lead his administration to adopt policies of so-called increased competition by doling out $1 billion in taxpayer money to encourage smaller, less efficient, and less effective meat production systems. Just as the Solyndra solar panel manufacturer collapse cost taxpayers $500 million in loan guarantees, this approach will temporarily prop up several small companies—many of whom will then go broke. Big Government Socialists refuse to believe they are bad investors, and the market is smarter than bureaucrats. They consistently take your tax money to subsidize their pet projects, and the net result is often a disaster.

BIG GOVERNMENT SOCIALISM NEVER WORKS

The amazing thing about the American intellectual community's passionate commitment to Big Government Socialism is that it never works. No matter how bad socialism's track record is, intellectuals love the concept because it shifts power from successful entrepreneurs, wealthy business leaders, and ordinary Americans to the elite intelligentsia. In a Big Government Socialist system, it is the intellectuals who have real power. They get to dictate to everyone else how to behave and what to do.

In some ways, Big Government Socialism is like the rise of the pigs in George Orwell's classic anti-Marxist novel *Animal Farm*. In the beginning, the Animal Farm was a revolution for fairness for all animals. Equality was the great value of the early animal revolution in Orwell's amazing fable. Then, gradually, the pigs—because they were smarter—took power and shifted the system until it was a new dictatorship with pigs rather than humans in charge. All the other animals were subservient. As the essential quote goes, "All animals are equal, but some animals are more equal than others." By the end, the pigs were occasionally picking out lesser animals to be sold to the butcher to finance their lifestyles. Everything had come full circle.

Historically, intellectuals are the pigs of *Animal Farm*. They know they are really smart. They read books, and they get degrees from famous institutions that promise them status and authority. They operate as petty dictators in their classes, where the students have a huge incentive to smile and flatter professors who have the power to pass or fail them. Imagine the disgust that world-class intellectuals face at family dinner with relatives who have less education, often fail to read books, but somehow are wealthier and more powerful than they are. The professoriate has a deep class interest in developing a mechanism that transfers power from their supposed lessers to themselves. Given their IQs (self-ascribed) and their learning (self-touted), it is only natural that they should dominate those who have money and power but no knowledge or culture.

From the French Enlightenment assault on the aristocracy and the church, to the Russian intelligentsia rallying around Vladimir Lenin and communism, to Chinese librarian Mao Zedong leading a bloody Cultural Revolution, history is filled with arguments for government control over the lesser, uneducated parts of the population. The language of Big Government Socialism always condemns an inadequate present and promises a remarkably better, almost utopian, future. Thus the popular analysis and promises of Big Government Socialism with its alluring transfer of power to politicians and bureaucrats has been attractive for people pursuing power throughout the third world.

Paul Johnson, in *Modern Times: The World from the Twenties to the Nineties*, emphasizes the unusual role of the London School of Economics in destroying progress in Africa. The number of African leaders who applied socialist models to their countries was astonishing. Yet socialism never worked. In country after country, with great potential in mining, agriculture, and in some cases in oil and gas, the potential for growth and prosperity was simply dissipated. A combination of bad socialist policies discouraged investment and growth—and sheer corruption frightened away investors who relied on honesty to safeguard their investments.

Corruption, specifically, is the enemy of economic growth. People refuse to invest in a country where the politicians may take their property through taxation or confiscation. The result is a steady outflow of money and talent seeking countries in which the rule of law guarantees opportunity and the right to keep the fruits of your efforts. Lee Kuan Yew, the extraordinary former leader of Singapore, who led that island country into becoming one of the richest and most technologically advanced countries in the world, understood thoroughly the dangers of socialist thinking. He had been a graduate student in England after World War II at the time of the Labor Government's efforts to create a government-dominated socialist system.

We were together one weekend when I was Speaker, and I asked him what principle he applied to create such a dynamic, modern, and wealthy country in one generation. "It was very simple," he replied. "Every time I faced a major decision, I asked myself what [former British prime minister] Clement Attlee and the socialists would have done. I then did exactly the opposite and it worked one hundred percent of the time." You can legitimately ask why would doing the opposite work. The answer lies in the nature of human beings—and the antihuman requirements of Big Government Socialism.

The deepest difference between Big Government Socialism and the American constitutional system built around the practicalities of human nature is this question of how the world really works versus how the intellectuals would like for it to work. Ultimately, you either design a system that reinforces and supports how people actually behave, or you design a system that imposes change on people whether they want it or not.

The American constitutional system was created by a group of wise, practical politicians who had spent their lifetimes studying various government forms and principles going back to ancient Rome, Greece, and Jerusalem. They were trying to deduce a set of principles about how people could maximize freedom by governing themselves—while remaining organized enough to defend society from outside and domestic efforts to take over and control the people. Virtually all the Founding Fathers were practicing politicians, who had spent time winning office and working with other people who had won elections. They were virtually all successful farmers or businessmen, so they had a lot of practical knowledge about how the world worked and how people behaved. They designed the structure of government based on this combination of historic knowledge, practical knowledge, and real-world experience.

In Abraham Lincoln's words at Gettysburg, the Founding Fathers wanted "government of the people, by the people, and for the people." By contrast, Big Government Socialism seeks government over the people, controlling the people, and defining the rights of the people. The contrast could hardly be greater. The first key difference is: "Who controls?" In a free society, you must largely control yourself. As many of the Founding Fathers wrote, self-government starts with governing yourself. They emphasized the importance of a moral (and often religious) basis of freedom. They believed that self-government required first literally governing self.

But in a Big Government Socialist system, government controls you. This is why Friedrich Hayek, in his classic, *The Road to Serfdom*, argues that centralized planning inevitably leads to tyranny. Forcing people to do what the bureaucracy wants ultimately leads the bureaucracy to impose more controls. The recent experience with masks and vaccinations is a classic example of government reaching deeper and deeper into your life. After all, if a government can determine what you will put in your body, and what you will put on your face, you have surrendered a lot of liberty to a faceless, nameless bureaucracy. To be clear: I support vaccinations and wearing masks for the sake of public health.

I don't support a federal government imposing vaccines and mask-wearing upon me.

Because governments inherently have the power to use force, the danger of a strong government micromanaging people and censoring people represents a real threat to the concept of freedom. There is a steady drift in Big Government Socialism toward more controls and a greater willingness to use force against your own people. This is how charismatic socialist leaders such as Benito Mussolini in Italy, Hugo Chavez in Venezuela, Fidel Castro in Cuba, Daniel Ortega in Nicaragua, and Robert Mugabe in Zimbabwe gradually acquire power and then ally themselves with the forces of repression (military and police) against the general public. Again and again, the dissidents, who are usually the middle class, find themselves crushed by police and military who are prepared to use force. The argument of the gun defeats the argument of reason, through sheer brutality.

In order to sustain their power, the leaders of socialist regimes find themselves forced to shift resources to take care of those who defend them and crush dissent. One of the reasons embargoes don't work well against dictators is that they simply take more of the dwindling resources to pay generously for their security forces. The people who prop up the regime not only fail to feel the impact of the foreign embargoes, they are strengthened by their relative wealth and comfort compared to those in the general public who are suffering but politically impotent.

Even in nondictatorships, governments have a constant pattern of favoritism and cronyism. As I mentioned before—and will bring up again—there is a profound reason Lord John Dalberg-Acton in 1887 warned, "Power tends to corrupt and absolute power corrupts absolutely. Great men are almost always bad men, even when they exercise influence and not authority: still more when you superadd the tendency or the certainty of corruption by authority. There is no worse heresy than that the office sanctifies the holder of it."[8]

The pattern of the Hunter Biden laptop; the Biden contracts with Ukraine, Russia, and China; and the ongoing fraud of Hunter's artwork, which will be priced vastly higher because he is the president's son, are clear examples of corruption at the highest levels. The parallel exploitation of the Biden name by the president's brothers—and the clear references to influence peddling—is outlined in painful detail in the book by Miranda Devine: *Laptop from Hell: Hunter Biden, Big Tech, and the Dirty Secrets the President Tried to Hide.*

The general corruption of the American system is evidenced in the desperate efforts of the left-wing propaganda media to avoid covering any examples of Biden family corruption. This effort includes the banning from the social media the fourth largest and oldest newspaper, the *New York Post*, founded by Alexander Hamilton, for the last few weeks before the 2020 election. The *Post* first broke the story about incriminating evidence on Hunter Biden's lost-and-found laptop. The propaganda media could not allow this information to come to light ahead of the election.

Corruption is all too often narrowed down to specific overt acceptance of bribes. Yet the much more dangerous corruption is the systemic willingness to reallocate resources and power for political and personal reasons rather than in implementation of legitimate public policy. The great American historian Gordon Wood dealt extensively with the alienating and corrosive impact of corruption in the British government on the American colonists in *The Creation of the American Republic*:

When the American Whigs described the English nation and government as eaten away by "corruption," they were in fact using a technical term of political science, rooted in the writings of classical antiquity, made famous by Machiavelli, developed by the classical republicans of seventeenth-century England, and carried into the eighteenth century by nearly everyone who laid claim to knowing anything about politics. And for England it was a pervasive corruption, not only dissolving the original political principles by which the constitution was balanced, but, more alarming, sapping the very spirit of the people by which the constitution was ultimately sustained.[9]

Wood describes the growing sentiment in colonial America that its mother country was corrupt. Despite the reforms of the Glorious Revolution of 1688, the Crown had still found a way to corrupt the supposedly balanced English government:

England, the Americans said over and over again, "once the land of liberty—the school of patriots—the nurse of heroes, has become the land of slavery—the school of parricides and the nurse of tyrants." By the 1770's the metaphors describing England's course were all despairing: the nation was fast streaming toward a cataract, hanging on the edge of a precipice; the brightest lamp of liberty in all the world was dimming. Internal decay was the most common image. A poison had entered the nation and was turning the people and the government into "one mass of corruption." On the eve of the Revolution the belief that England was "sunk in corruption" and "tottering on the brink of destruction" had become entrenched in the minds of disaffected Englishmen on both sides of the Atlantic.

This sense of ubiquitous corruption and lawbreaking is a widespread but generally unspoken and unexplored part of what is happening to America today. Remember, if California lost $20 billion in unemployment compensation funds,[10] that means there were a lot of people willing to steal from the state of California. When you see a video of a gang of eighty people robbing a Nordstrom department store near Los Angeles,[11] you are watching eighty Americans willing to break the law methodically and flagrantly. The illegal drug economy may be one of the largest centers of lawbreaking in the United States. When the Centers for Disease Control and Prevention estimates more than 100,000 Americans died from drug overdoses in a twelve-month period,[12] that means a lot of people were making money by breaking the law and selling drugs. The homeless settlements need to be studied for the level of illegal activity that sustains their economies. In some cases, they may turn out to be open-air drug markets.

Law-abiding Americans are in many ways under siege by a wide range of dishonest people engaging in a wide range of illegal and corrupt activities. The steady spread of corruption and dishonesty is just one component of a phenomenon the late senator Daniel Patrick Moynihan, a liberal Democrat and a great sociologist, wrote about in an essay in 1993 called "Defining Deviancy Down."[13]

Moynihan was identifying a series of patterns three decades ago that have grown in power and pervasiveness since he first wrote. Drawing on the work of the great nineteenth-century French sociologist Emile Durkheim, Moynihan reasoned that we had entered a phase in which society was accepting more deviancy, because it was so common people had to normalize it.

Moynihan's essay was summarized in a brilliant column by Charles Krauthammer in 1993 analyzing Moynihan's theory. In addition to explaining Moynihan's point about defining deviancy down, Krauthammer illustrated its impact brilliantly.[14]

Krauthammer pointed out that single parenthood tripled from 1960 to 1993, and that fatherless households are closely related to increases in crime, addiction, and a slew of societal issues. Yet, as he said, the intelligentsia of modern culture has ignored this problem and redefined single parenthood as a benign, alternative life choice. Krauthammer then pointed out that crime—and specifically homicide—has become so commonplace that "[w]e have come to view homicide as ineradicable a part of the social landscape as car accidents." Finally, he pointed out that rates of mental illness have not greatly changed, but as a society we have stopped dealing with it in a meaningful way. He pointed out that there were 93,000 patients in New York State's asylum system in 1955 and only 11,000 in 1992. As he put it:

> Where have the remaining 82,000 and their descendants gone? Onto the streets mostly. In one generation, a flood of pathetically ill people has washed onto the streets of America's cities. We now step over these wretched and abandoned folk sleeping in doorways and freezing on grates. They, too, have become accepted as part of the natural landscape. We have managed to do that by redefining them as people who simply lack affordable hous-

ing. They are not crazy or sick, just very poor—as if anyone crazy and sick and totally abandoned would not end up very poor.

Mr. Moynihan's powerful point is that with the moral deregulation of the 1960s, we have had an explosion of deviancy in family life, criminal behavior and public displays of psychosis. And we have dealt with it in the only way possible: by redefining deviancy down so as to explain away and make "normal" what a more civilized, ordered and healthy society long ago would have labeled—and long ago did label—deviant.

Moynihan's and Krauthammer's thinking is important because every trend they identified as decaying has gotten steadily worse since they wrote the original papers in 1993. This may be one of the most important explanations of American decay that anyone has written. The collapse of the family and the rise of children raised without male influence has dramatically accelerated. The crime rate has exploded once again. The homeless shelters of the early 1990s have become ramshackle tent cities in places such as Los Angeles, Seattle, and San Francisco.

There was a second, even more threatening aspect of defining deviancy down as Moynihan described it. The more we tolerated destructive behavior, the more traditionally normal behavior became unacceptable. Krauthammer added to the Moynihan analysis with a new insight that has become chillingly real.

In the process of defining deviancy down, we have simultaneously begun defining normalcy as deviancy to balance the social equation. Consider what it means now to be a heterosexual, Christian, married person, who is pro-life, anti–drug use, and pro-police. In today's society, these characteristics likely mean you are homophobic, cis-gender-centric, intolerant, probably racist, and living on unearned privilege gained from your inherent systemic effort to oppress others.

Back in 1993, Krauthammer concluded:

> The rationalization of deviancy reaches its logical conclusion. The deviant is declared normal. And the normal is unmasked as deviant. That, of course, makes us all that much more morally equal. The project is complete. What real difference is there between us? . . .
>
> Defining deviancy up also fills a psychological need. The need was identified by Senator Moynihan: How to cope with the explosion of real deviancy? One way is denial: defining real deviancy down creates the pretense that deviance has disappeared because it has been redefined as normal. Another strategy is distraction: defining deviancy up creates brand-new deviancies that we can now go off and fight. That distracts us from real deviancy and gives us the feeling that, despite the murder and mayhem and madness around us, we are really preserving and policing our norms.

I have spent this much time on Moynihan and Krauthammer because they so clearly captured the trajectory of decay and decline that has accelerated over the last thirty years. I particularly included Krauthammer because his contribution to Moynihan's insights is much less well known and profoundly captures the shift in who is discriminated against, from the historically deviant to the historically normal. So, now normal is deviant and deviant is normal. None of these changes were totally unobserved.

In 1982, James Q. Wilson and George Kelling wrote an article titled "Broken Windows," which outlined how decaying conditions in neighborhoods make it psychologically easier to commit crimes, while well-kept neighborhoods of the same income and ethnicity make it psychologically harder to commit crimes.[15] They had a huge impact on reducing crime for two decades (New York City police commissioner Bill Bratton called this theory the most important improvement in policing in a half century). Then the left repudiated them as racist (largely because former New York mayor Michael Bloomberg corrupted their sound theory into stop-and-frisk, which gave police license to racially profile and harass people). Nevertheless, "Broken Windows" was driven out of media acceptability, leading us back to today's skyrocketing crime.

In 1983, the Reagan administration released a report, *A Nation at Risk*,[16] which warned that the collapse in education was a threat to individuals and to the survival of the country. After a lot of publicity, nothing was done and the decay continued. While some progress was made on school choice, the overwhelming weight of the teachers' unions remains. Their willingness to dumb down schools, focus on race rather than learning, and avoid teaching whenever possible has continued the decay of American education, with enormous national security and personal life opportunity costs.

In 1984, Charles Murray wrote *Losing Ground*.[17] This was the seminal work explaining that the Great Society's anti-work and anti-family reforms were shifting power from civil society (including religious and charitable institutions) to government bureaucracies. Murray pointed out these reforms had hurt the people they were supposed to help. According to Murray, we were losing ground on every aspect of life for the poor. His book was the key intellectual breakthrough leading to the Welfare Reform Act of 1996. Millions left poverty, got jobs, and created better futures for themselves and their families. The American left (which has become the Big Government Socialist system) has worked tirelessly to destroy the work requirements that were at the heart of the 1996 reform. The Biden administration has succeeded in re-creating precisely the kind of incentive-destroying, life-crippling, passivity-inducing system about which Murray had warned.

In 1992, Marvin Olasky wrote *The Tragedy of American Compassion*, which expanded on Murray's analysis and contrasted the work-oriented tough love of the traditional reformers with the exact opposite attitude and policies implemented by the Great Society under President Lyndon B. Johnson.

The warnings of decay and decline were there for all to see, but the Big Government Socialists and their woke allies were determined to ignore and reject them. The simple fact is that a decaying, declining America dominated by bureaucracies imposing destructive policies (while being propped up by the taxpayers) is far better for the left than a vibrant, dynamic, entrepreneurial, work- and achievement-oriented society in which government is small and opportunity is large. To understand the contrast, we will turn now to the principles that have worked historically and to which we must return.

CHAPTER TWO

DANGER AND OPPORTUNITY

The greatest challenge of the elections of 2022, 2024, and 2026 is for a majority of Americans to develop a replacement program capable of overmatching the threats we face from Big Government Socialism. Note that I didn't say Republicans. I said a majority of Americans. I include all three election cycles, because we will have to win all three to overcome, and totally defeat, the forces that are endangering our nation.

This book is about defeating Big Government Socialism and its allied destroyers of freedom. It is about defeating and replacing a set of century-old ideas that have proven to be disastrous for America. It is about breaking the cronyism and corruption that now infect our system like a rapidly spreading cancer. Again, let me be clear: This is not about defeating Democrats. It is not about simply electing Republicans. It is about ending the system that has dominated American politics and government for nearly a century. Today Americans face threats chillingly similar to those that were described by Orwell in *1984*—and his other anti-totalitarian novel, *Animal Farm*. The American ideals

37

of free speech, conscience, and freedom within the rule of law are being challenged by a totalitarian mentality of growing power and fanaticism. People now find themselves compelled to publicly apologize for using the "wrong words" or having the "wrong thoughts." It is like a contemporary re-creation of Mao Zedong's public confession groups from his brutal Cultural Revolution in China.

People can be canceled and fired from their jobs. They can be forced to avoid public places. They can be coerced to submit their bodies to the dictates of a corrupt, crony-ridden system of power. Thinking, saying, or doing the wrong thing can lead to ostracism and exclusion. The largest communication systems on the planet now arrogate to themselves the ability to erase people and institutions. In the interest of influencing an election, the fourth-largest newspaper in America (and the oldest) can be silenced for telling the truth about Hunter Biden's corrupt ties to China, Russia, Ukraine, and other foreign countries. A president of the United States can be regularly silenced for saying things that are unpopular with half of the country (but acceptable to the half that supports him). We are faced with crises of culture, bureaucracy, cronyism, and corruption. And if we do not solve these crises, we may be faced with the collapse of America as we have known it.

For instance, there is a real possibility that the current American bureaucracies and policies will be unable to meet the foreign and domestic challenges that are endangering the survival of our constitutional system of freedom within the rule of law. I mean this literally. We are in danger of defeat by China. We are in danger of catastrophic damage from North Korea, Iran, Russia, Islamist terrorism, or any combination of them. Our national security system is incapable of evolving to meet threats as rapidly as they are growing. Our politicians seem incapable of executing the investigations and policy changes necessary. Our news media is uninterested in upholding our rights—and is indeed more interested in upholding political narratives.

The combined systems of Big Government Socialism, woke ideological destructiveness, cronyism, corruption, and a big business–hyperrich collaboration to appease China and impose radical values and policies on America must be overcome and replaced for the United States to survive as a free country.

I have on my wall a Solidarity labor union poster given to Callista and me when we made a 2010 film about St. John Paul II's pilgrimage home to Poland in 1979 (*Nine Days That Changed the World* is available on iTunes and the Google Play Store). The poster says, in Polish, "For Poland to Remain Poland, 2 plus 2 must always equal 4." This simple phrase was a repudiation of the language relativism by which the communist dictatorship in George Orwell's *1984* defined reality and forced people to memorize the state's version of facts—even if they were demonstrably not true (such as $2 + 2 = 5$).

Until the last few years, I never fully appreciated the brilliant simplicity of asserting that 2 plus 2 must always equal 4 as an antidote to the cancer of totalitarian movements Now, I understand why Albert Camus, himself a rebel of great courage, wrote, "There always comes a time in history when the person who dares to say that $2 + 2 = 4$ is punished by death. And the issue is not what reward or what punishment will be the outcome of that reasoning. The issue is simply whether or not $2 + 2 = 4$."

If we are to survive, we must get back to a rational country that operates on a basis of objective truth and morality. Otherwise, America will perish.

REVERSING ROOSEVELT

The revolution led by President Franklin Delano Roosevelt is now in its ninetieth year (starting with the victory over Republican president Herbert Hoover in 1932). The financial redistribution-bureaucratic model of government dominating society (and Washington dominating government) has been steadily at work for nine decades. Each decade has seen government grow bigger, more central to defining life and facing problems, more bureaucratic, and more based on increasing power in Washington.

Republicans have been the cheaper, more cautious managers of the Rooseveltian revolution, but the steady shift in power and philosophy has gone on through both Democrat and Republican political victories. The speed has changed from time to time, but the direction has remained constant. Bureaucracies and Washington power grew. Government gained greater control of our society's total resources. The influence of civil society—families, neighborhoods, churches, and volunteer organizations—diminished. "Is it legal?" increasingly replaced "Is it right?" as a standard of judgment. Corruption and crime became more commonplace (and therefore tolerable). And news media steadily became more committed to serving as the propaganda arm of power holders. Essentially, Roosevelt's system has metastasized into what we now know as Big Government Socialism.

The scale of growth of government from the pre-Roosevelt world to today can be clearly measured by the share of the economy taken up by government—and by the shift in relative size of the local, state, and federal governments. In 1928, local governments were four times the size of state governments and twice the size of the federal government. Local governments made up 6.5

percent of gross domestic product (GDP), states made up 1.6 percent, and the federal government represented only 3.7 percent.[1] By 2019, the federal government's 20.7 percent of GDP dwarfed states (which made up 9.0 percent) and all the local governments combined (at 9.5 percent).[2] In fact, Washington now also spends more money than state and local governments combined. More astonishing, the changes in raw percentage of GDP understates the growth of government. In 2019 dollars, the GDP for 1928 was $1.47 trillion. In 2019, it was $21.43 trillion. So, the federal government is taking a much bigger relative slice of a much bigger economy.

Along with that spending, an even greater shift in regulatory power and bureaucratic oversight has naturally arisen. Washington mandates, oversight, and regulatory intervention represented an even greater shift than the growth of government suggests. Issues that in 1928 were clearly decided by local voters and elected officials—or by local voluntary groups and organizations—were by 2019 limited by the decrees of Washington bureaucrats who had never been in the towns and counties they were directing. Furthermore, citizens in 1928 could reach their local officials and force them to pay attention to local concerns. By 2019, the bureaucrats were so deeply entrenched in Washington that even House and Senate members often found it impossible to bring their citizens' complaints and concerns to the system's decision makers.

The nature of bureaucracy is to become self-protective and to grow constantly without regard to productivity or effectiveness. Because bureaucracies focus on self-protection and defending their prerogatives and habits against outside supervision, they grow less capable as technology and challenges evolve. In the

Pentagon, the political appointees (placed by the president) are seen as "the summer help."

As a freshman member of Congress in 1979, I had a private conversation with a senior naval officer who enthusiastically— and with self-satisfaction—told me that President Jimmy Carter wanted to reduce the United States Navy to a North Atlantic taxi service. He bragged that senior naval officers had blocked that from happening. It hit me that while I agreed with the outcome, I was being told the senior naval bureaucracy had deliberately and methodically undermined the elected commander in chief. I was deeply disturbed. This was one of many conversations that prepared me for fully understanding—and engaging with— the civil service culture of blocking politicians from "interfering" with the judgment of career bureaucrats.

A similar experience occurred when President George W. Bush brought in David Brailer to modernize the Department of Health and Human Services' (HHS) approach to health solutions. Brailer was a doctor and an entrepreneur in information technology who had pioneered breakthrough solutions in California. He was also a first-generation financial success with property in Napa Valley and Hawaii. He was the kind of brilliant, aggressive, highly educated person who could bring twentieth-century paper-based industrial-model bureaucracies into the twenty-first century. Brailer first came to Washington to work as a volunteer at the Bush White House designing the National Health Information Technology program. Then President Bush asked him to head up the office he had designed.

Meanwhile, HHS secretary Tommy Thompson had had great impact as governor of Wisconsin in developing innovations that still echo throughout our political system. He worked with

Wisconsin state representative Annette Polly Williams, a single mother who had been on welfare and sponsored the first school choice legislation in the United States (passed in 1989). Thompson had also helped create profound reforms of the welfare system, injecting work requirements and pioneering ideas that would be incorporated in the 1996 welfare reform bill (which is still the largest conservative values reform in modern times).

As an experienced reformer, Thompson was eager to work with Brailer in modernizing the use of information systems in health care. However, he was about to get a tough education in the difference between leading a relatively small state government in Madison, Wisconsin, and trying to move a gigantic bureaucracy in Washington (HHS spends more than the Department of Defense). To mark Brailer becoming National Health Information Technology coordinator, Thompson hosted an astonishing innovations meeting at the Willard Hotel. Key members of Congress, industry, academia, and the federal bureaucracy were there. For two hours, people came up with good ideas for reform and modernization. When he got back to his office in the Hubert H. Humphrey Building, Brailer was informed by staff that he had violated several laws involving open meetings, proper procedures, and making promises he could not procedurally make without going through elaborate and time-consuming bureaucratic processes.

At the same time, Brailer went to his first day inside the federal bureaucracy. That afternoon he called me and asked if he could come by immediately to discuss what he had just experienced. Arriving as a well-meaning entrepreneur who was going to bring modern information technology to help patients and doctors in the health system, his first morning was spent with

the counsel for HHS, who briefed him about all the legal limitations of his job. His entire morning was spent on hearing what
he *could not* do.

Brailer wondered if he should even stay, considering the limitations on his ability to innovate and the risks he would run if
he aggressively tried to use his entrepreneurial leadership skills to
change the bureaucracy. I sympathized with his frustration but
urged him to stay and do all he could to move the machine as far
as he could. He tried his best but eventually moved back to San
Francisco to make a lot of money in venture capital, specializing
in investing in private sector health innovations. The bureaucracy
had won again.

These kinds of stories happen every day throughout the
federal government. President Harry Truman commented on
the difficulties even a president faced when changing things in
government. As Jason Kelly noted in the *University of Chicago
Magazine* in September 2012:

> Harry Truman felt sorry for Dwight Eisenhower. If
> Truman, merely a failed haberdasher, after all, bristled at
> the obstacles to his presidential authority, imagine how
> aggravated his successor, a former five-star general, would
> be. Tapping on his desk in the Oval Office, Truman
> remarked, "He'll sit here and he'll say, 'Do this! Do that!'
> And nothing will happen. Poor Ike—it won't be a bit like
> the Army."
>
> A promotion to commander in chief, in Truman's
> estimation, would limit Eisenhower's power. His orders,
> delivered as an elected official, would lose the sir-yes-sir
> acceptance that they received in the military. To hear

Truman tell it, the president could do little more than implore: "I sit here all day trying to persuade people to do the things they ought to have sense enough to do without my persuading them. . . . That's all the powers of the president amount to."[3]

If even a president finds the bureaucracy unmanageable, imagine the odds against a local citizen, the mayor of a small town, or even a governor taking on the federal bureaucrats. It is an extraordinarily difficult uphill challenge. Because the federal, state, and local bureaucracies have become so large and unionized, they have become resistant to change. The entire system has been growing more inefficient, ineffective—and in many ways dishonest.

The bureaucracies we have inherited represent an industrial-era form of mechanistic organization. My favorite example is the Pentagon. This huge building was opened in 1943 so 26,000 people could use manual typewriters and carbon paper to manage a global war. Almost eight decades later, the manual typewriters and carbon paper have been replaced with laptops, iPads, and smartphones. Imagine what the information management potential of modern systems is compared to the carbon paper and manual typewriters they replaced. It must be on the order of 1,000:1. Yet there are still roughly 27,000 people working at the Pentagon.

The steady growth of bureaucracies combined with their declining adaptability and productivity should not be a surprise. More than sixty-five years ago, the natural tendency of bureaucracies to grow, protect themselves, and decline in effectiveness had been described as an inevitable development. In 1955, the British naval historian Cyril Northcote Parkinson coined what became known as Parkinson's law in an issue of *The Economist*.

The law goes: "work expands so as to fill the time available for its completion."[4]

In a BBC essay, Tiffany Wen suggested that Parkinson was trying to understand a "different kind of inefficiency—the bureaucratization of the British Civil Service." She explained:

> In his original essay he pointed out that although the number of navy ships decreased by two thirds, and personnel by a third, between 1914 and 1928, the number of bureaucrats had still ballooned by almost 6% a year. There were fewer people and less work to manage—but management was still expanding, and Parkinson argued that this was due to factors that were independent of naval operational needs. . . . Parkinson pointed to two critical elements that lead to bureaucratization—what he called the law of multiplication of subordinates, the tendency of managers to hire two or more subordinates to report to them so that neither is in direct competition with the manager themself; and the fact that bureaucrats create work for other bureaucrats.

Wen reported on a modern nongovernment validation of Parkinson's law:

> One scholar who has taken a serious look at Parkinson's Law is Stefan Thurner, a professor in Science of Complex Systems at the Medical University of Vienna. Thurner says he became interested in the concept when the faculty of medicine at the University of Vienna split into its own independent university in 2004. Within a cou-

ple years, he says, the Medical University of Vienna went from being run by 15 people to 100, while the number of scientists stayed about the same. "I wanted to understand what was going on there, and why my bureaucratic burden did not diminish—on the contrary it increased," he says. . . . [C]ompanies typically start with a flat hierarchy, perhaps two engineers. As the company grows, they hire assistants, who then get promoted and hire their own subordinates. "A pyramid starts to grow. One might add artificial layers that serve no purpose other than introducing hierarchy, that help you to promote people to please them and keep them motivated. When the pyramid gets very large and expensive it might eat up all the company's profits. If the bureaucratic body is not drastically reduced at this stage the company will die."[5]

Of course, when the growing bureaucracy is taxpayer funded it does not die, it just demands more resources. This demand for more money from the taxpayer is even greater and more intense when the government bureaucracy has been unionized. The teachers' unions have recently been a case study of using their political power to demand salaries for teachers who refused to teach—and for keeping on the payroll teachers who have clearly failed to educate the young people to whom they are assigned.

Just as bad as the resource consequences of growing bureaucracy, there are huge real-world consequences of growing bureaucratization. First is simply failure to succeed. Then, to cover up its failures, the system must lie to a larger and larger extent. As the lies compound and grow, corruption becomes more commonplace and easier to tolerate.

THE BIG GOVERNMENT PROBLEM

There are three recent case studies that reflect the scale of failure and dishonesty that is increasingly eroding the American system of achievement and replacing it with a system of underperformance, inaccuracy, and duplicity.

First, there is the scale of theft that is being uncovered in the various government bailout efforts—particularly in the unemployment insurance programs created as a response to government-imposed COVID-19 shutdowns. Estimates show that up to $400 billion of unemployment payments were fraudulent and stolen by foreign crime organizations (roughly half of all funds nationwide).[6] In California alone, at least $20 billion was stolen from the state unemployment system, according to prosecutors.[7] (Initial estimates had been as high as $32 billion.) Apparently a good bit of it was stolen by criminals who were already in prison and using the prison's computers to engage in identity theft. Their colleagues on the outside picked up the checks and deposited them. In Washington State, the state's auditor estimated the unemployment compensation system apparently lost more than $647 million to fraud.[8] Much of the ill-gotten funds from Washington State reportedly went to Nigerians who have become experts in stealing Americans' identities. Of course, that much stolen money means there were an enormous number of Americans willing to steal from their fellow countrymen. In Washington State, for example, one former Employment Security Department employee has been indicted for allegedly stealing $360,000.[9]

The second case study is the disaster that was the Afghanistan conflict. There appears to have been continuous dishonesty, disinformation, and cover-up in the twenty years of the Afghanistan campaign. It turns out that military leaders on the ground didn't have a mission or definition of success—and knew the campaign was doomed to fail. Yet rosy, hopeful reports continued coming to Washington from superiors, and the bloody war continued. In a stunning book, *The Afghanistan Papers: A Secret History of the War*, Craig Whitlock of the *Washington Post* uses the Department of Defense's own records of debriefing senior officers to outline at least sixteen years in which the military and government systematically misled—and at times outright lied to—the American people. Your faith in the integrity and capability of the Pentagon will be shattered by its own internal interviews and documents. You will also better understand the incompetence of the actual withdrawal from Afghanistan in 2021.

This is the most dangerous scandal we face, because a bureaucratized, self-deluding defense system (which focuses more on wokeness than military competence) will simply collapse when faced with a serious opponent such as the Chinese Communists or a combined effort of other adversaries. As one retired military leader with great credentials as a student of military history wrote me, we are in the process of creating the defeatist French generals of the 1920s and 1930s—who had no hope of defeating the Germans in 1940.

The third case study is the extraordinary failure of the public health system in attempting to deal with the COVID-19 pandemic. In many ways, this failure dwarfs the impact of theft from relief funds—and even the lies about the war in Afghanistan. More than two years after the first U.S. infection, there are still shortages for tests and vaccines. And there is still no permanent plan for overcoming or coping with the virus. If the United States was not mired in soap opera politics, a pathetically narrow and partisan-focused majority in Congress, and a news media that wants to protect its allies against critiques, we would currently be having astonishing congressional and media investigations into the scale of incompetence, dishonesty, and petty self-interest that made the response to the COVID-19 pandemic so much worse than it should have been.

Consider two early failures of the public health bureaucracies in the emergence of COVID-19: the inability to track the spread of the disease, and the inability to develop an inexpensive self-administered test that could have permeated the country. To understand the scale of failure in the public health system, first understand that there really isn't a public health system. There is a collection of local, state, and federal agencies with different scales of budget, expertise, and competence. Many operate on antiquated, totally obsolete models of gathering information by fax and routinely taking two weeks or longer to figure out what was going on two weeks earlier.

At the heart of this mound of disconnected activities is the Centers for Disease Control and Prevention (CDC). This vast research system had grown from the Army's Office of Malaria Control in War Areas during World War II. Prior to the COVID-19 outbreak, CDC was widely regarded as the preeminent research and analysis center for new diseases in the world. Its work on everything from Ebola to measles was historic and set the global standard. Unfortunately, in the great tradition of bureaucracies, the CDC came to believe its own publicity and grew jealous about its power and status. Increasingly, if an idea came from outside the CDC, bureaucrats reacted like an immune system attacking a foreign disease. Furthermore, if the new ideas required fundamental change in how things were done, the self-satisfied CDC leaders shrugged them off as unnecessary. They had dealt with dozens of health crises around the world, and they did not need to rethink their protocols and procedures.

At the height of the COVID-19 pandemic, a former CDC director, whom I admire greatly and who has an impeccable reputation as a medical expert, reassured me that the chaotic, uncoordinated, slow, and clearly not standardized system of local public health offices doing their own thing was the best we could do. The CDC was not really in the test-inventing business, but it arrogated to itself developing the tests for COVID-19. Blood tests in America are dominated by a few giant corporations. The big government–big company alliances have made testing at scale too difficult, expensive, and slow. Callista and I were in Italy at Christmas in 2021, and virtually every pharmacy had a real-time testing capability for about $8 (5 euro). In December, we had gone twice to an efficient, one-day testing office in Arlington, Virginia (first to go to the Kennedy Center Honors and then to fly to Italy). In contrast to the test at virtually every pharmacy in Italy, here we had to make an appointment, show up on time, still wait in line, pay more than $8, and then wait overnight to get the results.

From the day it was clear COVID-19 was a pandemic, anyone paying attention to Wuhan, China, or much of Europe by the end of February 2020 knew that we needed new thinking and systems. Unfortunately, the last few threatening potential pandemics had never materialized as real worldwide threats. There was considerable caution about panicking and a bias toward suggesting normalcy. I had done a podcast with Dr. Anthony Fauci in February 2020, and he clearly thought it was going to be manageable and not something that would jar our entire system.[10]

The number of different failures at the CDC, the National Institutes of Health, the Food and Drug Administration, and the general public health environment should have led to in-depth, serious investigations with analyses of what went wrong and what needs to be fixed. As of this writing, none have taken place.

These are such powerful examples of how our bureaucracies are failing and weakening the nation that they are worth studying. We have seen hundreds of billions of taxpayers' dollars stolen. For two decades, we have seen a war dishonestly and incompetently led. A virus killed hundreds of thousands of Americans unnecessarily, and the entire economy was wrecked (especially for small businesses) by the government. The common thread with all these calamities is bloated, ineffective bureaucracy. There should be a call for deep investigations that get to the root of the problem and help develop powerful reforms.

Without this introspection and correction, these problems will compound and get much worse. At the present time, our news media–political–bureaucratic–interest group system is simply incapable of dealing with reality and getting to an acceptably better future response.

To survive, America must replace the systems that are failing. If we cannot break out from the straitjacket of ninety years of Rooseveltian, bureaucratic, and ideological evolution, we will find it impossible to compete with Communist China. The result will be a Chinese-defined and dominated system within a generation (something we can already see as many of our biggest corporations kowtow to Beijing and say patently false things to placate the Chinese Communist dictatorship).

Because the threat to American freedom and safety is so great, the goals of the elections of 2022, 2024, and 2026 must be dramatically greater than normal. We must campaign to mobilize public support for the replacement of the entire system of Rooseveltian government.

In effect, we need ideas—not personalities—to change. Simply changing personalities within the current idea framework will at most only slow the rate of decay. There are three possible outcomes for the elections of 2022, 2024, and 2026. Two of the three represent extraordinary dangers for America. Only one of these potential futures will enable America to survive the foreign and domestic threats to our freedom, prosperity, and safety—and to thrive beyond them.

A BIG GOVERNMENT SOCIALIST COMEBACK

The first disastrous outcome would be a Big Government Socialist comeback. This is unlikely—but possible.

No matter how bad things seem to be now, there is always the possibility that the Big Government Socialists (who are masquerading as the current Democratic Party) can make a comeback. The greatest recovery in modern times was President Harry Truman in 1948. Truman seemed so far behind that polling firms gave the election to the Republican nominee, New York governor Tom Dewey. In fact, most polling firms quit polling the presidential race in September because they were convinced Truman's position was hopeless.

Given the state of the country—and Joe Biden's approval ratings—the 2022 election appears to be strongly against the Big Government Socialists, unless something wildly unexpected happens. However, an off-year election may or may not lead to a presidential victory in 2024. Huge Republican congressional victories in 1946, 1994, and 2010—when Republicans gained

55, 54, and 63 House seats, respectively—were immediately followed by Democrat presidential victories. And it works both ways. Democrat congressional victories in 1982 and 1986 did not lead to Democratic presidential victories in 1984 and 1988.

No one should take for granted that President Biden's low ratings, Vice President Kamala Harris's lower ratings, or the Big Government Socialists' rampant failures will automatically lead to a Republican presidential victory in 2024. Political time moves fast. One year—even one weekend—can be a long time in politics.

It is unlikely that the Big Government Socialists can recover from a presidential performance that is beginning to make President Carter's collapse look normal (Carter lost in 1980 to Ronald Reagan in the largest Electoral College defeat for an incumbent in modern times, and the Democrats lost control of the Senate while Republicans gained thirty-four House seats). However, unlikely is not the same as impossible. Since eight years of Biden-appointed Big Government Socialists to the bureaucracies and courts would be a disaster for America, this possibility must be carefully analyzed. The GOP-led American majority campaign activities in 2023 and 2024 must start with planning to keep the House and Senate while also developing a broad coalition of Americans extending far beyond the Republican base to ensure a GOP victory at every level in 2026. Instead of "base mobilization" campaigns, we need "base-broadening" campaigns.

A STANDARD GOP MUD FIGHT

The second disastrous outcome would be a Republican victory that is entirely negative, myopically Republican, and devoid of momentum or understanding of the scale of threats to America's future.

Over the last few decades, Republicans have slowly lost their focus on creating better futures for Americans—the core of the Contract with America (the program of successful reforms we passed in the 1990s). We have instead fallen into a habit of simply beating our opponents to stay in office. As former political director for the Republican National Committee Gentry Collins recently told me, many Republicans have forgotten how to be "for something" and have defaulted to being "against someone."

This has made it easier for the media to attack us and harder for us to attract new Americans to the party—including minority voters who culturally share many of our ideals. In fact, the extensive polling and focus groups we have undertaken in the American Majority Project clearly indicate that Latino American and Asian American voters are being driven away by the Big Government Socialists in steadily growing numbers. Black women are moving toward Republicans over the issue of school choice, and Black men are moving toward the Republicans in response to the Biden-led economic disaster. So, an entirely negative, shallow Republican campaign victory is the most likely outcome—but it would have disastrous consequences for America.

There is an anti–Big Government Socialist tsunami building. Anyone paying attention can feel it. If the 2022 election is a referendum on inflation, lawless borders, failed COVID-19 policy, high energy prices, supply chain disruptions, weak foreign and national security policy, growing crime at home, out-of-control homelessness, rampant addiction, widespread mental health problems, and a host of other crises, the party in power is going to be punished by frustrated, disappointed voters.

A simple "Big Government Socialism isn't working" campaign is probably enough to win the 2022 election. But it's not enough to save the country. Winning the election because the party in power failed does not set the stage for the scale of change we need. It would be a continuation of running against Democrats rather than for our optimistic principles of freedom, prosperity, security, and hope—which are widely popular.

There is a deep Republican institutional bias against trying to develop ideas-oriented campaigns. Most Republican consultants and committees are comfortable keeping score by simply winning. They have developed an instinct for opposition research and developing a "not them" campaign system. The dominance of FDR's New Deal, big-government model makes it difficult to break through with new ideas and language outside the existing, near century-old system. For nine decades, politics and government have largely operated within the New Deal consensus. The largest changes were in President Lyndon Johnson's Great Society, which involved even bigger bureaucracies, more government, and greater redistribution from the rich and middle classes to the poor.

The intensity of the news media bias in favor of the dominant, big-government model—and deep hostility to ideas that would break from it—is also a tremendous hurdle. The modern news media grew up within the Roosevelt-Johnson consensus that big government and the redistribution of wealth are good, and the ideas and language of liberal Democrats are the natural solutions to America's problems. It is a lot harder to articulate and develop bold new solutions outside the big-government consensus. So, most of the news media is going to be hostile. It is much easier to get reporters and analysts to cover a negative campaign and communicate why the Democrats have flaws than it is to get them to communicate new ideas and new language that is challenging the liberal consensus.

Recall the collapse of Barry Goldwater's 1964 effort to break out of the dominant model. It was shattering. Goldwater's fall seemed to be proof that timid ideas within the Roosevelt system were acceptable, but bold efforts to break out of big government would be assaulted by the media and punished by the public. Even President Reagan, arguably the best communicator as president since FDR, was careful to avoid or initiate ideas outside the consensus that had grown up. Reagan had been an FDR Democrat. As late as 1948, he was making commercials endorsing President Truman for reelection and Hubert H. Humphrey for the United States Senate.

Reagan had a small set of big specific proposals, such as the three-year tax cuts to get the economy moving and methodical opposition to the Soviet Union in favor of freedom. He was cautious about a wide range of conservative proposals that he intuited were not ready for prime time. When we developed the Contract with America, we were careful to include only issues that had 70 percent or more approval—and we were determined to avoid issues that were strongly conservative but would be assaulted by hostile media.

So, the evolution from the FDR, New Deal model to the Big Government Socialism model that now dominates the Democratic Party—and the obvious decay of bureaucracies and policies that just don't work—presents an opportunity to develop a new generation of ideas. However, the underlying habits and biases of nine decades of left-wing idea dominance means that most Republican candidates and consultants are not in the habit of competing at the idea level. They don't quite understand the late British prime minister Margaret Thatcher's rule that "first you win the argument, then you win the vote." To win the argument, you must have a positive idea to advocate. That is a big jump from the traditional Republican campaign, which focuses on winning the attack.

Developing ideas requires candidate-centered campaigns, because the candidates must understand what they stand for—and must be prepared to *cheerfully* defend their ideas against opposition attacks, hostile news media, and citizens who may disagree with them. By contrast, a consultant-centric system inherently has a bias for attacking the opponent, minimizing risk of public debate, and keeping the other side on defense. The result is the consultant's candidate may win—but voters don't really know much about them. Importantly, their candidate hasn't been forced to think hard enough about his or her positions to successfully fight for them in Congress.

Developing ideas takes time. It also requires strategic discipline to communicate and defend proposals. A negative attack campaign simply doesn't. Attack campaigns are inherently tactical and opportunistic. Idea campaigns are inherently strategic and require staying on message. An amazing example of strategic development of ideas is Reagan's brilliant October 1964 nationally televised speech for Goldwater called "A Time for Choosing."[11] When you read the speech, you realize you are encountering most of the ideas on which Reagan would focus his presidency sixteen years later. As a practical outcome, we were able to pass welfare reform in 1996 because Reagan had proposed it in his first gubernatorial race in 1965. Welfare reform was an idea that had been germinating for thirty years and had grown steadily more popular.

Despite the difficulties inherent in a positive, idea-oriented campaign, it is the only way to really move the nation decisively. If you win a clearly negative campaign, you have not built popular support for anything. The public, your supporters, your allies in office, and even your own team will not really know what you are going to do.

By contrast, if you win a positive, ideas-oriented campaign, you have defended your ideas, learned from the popular reaction to them, let your allies in elected office know what you value, set the stage for positive action, and hopefully inspired like-minded leaders to come along. A 2022 campaign that avoids ideas and focuses on the negative Democratic performance will be a grave disservice to the country. Republicans can probably win that negative campaign, but they will simply have set the stage for two more years of intense partisan bickering and personality attacks. The news media will focus on savaging the Republicans, and America will continue to decay. Meanwhile, the collapsing Big Government Socialist system will continue to absorb resources and fail to develop a better American future.

THE AMERICAN MAJORITY

Only one outcome will meet and overcome the threats that endanger us. We need an informed, positive, *American* campaign that reaches out to Republicans, independents, and Democrats who are worried about the country's future. We need to reach everyone who does not believe that Big Government Socialism and obsolete bureaucracies can develop a safe, prosperous, free future for all. We must build a massive American majority. We need a decisive victory against the ideas of Big Government Socialism— paired with a program of reform and replacement powerful enough to enable America to defend itself and solve major domestic challenges for generations to come. Only a fully developed, positive, American program that pledges to replace failed systems and reform salvageable ones can meet the real challenges. At the American Majority Project, we have an enormous amount of data that indicates a national consensus could be developed around big solutions and a vision of a better American future.

The positive American campaign must start now. First, House and Senate Republicans should announce they favor focusing on the nation's needs over partisan wants. They must mean it. They must refuse to engage anything—either in Congress or the media—that doesn't meet that standard. They should describe an American future—not just a Republican future.

Incumbents and candidates should be encouraged to hold town hall meetings and listen for ideas. When he ran for Speaker of the Florida House, Marco Rubio got his members to hold "idea raisers" as well as fundraisers. At the meeting that elected him Speaker for the next session, he held up a book with blank pages and challenged his colleagues to fill in the book with solutions from their constituents. This is a great model that could be adopted.

In 2020, one of the keys to the House Republicans running 40 seats ahead of the experts' predictions (they were supposed to lose 25 and ended up gaining 15) was Leader Kevin McCarthy's "Commitment to America." It was a positive vision that gave House Republicans a better approach to reaching new voters and converting the undecided. House and Senate Republicans should launch a series of ad hoc hearings on national issues—not partisan issues. There are a wide range of think tanks that have people developing positive solutions. They can hold hearings, publish papers explaining and supporting reforms, and engage in positive public debate as the Big Government Socialists try to defend their failing system and attack the new, hopeful approaches. The Democrats, especially under Speaker Pelosi in the House, have been so mean-spirited, negative, and arrogant that it would be tempting to focus Republican time and energy on matching their partisan nastiness. That would be a historic mistake.

America faces many challenges as a country, and Americans face many challenges personally. They want leadership that is trying to solve their country's problems—and give them the tools to have a better chance of solving their own. They don't want to track political points. They want to live more successful lives. House Republicans should set a 10 percent rule for partisan-focused hearings. Ninety percent of their time and effort should be focused on understanding, discovering, developing, and communicating solutions to America's problems.

Even members in the minority can have a huge impact if they focus on big ideas and pursue them with cheerful persistence. I watched Jack Kemp steadily develop and implement supply-side economics, which led to powerful tax cuts that helped put millions of Americans to work. I saw Dick Armey develop the concept of a Base Closing Commission. In both cases, the idea leader was in the minority—and they were on the wrong committees for their ideas. Kemp didn't serve on Ways and Means, which was the committee dealing with taxes. And Armey didn't serve on the Armed Services Committee, which was the legislative point of origin for the bill that implemented his idea. Their entrepreneurial drive and willingness to tirelessly remain focused carried them to victory despite the odds and the structural difficulties.

In an open, solutions-oriented, American majority–focused Republican Party, there will be plenty of opportunities for scores of energetic members to pick topics they care about and work to turn them into winning issues and positive legislative initiatives. A solution-oriented party also needs lots of "product champions" and must create space for many people to become stars in their own right. As soon as possible, Republicans should introduce the bills they believe would make America better. They should focus most of their time on explaining why their solutions will lead to a better American future. In the process of this dialogue, they will learn about things that need to be modified—and omissions that need to be corrected. Developing new solutions is a process, and the first bold step often must be modified and improved until it is widely acceptable and practically implementable. (This is how the legislative process is supposed to work.)

When Republicans attract independents and concerned Democrats to become an American majority, they should pass those bills. If Biden wants to veto them, that is his prerogative. He would then be shaping the agenda for the 2024 campaign around issues Republicans can defend—and drawing a sharp contrast between his defense of failing Big Government Socialism and new ideas that would improve people's lives and help America survive. Now, there would be a real argument for the American majority to win.

Ultimately, it would be good for Republicans to adopt something similar to the Contract with America in September 2022—and again in September 2024. These contracts need to have no more than ten big, bold proposals around which a strong national majority can be rallied. There can be hundreds of useful bills developed and introduced. But the campaign should focus on the biggest, most powerful, and most popular new proposals—and they should be passed first.

This is the only way we can save the country. We must do it.

CHAPTER THREE

WHAT WORKS: HISTORY, STABILITY, AND STRENGTH

So, Big Government Socialism does not work. If we are going to break out of the massive cycle of self-reinforcing failure it has created, we need to understand the basis for positive policies and solutions that do work.

There are myriad immediate solutions to current problems that could be implemented to rapidly create a much better American future than the one Big Government Socialism offers. But, in the current political-media climate, pushing for these solutions ad hoc or haphazardly will potentially create a multitude of disconnected, individual fights that have no common basis or strategy. Some of these efforts will ultimately fail due to egos or infighting. The rest will be picked off one by one or ignored by the media, which is intransigently hostile to anything that approaches common sense.

So, we must start with a set of underlying patterns and principles for success, which combine into a larger theme. These can—and should—be applied to virtually every aspect of American life and every level of American self-government. Indeed, these ideas could be applied to virtually every level of civic and private life as well. The first are elemental principles from which all other solutions can be built and made more effective. They are: history, stability, and strength.

Almost everywhere you look, from the poorest neighborhoods to the most elite echelons of high society, the values, policies, and institutions of Big Government Socialism are failing. The Big Government Socialists reject American history, stability, and strength, the principles that produced two and a half centuries of success for America. That has led them into a hopeless commitment to ideas that simply do not work. A true-believer Big Government Socialist will find this book completely unacceptable—and even absurd. After all, in their world, America's past is the problem. It can't possibly be the solution. I hope more open-minded folks—especially those who do not consider themselves Republicans or even conservative—look at these patterns and ask themselves a simple question: If, at a practical everyday level, the historic principles of American civilization are bad, how have they produced the wealthiest, freest, safest, and most inclusive society in history?

Unlike every other country on the planet, you can come from anywhere and learn to be an American. In a few short years, you can find levels of success you could never have achieved elsewhere. Especially today, when so many in academia, media, and the political left are decrying perceived systemic faults in our society, America continues to attract millions from all over the world. The reason is simple: For the average person, it is far better to be here than any other place on earth.

SUCCESS BEGINS WITH HISTORY

History is at the heart of the American experience. For nearly three centuries, Americans have looked to history for lessons about what to do and what to avoid. Precisely because the lessons of history tend to lead one toward conservative values (hard work, perseverance, entrepreneurship, limited government, etc.), the Big Government Socialists hate history—and especially American history. After decades of looking at what is failing with the welfare state, it is obvious that the real problems exist at the fundamental level of how people see life and what lessons they learn.

In 1993, I began teaching a course, "Renewing American Civilization," which outlined the principled differences between the Great Society approach to bureaucratized dependency and the lessons of limited government and independence, which had previously worked for all American history. That course evolved into the number one best seller, *To Renew America*, and formed the basis for the Contract with America in 1994. It was the underpinning for the 1996 welfare reform bill. Today, almost thirty years after first teaching the course, the accuracy and power of American history seems more useful than ever in providing principles for success. It's clear that if we want to survive, we must study the ideas, systems, and principles that have made America the freest, most prosperous, powerful, and culturally integrated nation ever founded.

The Big Government Socialist bias against America's past makes it especially hard for its members to study history without contorting it. But from the Founding Fathers on, there has been a surprisingly strong pattern of American leaders learning from honest history. During the Revolutionary War period (and the following effort to write a Constitution and create a citizen-controlled government that could protect Americans from foreign dangers *and their own government*), the leaders turned repeatedly to history.

In making the case against the British Empire, the new Americans cited British history and the principles of law embodied in that tradition. The early Americans saw themselves embodying the traditional rights of the British citizen going back to the Magna Carta in 1215. In writing the Declaration of Independence—and in the disagreements with the English Crown leading up to its drafting—the Founders believed they were simply reasserting these rights.

As the early Americans wrestled with establishing a government strong enough to defend the new country while maximizing freedom and limiting government, they turned to the histories of Greece and Rome. Greek history convinced them that mass democracy was dangerous. Pure democracy risked mob rule and destructive, reactionary, shortsighted policies (a lesson for many today who want to abolish the Electoral College). As James Madison wrote in Federalist 55, "if every Athenian had been a Socrates, the Assembly would still have been a mob."[1] Rome's history convinced them that even republics could decay into corruption and factionalism—ultimately replacing freedom with imperial tyranny.

The other focus of study was the English Civil War (1642–51). That conflict led to Oliver Cromwell establishing a brutal dictatorship and dissolving Parliament (1653–58). One of the greatest fears the Founding Fathers had was that their freedoms, hard won in an eight-year war with the British Empire, would be crushed by a future Cromwell-like leader in America.

So, the key lesson of history for the Founding Fathers was that the government they were creating could become an even greater threat to American freedom than any foreign power. This is why they insisted on passing the first ten amendments to the U.S. Constitution as a Bill of Rights. They knew they needed to protect citizens from their own government.

This passion for studying history and learning its lessons did not stop with the Founders. Abraham Lincoln personified the commitment. Lincoln's earliest political reading was in American history through texts such as *The American Speaker*, *The Columbian Orator*, and *The Kentucky Preceptor*. Lincoln absorbed Parson Weems's famous biography of George Washington (the most common idealized introduction to Washington for several generations). When it was clear the United States was drifting toward a civil war, newly elected President Lincoln borrowed the Library of Congress's books on war history and war fighting to prepare himself. A year earlier, he had immersed himself in the history of the early republic in developing his key campaign speech at Cooper Union. Delivered in New York, the speech was a seven-thousand-word summary of the history of slavery, the thinking of the Founding Fathers, and their desire to ultimately abolish slavery. It was so compelling, the speech was reprinted in newspapers throughout the North and made Lincoln a viable national candidate for president.

A generation later, in 1882, a twenty-four-year-old Theodore Roosevelt wrote *The Naval War of 1812*. His vivid description of the importance of naval battles for the survival of America had a huge impact and helped lead to the development of the modern navy. The book is still considered a classic on the topic 140 years after it was published. Woodrow Wilson was a professor-president who studied history and wrote books on government before becoming commander in chief. Franklin Delano Roosevelt had a deep interest in history and was extraordinarily knowledgeable. Harry Truman spent a lifetime studying history. When he suddenly rose from being an obscure vice president to succeed President Roosevelt, he found his knowledge of the past was a key advantage in trying to deal with a complex and rapidly changing world. Dwight Eisenhower graduated first in his class at the Command and General Staff College at Fort Leavenworth. He wrote a history of American military cemeteries from World War I and spent the rest of his life studying history—and making it. The trend continued in the modern era. John F. Kennedy wrote two books about historic events, *Why England Slept* and *Profiles in Courage*. Ronald Reagan studied history and despite his public style as an affable actor was in fact an amazingly widely read scholar.

History is valuable because it grounds you in the virtues and weaknesses—and accidents and planned events—that swirl together to create the human experience. The Big Government Socialists hate the facts of American history, because they teach the limitations of government and the openness of individual opportunity that have made America the most desired country in which to live and pursue happiness.

Similarly, history teaches the failure of utopian thinking, the dangers of fanaticism, and the corruption of centralized power. Big Government Socialism is dedicated to creating a supposed utopia (by imposing its values and beliefs on every person in the country). It is driven by fanaticism, and it absolutely requires centralized power to function. The lessons of history invalidate the core tenets of Big Government Socialism—and warn citizens against the inevitable dangers and failures it brings.

Meanwhile, history validates the patterns and principles of classic American common sense—and highlights the failure of past radical experiments in creating a utopian society. A clear example of the tension between the lessons of history and the theology of radical utopianism is in fighting crime. Historically, we know what works. As I mentioned previously, "Broken Windows" became the basis for a revolution in policing led by Bill Bratton in his career as police chief and commissioner in New York, Boston, and Los Angeles. Bratton described the revolution in policing and the dramatic decline of crime in his 1998 book, *Turnaround: How America's Top Cop Reversed the Crime Epidemic*. Every time Bratton's principles are applied anywhere, crime goes down.

But the radical woke utopians of Big Government Socialism are committed to an anti-police, pro-criminal worldview in which police are always bad and criminals are always victims of oppression. This goes back to the 1960s, when protesters chanted that police were pigs, the Black Panthers promoted assassinating policemen, and the Weathermen waged a campaign of violence, with more than 1,200 domestic bombings from 1969 to 1970. This worldview also holds that criminals, no matter how brutal their rap sheet may be, always deserve another chance. This is the key position of the roughly two dozen George Soros–supported district attorneys who have ushered in an enormous rise in crime in Baltimore, Chicago, Philadelphia, and other American cities.[2] Every time radical district attorneys who refuse to execute the law release criminals—and politicians adopt anti-police, pro-criminal rules—crime rises. The cost of this insanity is borne by the poor, struggling, and innocent.

History can almost always provide useful insights that liberate and also restrict the mind. This process undermines the deepest values and hopes of the radical woke utopians. The result has been a deliberate effort to undermine historic studies, insist on falsifying them to produce the supposedly correct outcomes, and ignore them when necessary.

My advice to any candidate or active citizen is simple: When you encounter a new problem or opportunity, take time to study the history of those who have already solved that problem or developed that opportunity. What did they do that worked? What did they do that failed? When they looked back on their own lives, what did *they think* had succeeded? A few hours of studying history can save you years of going down roads that simply don't work. This is the first thing a would-be problem solver should do. The lessons of history matter because they apply to your life, community, and country. Virtually every challenge has been solved by people in the past. The crisis for the Big Government Socialists is that these solutions almost always validate conservative fundamentals and repudiate left-wing dogma.

The Founding Fathers understood this. They understood it while rebelling against the greatest empire in the world. And they understood it while writing a self-governing document that has lasted 231 years and enabled the nation to grow from the eastern seaboard to cover more than a continent. Applying the lessons of history has led America to grow from 3 million people to 330 million people—and created opportunities for every American to prosper and live in freedom. It is this historic truth that the Big Government Socialists must undermine or else lose all credibility.

HONEST, STABLE CURRENCY

A stable, prosperous society must be based on keeping your word. And a key part of keeping your word must be sound money. If you loan me money, and then it is devalued, so that I pay you back less in purchasing power than you loaned me, that is a form of cheating. If government can spend beyond its means, it will grow. Politicians will use borrowed money to increase their powers and pay off their allies. This constant can-kicking ultimately leads to insolvency.

The Founding Fathers were virtually all economically successful. They owned property. They knew how to invest. They viewed life as a motion picture, not a snapshot. They knew that things could grow or decline over time. They valued the work ethic, and they thought people should be allowed to keep the fruits of their labor.

The economic stress of the Revolutionary War had left behind a huge debt, given the size of the economy. In addition, the money printed by the Continental Congress had suffered such severe inflation that the phrase "not worth a Continental" became commonplace. For those of us who regard today's 7 percent inflation as painful, consider the collapse of the dollars issued by the Continental Congress. In 1777, the Continental bills were on a par with the Spanish silver dollar (which was the internationally recognized standard currency of the time). By 1780, the Continental currency had collapsed to 40:1 Spanish dollar. The Continental Congress had to stop printing them.

In 1786, when the state of Massachusetts tried to pay off its war debts by raising taxes on land, the farmers in the western part of the state rose in what became known as Shays's Rebellion. The combination of collapsing currency and growing anarchy were major factors in convincing the Founding Fathers that the Articles of Confederation were simply too weak and had to be replaced by a much stronger system. Ultimately, the

Constitutional Convention in Philadelphia moved from amending the Articles of Confederation to replacing them with what would become the U.S. Constitution.

As property holders themselves, the Founding Fathers saw property as the bedrock of a healthy society. In their view, a man's home could only be his castle if he truly owned it. So, English judge Sir Edward Coke's famous quote from 1644 that "the house of every one is to him as his Castle and Fortress as well for defence against injury and violence, as for his repose"[3] could only be effective in a society that had wide property ownership.

Since bonds and paper money were also property, the Founding Fathers had a deep bias in favor of protecting them and keeping them stable and reliable. Thus they had an abhorrence of inflation (which cheapened money) and debt repudiation (which would bankrupt those who had worked and saved in favor of the indolent and debtors who had failed to provide for their own well-being).

We need hard money that retains its value for another reason: The easy-money policies of the Federal Reserve enable corruption to the benefit of the ruling class. This is because of the mechanisms that the Fed uses to increase the number of dollars in circulation and because of the nature of inflation. The Federal Reserve has several tools to increase the supply of money. One way is to reduce reserve requirements for banks. This allows the banks to lend more money. Another way is to lower short-term interest rates. This allows banks to borrow more money from the Fed, which allows for more lending. Finally, the Fed can purchase Treasury bonds from private brokers. All three of these methods have one thing in common: The first people to receive the new money or the benefit thereof are banks and private brokers—the most well connected to the financial system. The first people the banks will lend money to are large corporations and other financial institutions. They'll use that money to buy back stock or purchase stock, respectively. This is partly why despite the economy bottoming out during the COVID-19 pandemic, the stock market hit record highs. The economy was flush with cash, and it was dumped into the stock market.

Easy-money policies free up money for midsize and small businesses to borrow—and people to purchase homes with new loans. But they're still paying interest to the banks who lent the money either freed up or given to them by the Fed. Again, it's the financial system and those connected to it who make the most money. In addition, being the first to utilize new money circulated into the economy is an enormous advantage. It allows the most well connected to use the dollars before inflation is felt. They get all the benefits of having increased capital without any of the downsides. Who does suffer all the downsides? It's members of working class who don't have investments and rely on savings instead of stocks. Their savings and paychecks get devalued as they are left out of the Wall Street boom.

The historic depth of this commitment to stable property (and therefore stable currency and debts) can be seen in the Article VI constitutional provision that "All Debts contracted and Engagements entered into, before the Adoption of this Constitution, shall be as valid against the United States under this Constitution, as under the Confederation."[4] This commitment to honoring debts was still powerful eight decades later, when the Fourteenth Amendment was adopted with a Section 4 that asserted: "The validity of the public debt of the United States, authorized by law, including debts incurred for payment of pensions and bounties for services in suppressing insurrection or rebellion, shall not be questioned."[5]

Advocates for the newly proposed Constitution made clear the importance of money. In Federalist 30 they asserted, "Money is, with propriety, considered as the vital principle of the body politic; as that which sustains its life and motion, and enables it to perform its most essential functions. A complete power, therefore, to procure a regular and adequate supply of it, as far as the resources of the community will permit, may be regarded as an indispensable ingredient in every constitution."[6]

Alexander Hamilton, the first secretary of the Treasury and the man who created a system of stable American currency and credit, explained: "Credit, private or public, is of greatest consequence to every country. Of this, it might be called the invigorating principle."

To have a stable currency and a limited national debt, the Founding Fathers developed a strict habit of government frugality. As Thomas Jefferson wrote: "I, however, place economy among the first and most important republican virtues, and public debt as the greatest of the dangers to be feared."[7] Jefferson argued in his first inaugural address that "[a] wise and frugal government, which shall restrain men from injuring one another, shall leave them otherwise free to regulate their own pursuits of industry and improvement, and shall not take from the mouth of labor the bread it has earned."[8]

This system of stable money, low taxation, and a deep bias toward allowing people to keep the money they earned came to define the American system. Except for wartime spending, government frugality was the norm from 1789 to the election of Franklin Delano Roosevelt in 1932. Only with Roosevelt's New

Deal and the massive growth of government did deficit spending in peacetime become typical. Today the difference between those states that have limited bureaucracies, lower taxes, and less debt and the states with huge bureaucracies, enormous budgets, and massive regulations is remarkable. It is not an accident that Nebraska—a state with a tradition of frugality that is led by businessman-turned-governor Pete Ricketts—has a 1.7 percent unemployment rate.

The lessons of history are clear: Money should be stable (with little or no inflation). Budgets should be frugal and balanced. Individual opportunities to work, earn, and save should be maximized. President Biden and the Big Government Socialists are presently rejecting this lesson. The United States is set to pay about $560 billion in interest on the debt in 2022. This is roughly one-tenth of the entire budget. This number will only increase as we continue to add debt. Then consider that the Federal Reserve plans to raise interest rates multiple times in 2022. This could become a real problem for the U.S. Treasury, and therefore the American taxpayer. We will get into a cycle where we are forced to choose between runaway inflation or paying even more interest, which will only increase the deficit, adding more debt. When we did the Contract with America, we included a provision that would allow people the option of using a percentage of their tax bill to pay down the national debt. This could be an idea worth revisiting.

ESSENTIAL STRENGTH

The world has always been perilous—locally and globally. There are criminal elements, terrorist cells, and foreign governments that are dangerous and mean us harm. Hopeful, idealistic weakness is an invitation to disaster, whether in dealing with murderers, rapists, and carjackers at home or dealing with those who would kill us and destroy our country from overseas. As Texas senator Phil Gramm said when he announced his presidential candidacy in 1995, "even in a world where the lion and the lamb are about to lie down together, I want America to always be the lion."[9]

As President Washington wrote in his Farewell Address, it was vital for America "to progress without interruption to that degree of strength and consistency which is necessary to give it, humanly speaking, the command of its own fortunes."[10] The Founding Fathers had learned the hard way in the Revolutionary War that they needed to establish a tradition of self-reliance and strength. It took courage—moral and physical—to cross the stormy Atlantic in small ships. It took bravery and an enormous amount of work to carve a way of life in the wilderness. The constant skirmishing with Native Americans, and the seven years of the French and Indian War (as it was called in the New World), took relentless strength. Being unprepared or unwary could easily lead to torture and death. When the soldiers and settlers at Fort William were disarmed and then attacked by the Native American allies of the French, it was termed a massacre in popular reporting. The concept that being vulnerable could be fatal was further driven into the colonial American culture.

The Founding Fathers knew that without armed strength, their protests would have been crushed in 1775 at Concord and Lexington. The War of Independence depended on their ability to equip, train, field, and finance an army for freedom to succeed. The participants in the Constitutional Convention and the first several Congresses were all deeply worried by the scale of the European war over the French Revolution. It exploded in

1792, continued until the Treaty of Amiens in 1802, and then was resumed in 1803. The Napoleonic Wars lasted until 1815. Those wars were large and involved many men and resources. The Founding Fathers were watching and knew they had to be armed enough to deter attacks by the Europeans—and also avoid getting involved if possible.

While avoiding the European war between great powers, the American experience continued to involve violence and strength. At home, there was constant skirmishing on the western frontier (then Ohio and Indiana). This included the historic battle at Fallen Timbers in 1794. Domestically, there was deep resistance by western farmers to a tax on whiskey designed to help pay off the Revolutionary War debt. Ultimately, President Washington raised an army of thirteen thousand to make resistance by the farmers impossible. Note the willingness to use force even against Americans—and the determination to make that force overwhelming.

While the United States sought to avoid entanglement with Britain, France, Spain, and others, the leaders decided the Barbary pirates of North Africa were intolerable. The pirates raided peaceful commerce in the Mediterranean, seized people, and sold them into slavery. President Jefferson, while professing a desire to avoid conflict, sent a naval expedition with Marines to punish the pirates and force a treaty that would end their depredations. The war lasted five years and ended with an American victory. It is why "the shores of Tripoli" are mentioned in the Marine Corps Hymn.

When the United States finally drifted into war with Great Britain in 1812, largely over British naval seizure of American sailors, the lack of preparation led to a generally poor performance by American forces, with three historic exceptions.

First, Fort McHenry in Baltimore Harbor withstood a siege, as witnessed by Dr. Francis Scott Key. From that experience, he wrote the national anthem. It was no accident that the close of the first stanza is "the land of the free and the home of the brave." Key was reflecting on the reality that without bravery, freedom would be rapidly lost to the more powerful and the more courageous.

Second, in one of those mythical accidents that create legends, the British decided to attack New Orleans even though it was well defended. The attack occurred after the Treaty of Peace had been signed. However, given the slow communications of that era, neither side knew that peace had been brokered. What made New Orleans unique on the American side was the aggressiveness and military capabilities of its commander, then-general Andrew Jackson. He had a long history as a tough campaigner against Native Americans, and he was an aggressive, even pugnacious personality. For a young country that had been badly battered in the War of 1812 (the White House was burned and the capital occupied), the victory of New Orleans came as a lightning bolt of hope. It led to Jackson ultimately becoming an extraordinarily tough president whose victory represented the victory of a grassroots populism over the establishment that had dominated the government for forty years.

Third, in the war at sea Americans did surprisingly well despite the overwhelming power of the British Royal Navy. American ships and captains did far better than their compatriots on land and gave the country a belief that preparedness in training men and equipment was essential in naval matters.

The result would be a consistent favoritism for naval expenditures over army expenditures in peacetime.

This pattern of strength mattering and the world being dangerous has continued throughout American history. President Lincoln had to mobilize the entire North. For four long years he had to sustain support for a campaign to crush the South and force it back into the Union despite enormous casualties (the most in American history).

The sense of the importance of strength in a dangerous world was also present in the frontier traditions that ran from the mountain men to the cowboys. Gunfights in which the good guys defeated the bad guys (the gunfight at the OK Corral being the most famous) became an American archetype. In the twentieth century, the movies deepened and made vivid the importance of strength in defeating evil (think of *On the Waterfront, High Noon, The Untouchables,* or even *Star Wars*). The ideology of the American intelligentsia may be a pleasant, safe world in which force is unnecessary. But the deeper cultural belief is that evil exists, danger lurks, and you had better be prepared and capable of defending yourself and your loved ones at home and abroad.

The woke elements of Big Government Socialism want you to think *The Lion King* is a documentary and that lions and zebras sing and dance together. But most Americans realize that protecting zebras means stopping lions—and that may make the lions pretty unhappy. Strength in a dangerous world is a core value of American civilization.

Whether dealing with crime at home or violence abroad, strength is a necessary prerequisite. Consider whether Vladimir Putin would have invaded Ukraine if U.S. leadership had been willing to use our strength decisively. All planning should start from a recognition that evil and danger exist—and they have to be overmatched by whatever kind of strength is necessary to defeat them and protect the innocent. Again, these are not specific solutions for the problems we face today, but they are where we must start.

CHAPTER FOUR

THE ROT AT THE TOP

Big Government Socialism corrupts.

It corrupts rich, multimillionaire CEOs lobbying for taxpayer bailouts. It corrupts poor, part-time hourly workers hiding their income from the government so they can keep getting welfare benefits. It corrupts the bureaucrats and administrators whose job it is to decide who gets money and who doesn't. It also corrupts the news media, academia, and all the institutions and people who interact with it.

Big Government Socialism corrupts because its primary function is to take money from one group and give it to another. This means that the more a society embraces Big Government Socialism, the more the people of that society focus their creative energy on manipulating government rather than being productive.

Of course, it's not just about money. It's about power. When government is more powerful, elections and the decisions made by government leaders become more consequential. The higher the stakes, the more willing political leaders (elected officials, campaign staff, or activist news media personalities) are to do anything to win. Once they win through dishonesty and deceit, they govern in the same corrupt way. It's worth it, they justify to themselves, because the stakes are so high for the country that worrying about the morality of your actions is an act of silly vanity. The powerful, the elite, those who benefit from the Big Government Socialist system, begin to believe they should be held to different standards than normal people because of the great responsibility they wield.

As promised, I again bring up Lord Acton. This corruption is exactly what he warned about in 1887 in his famous series of letters to Bishop Creighton concerning how historians should write about the Spanish Inquisition:

> I cannot accept your canon that we are to judge Pope and King unlike other men, with a favourable presumption that they did no wrong. If there is any presumption it is the other way against holders of power, increasing as the power increases. Historic responsibility has to make up for the want of legal responsibility. Power tends to corrupt and absolute power corrupts absolutely. Great men are almost always bad men, even when they exercise influence and not authority: still more when you superadd the tendency or the certainty of corruption by authority. There is no worse heresy than that the office sanctifies the holder of it.

The most famous phrase from those letters is that "power corrupts." But the last sentence in the highlighted paragraph is possibly more profound. "There is no worse heresy than that the office sanctifies the holder of it."

Earlier, I wrote about Senator Daniel Patrick Moynihan's concept of "defining deviancy down" and Charles Krauthammer's corollary that doing so makes normal behavior seem deviant. But Moynihan and Krauthammer were mostly talking about problems affecting poorer areas, such as inner cities.

Their analysis is correct, but the same problem is affecting the elite of America—and the world. In some ways, defining deviancy down for the elite is worse than doing so for the poor. The main victim of deviant behavior by the poor is themselves and those immediately around them. This is a tragedy. Meanwhile, the corruption of the elite affects the entire country because of the massive power they wield. That is a crisis, one similar to that which the Founding Fathers perceived in England that led to the revolution. As Gordon Wood wrote:

> England, the Americans said over and over again, "once the land of liberty—the school of patriots—the nurse of heroes, has become the land of slavery—the school of parricides and the nurse of tyrants." By the 1770's the metaphors describing England's course were all despairing: the nation was fast streaming toward a cataract, hanging on the edge of a precipice; the brightest lamp of liberty in all the world was dimming. Internal decay was the most common image. A poison had entered the nation and was turning the people and the government into "one mass of corruption." On the eve of the Revolution the belief that England was "sunk in corruption" and "tottering on the brink of destruction" had become entrenched in the minds of disaffected Englishmen on both sides of the Atlantic.[1]

The true target of the Founding Fathers' ire was not the common English citizen. It was leadership, the elite, from whom the corruption sprang. The Declaration of Independence is a catalog of the corruption of the British ruling elite justifying the colonies' break from England.

Today, a similar rebellion is brewing against the elite of America—and indeed the world. They insist that simply because of their wealth or power, they should be held to different standards than the rest of us. They also believe their status confers on them the right to make decisions that should be left up to all of us, the people, via democratic and republican systems under the rule of law.

STAKEHOLDER CAPITALISM, THE GREAT RESET, AND THE AUTHORITARIAN IMPULSE OF THE ELITE

In his book *The Wealth of Nations*, Adam Smith warned: "People of the same trade seldom meet together, even for merriment and diversion, but the conversation ends in a conspiracy against the public, or in some contrivance to raise prices."

The quote is often taken out of context to be a warning against unfettered capitalism. In fact, Smith was warning against the collusion of government and the merchant class. He goes on to say that preventing such meetings would be "inconsistent with liberty and justice," so government "must do nothing to facilitate such assemblies; much less render them necessary."

In our public opinion research with the American Majority Project, we have consistently seen that Americans have the highest levels of dissatisfaction with industries such as health care, higher education, energy, and telecommunications. All these industries share a common characteristic: They are intimately intertwined with government. They are all partly paid by the government, partly protected from competition by government, and have government programs and regulations intimately tied into their business models. They are as much an example of free market capitalism as a fishbowl is an example of a coral reef.

Alarmingly, there is a global movement afoot to further intertwine big business and big government. If it is not stopped, the result will be far worse than more dissatisfied customers. It risks destroying democratic governance itself and the transforming of free, democratic societies into authoritarian regimes more like China than the United States.

The movement is called "stakeholder capitalism" and it is the latest craze of the global elite that gather at places like the World Economic Forum (WEF) in Davos, Switzerland. WEF is a club of billionaires and powerful government officials united in the lofty goal of being "Committed to Improving the State of the World." They spend a few days attending seminars on issues such as climate change and global poverty and then fly home on their private jets or to their yachts parked off the Amalfi Coast. Attendance at the forum can cost hundreds of thousands of dollars, thus making an appearance at the annual event possibly the most expensive act of useless virtue-signaling available today. No wonder it is so popular.

The Davos crowd wants to appear as if they are acting for the good of the world, but they keep inadvertently revealing their autocratic tendencies. In 2020, WEF branded its annual meeting with the creepy theme "The Great Reset." Then it released an equally creepy video promising that by 2030, under the guise of the visionary leadership of the world's elite, we will all "own nothing and be happy." Somehow I doubt they were including themselves as owning nothing. The most recent conference featured Bill Gates and WEF head Klaus Schwab praising Chinese Communist Party general secretary Xi Jinping for the country's magnificent economic growth and supposedly brilliant response to the COVID-19 pandemic.

It is clear that many of the attendees would prefer a Chinese Communist Party system of authoritarianism that cleared the way for them to enact their agendas. This is where stakeholder capitalism comes in. Stakeholder capitalism is the vehicle by which the Davos crowd hopes to achieve their goals of solving global problems while maintaining their own power and prestige. Understanding stakeholder capitalism and why it is so different than traditional free market capitalism is vital to understanding much of what is happening in the world today. It is a big reason why in democratic countries around the world, citizens vote for change again and again, and so little actually changes. It is why government is so unresponsive to the people, and why corporate America is increasingly unresponsive to its customers.

Stakeholder capitalism presents itself as an alternative to "shareholder capitalism." Instead of a corporation being primarily responsible to its shareholders (the owners), stakeholder capitalism is supposed to make corporations responsible for meeting the needs of everyone impacted by its actions.[2] This goal may sound appealing but in practice it is a vehicle for corruption.

There are some downsides to shareholder capitalism. Critics argue it tends to promote short-term thinking, and there may be something to this. However, shareholder capitalism has one big advantage: its simplicity. By meeting the demands of the customer, a corporation earns more money and maximizes value for shareholders. Furthermore, the company has a simple way of knowing whether it is meeting customer demand: sales. If the customer is happy, the shareholder is happy.

This simple arrangement, however, requires a free market to work to mutual benefit. When the government grants businesses artificial monopolies and creates barriers to entry for competition with excess regulations, corporations can ignore the needs of their customers and keep making money. This collusion is exactly what Smith warned would become conspiracies against the public.

This type of collusion between big business and big government is at the heart of the stakeholder capitalism model. It is a natural outgrowth of the Big Government Socialist model of more regulations benefiting the most powerful and well-connected corporations. In stakeholder capitalism, corporate and government leaders drop the pretense of an adversarial relationship and "cooperate" to supplant meeting the needs of the customer with meeting the needs of the "global good"—as defined by the values and priorities of the global elite, of course.

In exchange for subordinating the demands of customers with the elites' perception of what is good for society, corporations are offered protection from consumer backlash via guaranteed market share and other forms of protection. If we think the power of lobbyists and insider corruption is bad now, wait until "stakeholder capitalism" becomes the norm.

The dirty secret of the corporate and governing elite is that they look down on the rest of us. They hate having to meet the demands of the customer, which includes voters. This is because they view the priorities and values of the people as self-interested and narrow-minded, while they convince themselves that their priorities are global and virtuous. Even if you assume the good intent of the elite, the fact is that they are so disconnected from the lives of normal people that they are incapable of acting in the best interest of all.

In recent years, we have seen two vivid examples of stakeholder capitalism in action. The first is in energy. For years, the focus of the Davos crowd has been lowering greenhouse gas emissions to fight climate change. Their method of doing so is to reduce energy use and switch power generation over to wind and solar. This is even though global energy demand is skyrocketing globally, and fossil fuels are still the most reliable and least expensive form of energy on the planet.

In the shareholder capitalism model, if energy companies were to switch to less reliable forms of power, they would be punished by their customers. However, because power industries are so heavily regulated by governments across the world, and many have practical monopolies already, government leaders and private industry have been willing to work together to switch to renewable forms of industry despite the reduction in capacity.

The result is most vivid in Europe, which is experiencing a severe energy crisis that is ironically causing them to purchase more natural gas from Russia. We also see it in California, which has aggressively switched to renewable energy only to find itself with regular "brownout" problems in the summer, when energy usage is high.[3, 4] This is stakeholder capitalism working exactly as intended. The customer suffers for the good of the world, but the company and its wealthy leadership are protected from consumer backlash or financial hardship.

That protection goes both ways. Just as corporations can escape accountability from their customers, stakeholder capitalism gives governments a mechanism to escape accountability from their citizens. If government leaders want to restrict consumer choice for the good of society in a traditional democratic society, they need to pass laws doing so, and then justify their actions to the voters in elections. But stakeholder capitalism allows government leaders to use corporate power to limit consumer choice in back rooms, in secret, without needing to ever write legislation.

BIG TECH CENSORSHIP: STAKEHOLDER CAPITALISM IN ACTION

Worse, stakeholder capitalism allows the governing elite to trample on citizens' rights by using corporate power to do things that are illegal for governments to do in free societies. The clearest example of this phenomenon is big tech and major media censorship of content that the government or other elite powers find objectionable.

The idea that this could happen in the United States of America, which prides itself on the protection of basic liberties enshrined in the Bill of Rights, starting with the freedom of speech, is both a tragedy and a crisis of identity for our country.

Alexis de Tocqueville, the great chronicler of American exceptionalism in the mid-nineteenth century, marveled at our protection of speech as a defense against "the tyranny of the majority over the minority." Critically, he was not just talking about the danger of the majority using the machinery of government to suppress minority views; he was talking about a social phenomenon. He argued that in democracies, before a majority opinion is formed, there is "great liberty of debate." However, once majority opinion crystallizes, the tolerance for minority opinion can evaporate. For those on the outside, "your fellow creatures will shun you like an impure being, and those who are most persuaded of your innocence will abandon you too, lest they should be shunned in their turn."[5]

Consider how perfectly this warning from the nineteenth century describes the cancel culture of today. For Tocqueville, the protection of speech was not just essential for government, but as a national value. He deeply influenced John Stuart Mill, who in *On Liberty* wrote:

> Protection, therefore, against the tyranny of the magistrate is not enough: there needs protection also against the tyranny of the prevailing opinion and feeling; against the tendency of society to impose, by other means than civil penalties, its own ideas and practices as rules of conduct on those who dissent from them; to fetter the development, and, if possible, prevent the formation, of any individuality not in harmony with its ways, and compel all characters to fashion themselves upon the model of its own. There is a limit to the legitimate interference of collective opinion with individual independence: and to find that limit, and maintain it against encroachment, is as indispensable to a good condition of human affairs, as protection against political despotism.[6]

The big tech oligarchs and major media powers who have gone all in on censorship of content that runs against the official narrative are failing this test and paving the way for political despotism. Whether it is criticism of woke racial and gender radical ideology, criticism of the 2020 election, or challenges to the government's response to the pandemic, big tech regularly suppresses and bans content that runs counter to the official government narrative.

Even when start-ups emerge that cater to those who value free speech, they are constantly under threat. The internet is a deeply interconnected system of services that all work together to create the experience we enjoy today. Many of these services, such as credit card processing, search, and hosting, are controlled by a small number of large companies. These big companies can effectively make it impossible for a start-up to do business by denying them access to the essential services that create the infrastructure of the online experience. Whereas the U.S. government, because of the protections afforded in the Bill of Rights, lacks the power to shut these companies down, the big tech Goliaths have it. Stakeholder capitalism creates the mechanism by which the elite of the world conspire to violate our rights without any checks on their power.

Ultimately, stakeholder capitalism is about avoiding accountability. It allows corporations to avoid accountability to their customers, replacing meeting their needs with the values of the corporate and governing elite. It also allows the governing elite to avoid accountability to the voters, because it uses corporate power to accomplish what government power cannot.

"MISINFORMATION," "CONSPIRACY THEORIES," AND THE DANGER WHEN DISHONESTY BECOMES EXPECTED

Of course, the ruling class has a pithy dismissal for justifying censorship, including concerns about stakeholder capitalism and their "Great Reset" type agendas: It's "misinformation" or a "conspiracy theory."

This is a clever retort because the truth is, there is a lot of false information to be found online, including some truly outlandish claims about Davos and the Great Reset agenda. This is a classic trick of politics and propaganda: Define all alternatives to the preferred narrative by the most extreme among them. In this way, legitimate concerns about the improper collusion of government and corporate power are lumped into the same category as claims that the Davos crowd planned the pandemic.

To be clear: I don't want to excuse the actions of people spreading nonsense on social media (or the lack of discretion of those who so easily buy into it) but the fact is that this country has always had cranks and conspiracy theorists. It's a grand American tradition. Just ask the guys who faked the moon landing (late trigger warning: sarcasm).

What is new and dangerous is the degree to which the institutions we are supposed to be able to trust, such as the mainstream news media and our public servants, have become so dedicated to the Big Government Socialist agenda that they are willing to spin, prevaricate, and sometimes outright lie to advance it. This is another example of stakeholder capitalism in action. Journalists, academia, and the scientific community have abandoned the mission of their professions—to find and tell the truth, no matter what the consequences—in favor of a commitment to a political agenda they view as being for the greater good. Instead of speaking truth to power, they're colluding with power—and feeling morally superior in the process.

The misinformation and spin coming from our own government and major institutions are a far greater danger to democracy than that which is coming from cranks on Twitter and Joe Rogan's podcast. In fact, you can make the case that it is the former feeding the latter, because when people get the sense that their own government and major news sources are lying to them, they will turn to alternative sources of information and be primed to believe those selling a fantastic tale of dark forces conspiring against them.

The spin, corruption, and lies from sources we should be able to trust are a mortal threat to civilization itself. Mutual trust is the foundation upon which civilization works. For millennia, humans evolved to live in small groups, where we knew by reputation whom to trust and whom not to. What allowed humanity to advance past this stage was the creation of laws and customs that allowed us to trust relative strangers. This trust is what allowed us to move from tribes to settlements to cities, and countries. The more lies that are told, the more our system of government and our institutions are corrupted by woke politics and self-serving agendas, the more the foundation of freedom in our society becomes cracked and unstable.

THE BRILLIANCE OF "LET'S GO BRANDON"

Americans are starting to fight back against the cavalcade of lies and woke nonsense emanating from the governing and powerful elite.

"Let's Go Brandon" was born from a weird—and funny—moment of live television. In the fall of 2021, many college football and other sporting events started returning to normal capacity at their stadiums. This led to a lot of predictable hand-wringing from the acolytes of Big Government Socialism, who, even after vaccines for COVID-19 were made available to anyone who wants one, were terrified of the idea that people might go back to living their lives.

This was also right after the Afghanistan withdrawal disaster. It was also around the time that most Americans realized that inflation and a broken supply chain were major problems (before the White House would admit it). The result of this frustration with President Joe Biden's leadership was a crude chant that began to be heard at many sporting events: "F*** Joe Biden."

On October 2, 2021, at the Talladega Superspeedway in Alabama, Brandon Brown won his first-ever NASCAR victory. As he was being interviewed live by NBC Sports Network after the race, a group of fans started yelling the anti-Biden chant in the stands. It was clearly audible on the broadcast. The reporter, perhaps trying to stay on message (or protect her employers from a Federal Communications Commission fine), chimed in: "As you can hear, the chants from the crowd—'Let's go, Brandon!'"

The absurdity of the obvious lie struck a chord because it reminded millions of Americans of how the news media refuses to report the news honestly. The clip went viral on social media, and at that moment the "Let's Go Brandon" movement was born. "Let's Go Brandon" is about more than President Biden's leadership. It is a declaration of defiance. It says: "We're on to your spin and your lies." Millions of Americans adopted the phrase on hats, bumper stickers, and other paraphernalia as an expression of defiance against the lies of the elite and powerful trying to shout down the common sense of normal Americans.

The lies that "Let's Go Brandon" calls out are replete. The following is hardly an exhaustive list, but they are some of the most egregious.

- Gender is independent from sex.
- Critical Race Theory is not being taught in schools.

- America is systemically racist.
- All white people are inherently racist.
- The Black Lives Matter riots across America were "mostly peaceful" and legitimate expressions of frustration.
- Every single one of the ten-thousand-plus people who gathered in Washington, D.C., on January 6, 2021, to protest the 2020 election wanted to violently overthrow the government.
- Follow the science. No, not that science, "the science."
- Masks? No masks? Only masks for the voters, not the leaders.
- Defunding the police will lead to less crime.
- Inflation is transitory.
- Russian collusion helped Donald Trump and stopped Hillary Clinton.
- Hunter Biden's laptop from hell was Russian disinformation.
- Hunter Biden selling his artwork for hundreds of thousands of dollars (potentially to foreign nationals) is not corruption.
- Killing America's oil and gas industry is worth the cost.
- Leaving Afghanistan was done brilliantly and a great success.
- Two million people a year illegally crossing our southern border is not a problem.
- Flying illegal immigrants into cities and towns around the country with no checks on public health status or criminal records is perfectly reasonable.

But by far, the most appalling lies of the last few years have centered on the pandemic.

A PANDEMIC OF LIES: HOW COVID-19 BROKE SCIENCE AND PUBLIC HEALTH

The past two years have revealed a clear difference between medical science and public health.

Medical science is slow, rarely conclusive, relatively narrow in its pronouncements, and humble about the possibility of new information changing what we know. Moreover, it is messy. Medical science rarely produces definitive conclusions, due to the incredibly complex and individualized nature of human biology.

Public health, in contrast, has an agenda—to convince Americans to act a certain way. Because of that agenda, public health advocates like to communicate absolute certainty, and they resist sharing information that might muddy their message.

There is also a big difference between public health and personal health. The latter is unique to you and your circumstances. In public health, your unique circumstances cannot be accounted for. Moreover, your personal health is less important than how your decisions impact society at large. These key differences between medical science and public health, and personal and public health, mean that public health has a lot more in common with politics than it does with science; and public health advocates behave a lot more like politicians than they do your doctor. The public health advocates we hear and see may have scientific and medical credentials. However, when they appear on television and at press conferences, they are not there in their capacity as scientists and doctors—they are there as public health advocates. They are politicians wearing a lab coat and stethoscope.

Aided by their allies in the mainstream media, who cast aside their obligation to be skeptical of information being fed to them in favor a stakeholder capitalism rationale of "saving grandma," the public health advocacy complex spent two years making misleading statements and peddling half-truths to an increasingly dubious American public. Anytime someone questioned what they were saying, we were scolded to trust "the science" and marginalized for questioning the dominant narrative. This may have been a viable strategy for a short period of time. But as the pandemic wore on, Americans began to see through the spin and recognize the politics. The more people began to speak up and question what we were being told, the more rigid, dogmatic, and arrogant the information arbiters and so-called trusted sources became. The result was a debasement of science and public health in service of a purely political power grab.

THE WUHAN LAB AND PARSING THE DEFINITION OF "GAIN OF FUNCTION" EXPERIMENTS

We now know that the pandemic began with a series of lies. We were lied to when we were told that the virus started in a wet market in Wuhan, China, and likely was transferred from a pangolin to a human. We were lied to when we were told that Chinese scientists were cooperating with the international community and sharing information. We were lied to when we were told that the idea that the virus could have come from the Wuhan Institute of Virology, which collects and conducts experiments on coronaviruses to see how they could become more lethal to humans, was a conspiracy theory and not supported by science. We were also lied to when we were told that the U.S. government does not fund these types of experiments, commonly called "gain of function." Importantly, we know we were lied to not *because* of the news media and scientific establishment's efforts to expose the truth, but despite them.

It was a spontaneously organized group of researchers on Twitter, who called themselves DRASTIC and spent countless hours poring through Chinese scientific databases, who exposed the truth about the Chinese government and scientific and public health community's efforts to cover up key facts about COVID-19's origins. DRASTIC discovered that the Wuhan Institute of Virology was collecting and conducting experiments on coronavirus samples, including one sample that is the closest known match to SARS-CoV-2 ever found in nature.[7]

They discovered that claims by the Chinese scientists and groups that work with them that this sample was never experimented on were lies.[8] They discovered that the three Chinese scientists who died collecting this—and hundreds of other samples—did not die of a fungal infection, as was claimed in official Chinese government reports, but instead from a "SARS-like virus."[9] They discovered that the first cases of COVID-19 occurred weeks before the outbreak in the Wuhan wet market, which was initially claimed to be ground zero of the infection.[10]

Additionally, it was Republican congressional investigations, not a crack investigative reporter at the *New York Times*, that revealed that the world's top virologists—including U.S. officials Anthony Fauci and Francis Collins—were saying one thing in public about a potential lab leak origin of COVID-19 but another in private. Notes from phone calls on January 30, 2020, and February 1, 2020, revealed that several of the scientists who just a few days later signed a letter in *The Lancet* praising China and calling the lab leak theory a conspiracy theory thought it was more likely than not that the virus was the product of experimentation.[11]

Furthermore, it was a Freedom of Information Act request filed by Right to Know—not a government inspector general—that revealed that this letter was organized by the head of EcoHealth Alliance, a group that received National Institutes of Health grants that were funneled to the Wuhan Institute of Virology. And that he went out of his way to hide the fact that he organized it.[12] It was other Freedom of Information Act requests filed by citizen groups that revealed that EcoHealth Alliance was funding "gain of function" research at the Wuhan Institute of Virology designed to increase the transmissibility of viruses found in nature to humans. And that government officials, including Fauci, were relying on a highly technical and specific definition of "gain of function" to falsely claim that the U.S. government could not have helped fund them.

From the assembled information from alternative news sources, which were later repeated by more mainstream outlets once they realized they were being made to look stupid, it is clear there was a conscious effort by the scientific establishment to suppress the lab leak theory—not because it was unlikely, but precisely because it was likely, and they feared the consequences.[13, 14] Namely, that it would hurt scientific cooperation with China, dry up funding for research, and increase distrust in science. Of course, all three of these consequences seem likely to happen anyway, and they only have their dishonesty to blame.

FREE SPEECH FOR ME, BUT NOT FOR THEE

The second great violation of the public's trust by the COVID-19 public health advocacy complex occurred in response to the

Black Lives Matter protests sparked by the murder of George Floyd by a police officer in Minneapolis, Minnesota. After months of Americans being told to isolate and that close contact with others—even outside—was dangerous, public health advocates suddenly changed their tune. More than 1,200 "health professionals" signed a letter explaining that protests against "the pervasive lethal force of white supremacy" were good for public health but other protests they didn't agree with—for example, against stay-at-home orders—were dangerous.

> [A]s public health advocates, we do not condemn these gatherings as risky for COVID-19 transmission. We support them as vital to the national public health and to the threatened health specifically of Black people in the United States. We can show that support by facilitating safest protesting practices without detracting from demonstrators' ability to gather and demand change. This should not be confused with a permissive stance on all gatherings, particularly protests against stay-home orders.

They even went so far as to say that the protests would help combat the pandemic:

> Instead, we wanted to present a narrative that prioritizes opposition to racism as vital to the public health, including the epidemic response. We believe that the way forward is not to suppress protests in the name of public health but to respond to protesters['] demands in the name of public health, thereby addressing multiple public health crises.[15]

Apparently, it doesn't take masks and vaccines to stop the spread of COVID-19. All it takes is being "on the right side of history" and we can become immune.

Former CDC director Tom Frieden got into the act as well. In March 2020, he wrote that responding to growing pressure to "resume social and economic activity" was not "informed by thoughtful analysis or public health expertise." Just a few weeks later he had a much more nuanced view in response to the BLM riots: "The threat to COVID control from protesting outside is *tiny* compared to the threat to COVID control created when governments act in ways that lose community trust."[16, 17] He's right: Government losing the trust of the community is a big problem. And hypocrisy and double standards are a big way to lose that trust.

The public health establishment's hypocrisy created the cover that politicians and activists needed.

In April 2020, Michigan governor Gretchen Whitmer said anti-lockdown protests were going to "endanger people's lives because this is precisely how COVID-19 spreads."[18] In June 2020, she participated in a Black Lives Matter protest, stating, "I felt it was an important moment to show my support."[19]

In July 2020, the state of California banned singing in church and required that they only be filled to 25 percent of building capacity but made no such restrictions on protests.[20] In April 2020, CNN analyst April Ryan asked if Americans protesting lockdowns should be required to sign a waiver refusing medical attention.[21] In June 2020 she tweeted support for the BLM protesters, calling them "Americans protesting human rights violations."[22]

The signers of the letter and the mainstream media voices who amplified the sentiment behind it were engaging in politics, not public health, and certainly not medical science. The American people knew it. No amount of letter-signing and credential-waving could convince normal Americans that protests for one cause would be safe from COVID-19 and another would not be.

To be clear, I'm not saying that they were wrong that the protests could be done safely. Most of us who were critical of the heavy-handed nature of the pandemic response focused on the absurdity of limiting outside gatherings, where there is plenty of natural ventilation. What they were wrong to do was arrogate to themselves the authority to define what exercises of free speech are worthy of government protection and what are not. They destroyed their credibility trying to concoct nonsensical rationales for their double standard.

THE ZERO-COVID FANTASY, VACCINE MANDATES, AND ONE-SIZE-FITS-ALL VACCINE POLICY

The third great violation of public trust between public health officials and the American people occurred at a moment that should have been a great victory. The development of the COVID-19 vaccines in less than a year was a remarkable achievement of both science and public health. It was arguably one of the only things that the government, in partnership with private industry, was able to do right in response to the pandemic. Then it got all screwed up because of the heavy-handed campaign to get everyone vaccinated. It was a perfect example of how public health subsumes the personal nature of health care underneath its agenda.

We have known from the beginning of the pandemic that the risk from COVID-19 varies greatly by age and other risk factors such as obesity and chronic illnesses. When the vaccines first became available, they were rightly prioritized for those over sixty-five and with certain comorbidities. However, the focus of the public health complex soon moved on from protecting those who were most at risk of serious illness to pursuing an impossible "COVID-zero" policy by getting every single person in America vaccinated. There was also rank political opportunism in the mix. The Big Government Socialists understood that Republicans were less likely to want to get vaccinated and were most strongly against lockdown measures and mandatory masking. So the Biden administration decided to polarize the issue further by issuing a vaccine mandate.

This was a political decision, not a health decision. The only legitimate rationale for mass vaccination against a disease is if vaccination successfully controls its spread. However, it has been clear since at least the middle of 2021, when the Delta variant spread throughout the United States, that the primary benefit of vaccination is not preventing infection and spread, but in greatly reducing the severity of the illness. In September 2021, the CDC even changed the definition of "vaccine" and "vaccination" on its website by removing the word *immunity* and replacing it with *protection*.[23]

The disconnects between the facts on the ground about breakthrough infections and the Democrats' desire to polarize the issue led the public health advocacy complex to settle on a fundamentally false narrative: the idea that the unvaccinated posed a risk to the vaccinated.

In announcing his vaccine mandate, President Biden promised to "[protect] vaccinated workers from the unvaccinated."[24] Ironically, this claim undercut the rationale for getting vaccinated, since it muddied the difference between getting a mild infection after vaccination and a more severe infection without one.

Some have tried to argue that the alleged drain on public health resources from the unvaccinated disproportionately needing hospitalization justifies a vaccine mandate. This is a dangerous precedent. Consider that obesity is also major risk factor for hospitalization. Should we mandate exercise? What other personal health decisions should be made mandatory in the name of conserving public resources? Health outcomes are a result of a combination of personal choices and luck, and the ratio of responsibility is unique in each person. One of the great dangers of socialized medicine is that once health spending is the responsibility of the government, there are few aspects of our private life choices that are not legitimately in the interest of the government to regulate. The same danger is to be found in a heavy-handed public health regime that tries to coerce individual behavior for the greater good. The one-size-fits-all vaccine policy manifested itself in many dishonest ways.

One particularly galling example that further eroded the public's trust in public health was ignoring the obvious fact that those who already contracted and recovered from COVID-19 did not need to get vaccinated. I say this was obvious because it fits everything we know about viruses and vaccines. The World Health Organization even explains how vaccines and getting the disease both help on its website. "Vaccines train our immune systems to create proteins that fight disease, known as 'antibodies,' *just as would happen when we are exposed to a disease* but—crucially—vaccines work without making us sick" (emphasis added).

This means that while it is certainly preferable to get vaccinated and avoid potentially serious illness, there is little to be gained from getting vaccinated after you recover. That is there is little to be gained from a personal health standpoint. From an authoritarian public health standpoint, however, there is much to be gained because it creates the imperative for the infrastructure that government needs to exert more control.

When you get vaccinated, there are official records created, like the vaccine cards that many of us received. The same is not true of getting COVID-19, even if you test positive, thanks to the wildly different and sloppy ways that state and local public health agencies keep records and transmit them to the CDC. Acknowledging natural immunity prevents public health officials from being able to exert control and impose restrictions such as vaccine requirements. This was Big Government Socialism in public health rearing its ugly head.

That's why the CDC and other public health officials decided that assuming recovered immunity was dangerous and thus signed a memorandum in October 2020 declaring that there was "no evidence for lasting protective immunity to SARS-CoV-2 following natural infection." Think about when this statement was issued and the word choice. It was issued just six months after COVID-19 came to the United States and talks about "lasting" protective immunity. In other words, there was no evidence because not enough time had passed.

In truth, there were many reasons to believe that recovered immunity was real. Studies on previous dangerous coronaviruses such as SARS and MERS showed robust recovered immunity. Studies in monkeys from May 2020 showed that those who recovered from COVID-19 didn't get sick again when exposed to the virus.[25] Later, when a massive Israeli study published in August 2021 showed that natural immunity was vastly superior to vaccinated immunity in preventing infection, the CDC stuck with its rigid stance of vaccinating everyone, even if they already recovered from COVID-19.[26]

Finally, in January 2022, the CDC released data on reinfection rates for COVID-19. It showed that natural immunity was 3.3 to 4.7 times as effective in preventing COVID-19 infection and 2.8 times as effective in preventing hospitalization as vaccination alone. The data also showed minimal additional benefit from getting vaccinated after recovering from COVID-19.[27] By then it was too late. Millions of vaccines were wasted on people who didn't need them that could have gone to developing countries, and an untold number of Americans were fired thanks to Biden's vaccine mandates, including many working in health care.

The rollout of booster shots also suffered from the Biden administration's one-size-fits-all vaccine policy, further eroding public trust. In fact, two top officials at the Food and Drug Administration (FDA) resigned over the Biden administration's booster shot plan, saying that the White House was ignoring FDA recommendations and processes for determining if boosters were appropriate for everyone.[28]

Despite this litany of overreach and the collapse in public support of our public health institutions due to shifting guidance and being repeatedly proven wrong, the Biden administration is still running full speed ahead with its one-size-fits-all vaccine mandate. As I am writing this, they are planning to make booster shots available to children—the group least susceptible to serious illness from COVID-19—despite little personal or public health benefit.

CHAPTER FIVE

HUMAN NATURE, GOVERNMENT, AND THE RULE OF LAW

At the most basic level, Big Government Socialism and its historic predecessors do not account for human nature. Importantly, they reject human nature for an idealized version of the people their government is trying to create. This is the opposite of the historic American system—and even the classically liberal representative republic.

President Ronald Reagan observed, "The trouble with our Liberal friends is not that they're ignorant; it's just that they know so much that isn't so." He was speaking to a fundamental issue at the heart of left-wing doctrine that prevents its adherents from bringing to fruition their ideal utopian concepts. In part, they fail because their ideas are based on a pattern of thought that is ideologically appealing, but realistically impossible. Simply put: The utopia can't work because it's not made for free, thinking human beings.

The left's idealized utopia is made for imaginary beings who have no self-interest, ambition, sense of fairness, or qualms with perpetually being exploited by their government—and the elites who run it. Because of this, the utopia is designed to have a government that perpetually grows in power (at the expense of its citizens) and follows a different set of rules.

ACCOUNTING FOR HUMAN NATURE

There are patterns of human behavior that have been around for all recorded time. That is why the stories of Homer, the plays of Aeschylus, the lessons of the Bible, and the tragedies, dramas, and comedies of Shakespeare all resonate within us today. *West Side Story* as a modern musical revisioning of *Romeo and Juliet* is a great example of the enduring human story. Big Government Socialism, with its roots in the French, Russian, and Chinese revolutions and its outlook in woke theology, believes humans are plastic, malleable, and easily reshaped. Just as the "New Soviet Man" collapsed in the Soviet Union, and Mao Zedong's efforts to create a permanent cultural revolution in China collapsed, the woke revolution will also collapse. Creating a better future and solving problems must be based on human nature to succeed.

The Founding Fathers were an amazing collection of men who lived practical lives. They were farmers, merchants, lawyers, and investors. They were also experienced in politics and the legislative process. They studied widely and thought deeply. Their lifetimes of experience collectively led them to a tough-minded view of human nature. The Founders all understood that centralized power leads to tyranny. And they would have thought it naive and silly to attempt to design a centralized system for some perfect model of humankind.

Indeed James Madison, in Federalist 51, makes the case for the inevitability of human nature and therefore human weakness:

> But the great security against a gradual concentration of the several powers in the same department, consists in giving to those who administer each department the necessary constitutional means and personal motives to resist encroachments of the others. The provision for defense must in this, as in all other cases, be made commensurate to the danger of attack. Ambition must be made to counteract ambition. The interest of the man must be connected with the constitutional rights of the place. It may be a reflection on human nature, that such devices should be necessary to control the abuses of government. But what is government itself, but the greatest of all reflections on human nature? If men were angels, no government would be necessary. If angels were to govern men, neither external nor internal controls on government would be necessary. In framing a government which is to be administered by men over men, the great difficulty lies in this: you must first enable the government to control the governed; and in the next place oblige it to control itself. A dependence on the people is, no doubt, the primary control on the government; but experience has taught mankind the necessity of auxiliary precautions.[1]

The great danger from the Big Government Socialists has been the stripping away of these auxiliary precautions—and a belief that people can be trusted even if they repeatedly prove to be untrustworthy. When someone has been arrested eleven times before killing a twenty-four-year-old woman as she worked in a furniture store, it is a consequence of the utopian rejection of evil and the need to guard against bad, destructive people.[2]

The rule of law is vital precisely because of the inherent weaknesses that exist at the center of human nature. That is the warning of Sir Thomas More in *A Man for All Seasons*, that if you knock down every law in pursuit of the devil, then the laws are gone when the devil turns on you. Soviet secret police chief Lavrentiy Beria's pledge to Joseph Stalin, "show me the man, and I will show you the crime," is a powerful example of the evil and danger inherent in a world in which the rule of law has been replaced by the rule of man.

So the U.S. Constitution was designed by people who expected normal humans to end up running the government. They assumed the structure had to be designed to preserve freedom by separating powers and pitting egos and interests against one another. In effect, rather than rely on goodwill and purity of intent, the Founding Fathers assumed everyone was self-interested and would seek power. Their goal was to construct a system that balanced different powers against each other. They did not naively think they could tame human nature. They thought they could channel the human pursuit of power in such a way that it would not threaten the survival of a free society. They followed the writings of the French political philosopher Montesquieu, who in his classic, *The Spirit of the Laws*, had advocated dividing up power between different institutions so they would balance each other, and freedom would survive in the balance.

The American model has three divisions in the federal government—legislative, executive, and judicial. They are all bounded by the Bill of Rights, the states, and by the provision that all other powers reside with the citizens. This was all designed to protect individuals, limit government powers, and minimize the risk of dictatorship.

This sense that human nature inevitably led to corruption and coercion was reinforced by the American perception of the British government. In the American view (which reflected the Whig view in Britain), the king and his ministers had corrupted British politics and government by giving away money and status to sustain their political machine at the expense of the public good. Corruption in this model was not merely limited to illegal bribery for specific acts. It referred to any allocation of resources or position for private rather than public ends.

Furthermore, the American colonists' experience of judges was that they were agents of the king and would pervert the law to implement the king's edicts. The result was that reforming the judges was the second most frequent demand of the colonists (after no taxation without representation). It was this fear of loyalist judges that led to the constitutional protections against judicial tyranny. Similarly, it was the general fear of government that led to the Second Amendment right to bear arms. Contrary to the modern left's interpretation, the Founding Fathers were not protecting the right to bear arms so Americans could go deer hunting. Madison, in Federalist 46, argues for the maintenance of militias for citizens to protect themselves. Madison wrote that state militias "would be able to repel the danger" of tyranny:

> Besides the advantage of being armed, which the Americans possess over the people of almost every other nation, the existence of subordinate governments, to

which the people are attached, and by which the militia officers are appointed, forms a barrier against the enterprises of ambition, more insurmountable than any which a simple government of any form can admit of.[3]

Madison further contrasted a free government's comfort with an armed citizenry with European kings who were "afraid to trust the people with arms."

The American belief in the right to bear arms went back to Lexington and Concord on April 19, 1775. As David Hackett Fischer notes in his book *Paul Revere's Ride*, the British Army had routinely overwhelmed peasant rebellions in England, Scotland, Wales, and Ireland. They marched out of Boston that day confident that this would be another mopping-up expedition against an unarmed rabble. However, the British encountered an armed militia that had been training. The militia decisively defeated the British column and sent it reeling back to Boston, leaving a trail of blood. That memory of the power of armed citizens was still vivid fifteen years later as the Bill of Rights was written.

The American left has routinely found it impossible to believe that the Founding Fathers were as suspicious of their own government as of foreign powers. However, their deep belief in the dangers inherent in human nature led them to a series of efforts to safeguard the citizenry from their own government. Those same tensions still exist more than two centuries later.

We learn from the Founders that human nature must be the bedrock on which any policy is built. When we design policies based on theories that do not fit human nature, we inevitably set ourselves up for failure. President Franklin Delano Roosevelt's New Deal was pro-work because Roosevelt believed work was central to a healthy life and a healthy society. By contrast, Lyndon B. Johnson's Great Society embraced radical ideas that assumed the poor were helpless and hopeless—and that government had to intervene to make their dependency more comfortable. Roosevelt understood human nature and built policies to reinforce it. Johnson had been talked into a philosophy that rejected the core principles of thousands of years of experience. Whether it is crime, welfare, education, or a host of other challenges, if the policy does not accept and reinforce human nature, it will fail.

THE DANGER OF BIG GOVERNMENT

The same governmental strength that is necessary to survive in a dangerous world is also a threat to liberty. If freedom is to survive while also being kept safe, it is vital to create a system in which the structure of government, and the rules it must follow, limit its ability to dominate and dictate to its own people.

Again, recall Madison's core argument in Federalist 51. If men were perfect, we wouldn't need government, and so long as government is made up of men, we need to limit it. The depth of the Founders' commitment to freedom from the seduction of power was illustrated by General Washington's determination to return his sword and commission to the Continental Congress when the war ended. The scene is captured in the Maryland state capitol, in Annapolis. Its unique symbolism of voluntarily giving up power was so powerful that King George III, on being told about Washington's relinquishment of power, said, "if he does that, he will be the greatest man in the world."

The Founding Fathers knew that over time, power would be acquired by people who lacked Washington's honor, integrity, and passionate commitment to freedom. They knew that eventually normal people—and even scoundrels—would acquire power. The challenge to the Founders was to design a system that would limit the ability of unscrupulous power seekers to undermine liberty in favor of corruption. Their goal was to design a government structure that would block the acquisition of unchecked power by any agency of government.

Their first step was to adopt the insights of Montesquieu in *The Spirit of the Laws* that a division of power would maximize freedom and minimize the danger of tyranny. As I mentioned, each branch of government would jealously guard its prerogatives and power against the other two. Within the legislative branch, the U.S. Constitution further divides the power between a popularly elected House directly representing the people (and being renewed every two years) and a Senate representing the states, only one-third of which would be elected every two years. The Founders were trying to replicate the division between the House of Commons and House of Lords in London. In the first six years, the effort to make the Senate different went so far as to have the sessions secret, with no recorded votes. Prior to the adoption of the Seventeenth Amendment in 1913, senators were elected by state legislatures. It was only after that amendment that senators were also chosen by popular vote. Specific powers of raising taxes, spending money, and approving presidential appointments were divided between the House and Senate to create two competitive institutions, further dividing power.

Thomas Jefferson felt that the rights of individuals were not sufficiently protected from government in the Constitution and insisted on the adoption of a Bill of Rights, which became the first ten amendments to the Constitution. Despite the gradual erosion of those rights in favor of government power, it is vital to remember that the Bill of Rights was designed to protect the individual *against* government. Furthermore, the Founders wisely reserved all power to the states and the citizens thereof that were not expressly granted to the federal government by the U.S. Constitution.

As an ultimate protection against tyranny, Jefferson often said every generation needed a revolution and the Founding Fathers insisted on the Second Amendment, so the armed citizenry would make a dictatorship impossible. These men were serious about applying the rules of history to sustaining and protecting the freedoms they had won through a generation of struggle and conflict.

The Founding Fathers worked overtime to create a system of limited government and personal liberty. While that system has been eroded by a century of intellectual elites who thought the American people were incorrigible or ignorant, the core of it is still designed to limit government and liberate the American people. It is essential for our long-term freedom that we reestablish the principles of limited power and the rule of law. Every warning the Founding Fathers felt about concentrating power and gradually losing our freedoms applies to our generation.

Again, power tends to corrupt today just as much as in Lord Acton's time. Absolute power still corrupts absolutely. Watch Speaker Nancy Pelosi, who has been establishing a dictatorship in the U.S. House while protecting and promoting members who clearly, blatantly lie even on national security matters.

Read Peter Schweizer's *Red-Handed: How America's Elites Get Rich Helping China Win* and reflect on all the warnings in the Federalist Papers. We need a generation of leaders and determined citizens dedicated to reestablishing the principles of freedom at every level—from Washington, to state capitols, to city and county governments, to school boards, to the activity of individual citizens, including the billionaire oligarchs, many of whom today routinely place profit above patriotism.

REVIVING THE RULE OF LAW AND
THE LEGISLATIVE PROCESS

The rule of law is the heart of protecting the weak from the strong. It creates safe conditions for investing and saving and ensures the continued liberty of the people against the inevitable encroachments of bureaucratic government and self-serving politicians. It also blocks the wealthy and powerful from gaining unfair advantages.

The legislative process is a key building block of engaging the society's consent and making "the consent of the governed" real. It is also through the legislative process that a community educates itself and finds agreements that the entire community is prepared to sustain. The Founding Fathers were deeply immersed in the law. Many of them were lawyers. All of them understood the importance of the law and had participated in writing laws in colonial legislatures before the revolution.

Their entire approach to key decisions revolved around a legislative process. They used that process for fact finding, discussions about possible solutions, building a consensus so that everyone would feel comfortable that the rules and decisions had been reasonably made (even if on occasion people might disagree with one conclusion or another). It is a process-oriented approach to self-government.

The recent breakdown of that legislative process in Washington has been antithetical to this approach. Power has centralized in a small number of people who draft laws in secret and ram them through without amendment or hearings. It is a real threat to the rule of law and the consent of the governed. It also guarantees that laws will be written with too little input and too little critical thinking. No one knows as much as some of the current congressional leaders seem to think. They routinely decide about issues in virtually total lack of knowledge. The results reflect that overly restricted, limited-input system.

The Founding Fathers had a practical reverence for the law. One of their greatest complaints about the British Empire was the replacement of independent judges with servants of the Crown who would distort and prostitute the law to do the king's bidding. All of the Founders understood that undermining the rule of law and replacing independent judges with lackeys to the Crown meant that no one and nothing was safe from the depredations of a tyrannical government.

When in *Henry VI, Part Two*, Shakespeare has a criminal and genuinely bad man say, "the first thing we do, let's kill all the lawyers," he is pointing out the degree to which the lawyers and the law deter criminals and crime. As we are discovering in many of our major cities, when the law is suspended by ideological district attorneys, evil men and women prey upon the innocent. The perversion of the law by George Soros–supported district attorneys has led to death, injury, loss of property, and a dramatic decay of decent society.

It would have been good for the members of the House select committee on the January 6 attacks to have thought deeply on maintaining the rule of law before they began trampling on the Constitution and the principles of liberty in the pursuit of their self-defined crusade. Instead, members of the committee have been spying on Americans without warrant or judicial oversight, using the power of Congress to attack political enemies, serving as a propaganda operation for Big Government Socialism, and operating without due process or any restraint.

The Founding Fathers' faith in the rule of law draws much of its strength from the writing of John Locke. Locke was a late-seventeenth-century philosopher and physician whose thinking and writing was a forerunner for pragmatism and a law-based society.

Locke was wrestling with the complex challenges of the English Civil War. The king was beheaded despite his presumably divine right to the throne. The republican commonwealth of Oliver Cromwell then arose. King Charles II was conditionally restored. Then there was the tumultuous reign of the Catholic King James II and his ousting in 1688 by the "Glorious Revolution," which brought the Protestants William and Mary to the throne. Since William came from the Dutch tradition of representative government, with limited power to the leaders, he had a different approach from the absolute monarchy in which James had believed. The Bill of Rights of 1689 was a parliamentary declaration of limits on the power of the monarchy and a key part of the pact that made William and Mary the rulers of the country with significant limits on their power.

As a champion of the new restoration of a limited monarchy with strong parliamentary power, Locke became the best-known early theorist of representative government under the rule of law. He wrote, "the difference betwixt a king and a tyrant to consist only in this, that one makes the laws the bounds of his power, and the good of the public, the end of government; the other makes all give way to his own will and appetite. Where-ever law ends, tyranny begins."[4] Remember that phrase as you watch the current out-of-control White House, House, and bureaucracy— "where-ever law ends, tyranny begins."

Jefferson studied Locke extensively and can be considered his successor in defending the rule of law. The Founding Fathers' insistence on the rule of law really stands out in the Declaration of Independence. Normally we only read the preamble and stop after we have been reassured that "we are endowed by our Creator with certain unalienable rights."

However, if you take a moment to look at the claims against King George III, you will see how much the Founding generation was offended by what they saw as a tyrannical effort to violate their legal rights as Englishmen. The claims criticized the king for barring the colonists from governing themselves—while also largely neglecting them and their needs. Through this neglect, the colonists saw constant obstacles to maintaining orderly, safe society. However, many of their grievances against King George III in the Declaration of Independence asserted violations of the rule of law and tyranny:

> He has obstructed the Administration of Justice, by refusing his Assent to Laws for establishing Judiciary powers.
>
> He has made Judges dependent on his Will alone, for the tenure of their offices, and the amount and payment of their salaries.
>
> He has erected a multitude of New Offices, and sent hither swarms of Officers to harrass our people, and eat out their substance.

He has kept among us, in times of peace, Standing Armies without the Consent of our legislatures.

He has affected to render the Military independent of and superior to the Civil power.

He has combined with others to subject us to a jurisdiction foreign to our constitution, and unacknowledged by our laws; giving his Assent to their Acts of pretended Legislation:

For Quartering large bodies of armed troops among us:

For protecting them, by a mock Trial, from punishment for any Murders which they should commit on the Inhabitants of these States:

For cutting off our Trade with all parts of the world:

For imposing Taxes on us without our Consent:

For depriving us in many cases, of the benefits of Trial by Jury:

For transporting us beyond Seas to be tried for pretended offences:

For abolishing the free System of English Laws in a neighbouring Province, establishing therein an Arbitrary government, and enlarging its Boundaries so as to render it at once an example and fit instrument for introducing the same absolute rule into these Colonies:

For taking away our Charters, abolishing our most valuable Laws, and altering fundamentally the Forms of our Governments:

For suspending our own Legislatures, and declaring themselves invested with power to legislate for us in all cases whatsoever.

These grievances were seen as so deeply threatening that they led formerly loyal colonists to wage an eight-year war for independence against the most powerful empire in the world. John Adams explained why Americans rejected government by a dictatorial regime and what Americans expected:

> Fear is the foundation of most governments; but is so sordid and brutal a passion, and renders men, in whose breasts it predominates, so stupid, and miserable, that Americans will not be likely to approve of any political institution which is founded on it. . . . so the very definition of a Republic, is "an Empire of Laws, and not of men." That, as a Republic is the best of governments, so that particular arrangement of the powers of society, or in other words that form of government, which is best contrived to secure an impartial and exact execution of the laws, is the best of Republics.[5]

Our current generation of politicians and news media would do well to think about Adams's later assertion that "the great political virtues of humility, patience, and moderation, without which every man in power becomes a ravenous beast of prey." His cousin Samuel Adams summarized the positive goal as "There should be one rule of justice for rich and poor, for the favorite at court, and the countryman at the plough."[6] That was the rule of law the Founding Fathers held as an ideal and were trying to build in America. Two generations later, in 1838, in a speech to the Lyceum in Springfield, Illinois, Abraham Lincoln reaffirmed the importance of the rule of law.

Lincoln called for "a reverence for the constitution and laws." He said:

> Let every American, every lover of liberty, every well wisher to his posterity, swear by the blood of the Revolution, never to violate in the least particular, the laws of the country; and never to tolerate their violation by others. As the patriots of seventy-six did to the support of the Declaration of Independence, so to the support of the Constitution and Laws, let every American pledge his life, his property, and his sacred honor; —let every man remember that to violate the law, is to trample on the blood of his father, and to tear the character of his own, and his children's liberty. Let reverence for the laws, be breathed by every American mother, to the lisping babe, that prattles on her lap—let it be taught in schools, in seminaries, and in colleges; let it be written in Primers, spelling books, and in Almanacs; —let it be preached from the pulpit, proclaimed in legislative halls, and enforced in courts of justice. And, in short, let it become the political religion of the nation; and let the old and the young, the rich and the poor, the grave and the gay, of all sexes and tongues, and colors and conditions, sacrifice unceasingly upon its altars.
>
> While ever a state of feeling, such as this, shall universally, or even, very generally prevail throughout the nation, vain will be every effort, and fruitless every attempt, to subvert our national freedom.[7]

A quarter century later, on the site of the bloodiest battle of our bloodiest war, in his Gettysburg Address, Lincoln captured this sense of the subservience of all of us to the rule of law when he said: "This nation, under God, shall have a new birth of freedom—and that government of the people, by the people, for the people, shall not perish from the earth."

As we watch the bureaucrats grow more arrogant, the lobbyists grow more corrupt, the politicians grow more lawless, and the news media grow more dishonest, we must come once again to Lincoln's understanding that without the rule of law there is no government by the people. That is how important the rule of law is to our freedom and our country. If America is to remain free, we must return to a much more serious enforcement of the rule of law—and a more open legislative process, in which every member has a fair opportunity to participate.

The excessive centralization of power in the presidency is a grave threat to freedom. Presidents are in effect elected kings, and any threat from a king can be replicated in the White House. Centralizing power in a handful of congressmen and senators violates the principle of legislating in a free society. Bureaucracies that can make up their own rules and impose their power on citizens are replicating exactly what the Founding Fathers accused the British monarchy of doing.

It will be a difficult, conflict-ridden, and controversial process to get back to the rule of law at every level of government—local, state, and federal—but it must be done if freedom is to survive.

CHAPTER SIX

POVERTY AND DESPAIR

A gain and again, we have seen how out of touch Big Government Socialists are with reality.

President Joe Biden repeatedly said his $1.75 trillion Build Back Better plan would reduce inflation. To the Big Government Socialists, the principles of economics—which have historically shown that more government spending brings higher inflation— are irrelevant. Facts don't matter to Big Government Socialists when they encounter inconvenient truths.

The Congressional Budget Office, heralded by then–vice president Joe Biden in 2010 as "the gold standard," was outright dismissed when it reported that the Build Back Better bill would cost a lot more than proponents said it would. After conducting an analysis that found the bill would add $3.01 trillion to the deficit, instead of the $365 billion that was initially advertised, White House press secretary Jen Psaki simply described the estimates as "fake."[1]

Big Government Socialism's solution to problems is to simply ignore or dismiss them until they eventually go away or until the mainstream media loses interest. They prioritize virtue-signaling toward unattainable goals over self-sufficiency and ingenuity when faced with tough challenges.

At the time of this writing, Americans are paying about $3.50 for a gallon of gas, which is approximately a dollar more than a year ago.[2] (In Beverly Hills, California, prices are as high as $6.25 for a regular gallon of gas, while the average in the state is nearing $5 per gallon.[3])

Under President Trump, the United States was energy independent. As the *Wall Street Journal* reported, when demand for oil crashed during the pandemic, so did supply. Even though demand has now been restored, supply hasn't returned to pre-pandemic levels.[4] But, in the name of stopping climate change, the Biden administration has not worked to restore American energy independence. Instead he is actively crippling the oil industry in the United States through policies such as suspending oil drilling leases and canceling the Keystone XL pipeline. The Biden administration's disassociation with reality was hit home when U.S. energy secretary Jennifer Granholm was asked about her plan to increase America's oil production. She laughed and said, "That is hilarious."[5]

Polling from the beginning of 2022, one year after Biden was sworn into office, reveals how dissatisfied Americans are with the current state of affairs. According to a CBS/YouGov poll, only 4 percent of voters think that things are going "very well" in America. The same poll found that the Biden presidency has made 50 percent of Americans feel frustrated, 49 percent disappointed, and 40 percent nervous. This concern stems from the Biden administration not addressing the issues that matter to Americans. The majority of Americans do not think that

President Biden is spending enough time focusing on the economy or inflation. Sixty-two percent of poll respondents disapprove of the administration's handling of the economy, while 70 percent disapprove of Biden's handling of inflation.

Importantly, the poll found that 67 percent of Americans said President Biden and Big Government Socialists are focusing on issues they don't care about or only care a little about. Big Government Socialists in Congress (formerly known as the congressional Democrats) were focused on passing the failed Build Back Better Act. Now, after it failed to pass, they are aiming to break it up and pass it in chunks.

But that's not what's top of mind for the American people. According to the CBS/You Gov poll results, 76 percent of respondents would not improve their opinion of President Biden if Build Back Better passed.[6]

The bottom line is that the Big Government Socialists' disassociation with reality ultimately harms Americans, our families, and our communities. The constant failure to recognize and distinguish fiction from fact, prioritize outcome over process, and reward achievement over participation leaves many Americans trapped in a cycle of poverty and despair.

INFLATION AND THE SUPPLY CHAIN CRISIS

The rate of inflation impacts every American filling up their cars at the gas pump, going to the grocery store to buy food, or purchasing necessities for their families. When inflation rises, it drives down consumer purchasing power by increasing prices and decreasing the value of the currency. Overall, inflation is a hidden tax baked into the price of goods and services on the middle and lower wage earners. The net result of inflation is that

Americans have less money in their pockets without even spending it.

Under the Biden administration, inflation has skyrocketed. In December 2021, the Consumer Price Index, which is a measurement of how much Americans pay for goods and services, jumped by 7 percent. It was the third month in a row that inflation rose above 6 percent.[7] This significant increase set a forty-year record (the last time inflation was this high was in 1982). But at that point, inflation was trending downward.[8] Now it is going up, and up, with no sound policies or solutions from the Biden administration on how to bring it down.

It is no surprise that Americans are concerned about the economy and the rise in prices. An Associated Press–NORC Center for Public Affairs Research survey found that the economy is the top concern for most Americans in 2022. In an open-ended question, 68 percent of Americans responded that they wanted the government to prioritize the economy in 2022. Compared to last year's findings, the results also found a significant increase in Americans' concerns about their personal finances, the cost of living, and inflation.[9]

Americans are feeling the squeeze of inflation every day. Prices for food at home rose by 6.5 percent, which is higher than any year-over-year increase since 2008. More specifically, all of the major grocery store food groups saw a rise in prices from 2020 to 2021. For example, the cost of meat, poultry, fish, and eggs increased by 12.5 percent, fruits and vegetables rose by 5.0 percent, and cereals and bakery products increased by 4.8 percent.[10]

This price strain stretches the energy sector as well. Unleaded regular gasoline in 2021 peaked in November at $3.48 per gallon—the highest price since November 2012.[11] The average price of electricity in 2021 also reached its highest point since the U.S. Bureau of Labor Statistics began recording this data in 1978.[12] Note, this jump in electricity prices makes driving electric cars more costly. For Americans across the country, it's getting harder to put quality food on the table, fuel in their cars, and keep the lights on in their homes. Meanwhile, President Biden is not confronting the inflation crisis or doing enough to stop it from getting worse.

There are a variety of factors contributing to the rise in inflation. As the Associated Press wrote on January 12, 2022:

When the pandemic paralyzed the economy in the spring of 2020 and lockdowns kicked in, businesses closed or cut hours and consumers stayed home as a health precaution, employers slashed a breathtaking 22 million jobs. Economic output plunged at a record-shattering 31% annual rate in last year's April–June quarter.

Everyone braced for more misery. Companies cut investment. Restocking was postponed. A brutal recession ensued.

But instead of sinking into a prolonged downturn, the economy staged an unexpectedly rousing recovery, fueled by vast infusions of government aid and emergency intervention by the Fed, which slashed interest rates, among other things. By spring this year, the roll-out of vaccines had emboldened consumers to return to restaurants, bars, shops and airports.

Suddenly, businesses had to scramble to meet demand. They couldn't hire fast enough to fill job openings—a near record 10.6 million in November—or buy enough supplies to meet customer orders. As business roared back, ports and freight yards couldn't handle the traffic. Global supply chains became snarled.

Costs rose. And companies found that they could pass along those higher costs in the form of higher prices to consumers, many of whom had managed to sock away a ton of savings during the pandemic.

But critics, including former Treasury Secretary Lawrence Summers, blamed in part President Joe Biden's $1.9 trillion coronavirus relief package, with its $1,400 checks to most households, for overheating an economy that was already sizzling on its own.[13]

In short, the American economy was met with a perfect storm: supply chain bottlenecks, a shortage of workers (due in part to restrictive coronavirus mandates), high energy prices (thanks to the Biden administration's attacks against American energy independence), and a demand surge.

Wages increased to lure laborers into job openings. This, coupled with other rising costs due to limited supply and rising gas prices, has led to higher costs that are reflected in the price consumers see on the sticker. (It is important to note that even though hourly wages have increased—at a rate of 4.7 percent— raises have not kept pace with the rate of inflation. As CNBC reported, 7 percent growth in inflation with an average raise of 4.7 percent nets an average pay cut of more than 2 percent.[14])

But while demand surged, supply chains simultaneously experienced significant disruptions—which, as an aside, has underscored the serious problem with America's overreliance on imports from Communist China (the top supplier of goods to the United States).[15] Rising demand has resulted in record amounts of cargo struggling to reach U.S. ports. In the Port of Los Angeles, 10.7 million twenty-foot containers passed through in 2021, surpassing the previous record by 13 percent.[16]

Shipping congestion, notably in Los Angeles and Long Beach, California, has caused backlogs, delays, and price increases. These two ports handle approximately 40 percent of container-ized imports to the United States.[17] On November 16, 2021, the Ports of Los Angeles and Long Beach instituted a new queuing system to ease congestion (under the guise of improving safety and air quality). After placement in an arrival queue, vessels are required to wait for an available berth approximately 150 miles from land, outside of the "Safety and Air Quality Area."[18]

But this ultimately doesn't solve the backlog problem—it prolongs it. In fact, this was merely a cover-up to mask the back-log itself. As Aaron Kliegman wrote for *Just the News*, "The new queuing system was ostensibly devised to lower harmful emis-sions and improve safety by dispersing ships more widely. It has alleviated congestion at the ports of Los Angeles and Long Beach as intended, but this achievement has no bearing on the supply chain crisis—except insofar as it removes from view the most striking and accessible material evidence of the distribution bottleneck."[19]

It doesn't matter how many ships are inside an arbitrary sea boundary; what matters is how many ships are waiting to off-load their cargo to be shipped to consumers across America. According to the Marine Exchange of Southern California, on January 21, the total container ship backup was 106. At the time of this writing, the record high was set on January 9 with 109 container ships backed up.[20]

President Biden and Secretary of Transportation Pete Buttigieg have been quick to claim they have been successful in easing the supply chain crisis by expanding port operations. In October, President Biden announced a deal that shifted the Port of Los Angeles to around-the-clock operations that had "the potential to be a game changer." The administration heralded a so-called "90-day sprint" to ease the supply chain crisis.[21] But nearly ninety days later, as Americans shared numerous images of empty shelves at stores across the country, #BareShelvesBiden was trending on Twitter. The "game-changing" plan to keep the Port of Los Angeles open longer—as well as the Port of Long Beach—"barely made a ripple," according to the *Wall Street Journal*.

As it turns out, truckers and warehouses don't work in the middle of the night. When the Port of Long Beach started staying open all night in mid-September, no trucks showed up.[22] Additionally, the transportation industry has been hit by the same labor shortages experienced across a multitude of sectors and industries. Many truck drivers retired and licensing classes for new drivers were stalled as a result of the pandemic, leaving a shortage of drivers to transport cargo.[23]

There have been threats of imposing container dwell fees, which are fines for containers sitting at terminals for extended periods of time, but as I'm writing in late February 2022, they keep getting delayed. However, if they were implemented, who would bear the cost of the fees? Consumers.

The Biden administration has been laser-focused on addressing one link in the massive supply chain (which now includes $4 billion to expand the largest ports in the United States).[24] President Biden has been operating under the illusion that keeping ports open longer and easing transportation bottlenecks will ease inflation. But this misses the much, much larger picture of how his policies have impacted prices across the economy. Slashing oil production and energy independence raises costs for consumers, businesses, and suppliers. Excessive (and as determined by the Supreme Court, unlawful) vaccine or test mandates harm American workers already fleeing the workforce. Failing to address the supply chain crisis minimizes economic growth. And flooding the economy with cash, in the form of government checks to individuals and approving trillions in federal spending, leads to surging demand for limited goods and services and thus even higher inflation.

President Biden is not easing inflation or solving the supply chain crisis. His policies are leading to more empty shelves, more empty bank accounts, and more challenges for the American people.

KEEPING AMERICANS DEPENDENT

Not only have Big Government Socialists made the cost of living much higher, but their policies have hurt the most vulnerable Americans. Because of Big Government Socialist policies, Americans in need become more reliant on the government rather than on their own self-sufficiency. For example, the Big Government Socialist approach to eradicating homelessness has *increased* the number of homeless people living in America. In 2013, the Obama administration overhauled the focus of the approach to combating nationwide homelessness by instituting a policy called "Housing First."

The idea behind this federal policy is just as it sounds. Housing First has two core principles. First, it proposes that providing permanent housing through government assistance and housing vouchers is the best solution for ending homelessness. Second, provided housing should be immediate and shouldn't have any preconditions (that is, sobriety or minimum income thresholds) or service participation requirements.

The focus shifted from helping the person to rapid placement in permanent housing. This resulted in changes in funding allocation and, consequently, the programs and priorities of local communities on the front lines. According to an October 2020 report from the United States Interagency Council on Homelessness:

> The [December 20, 2013, Notice of Funding Availability from the Department of Housing and Urban Development] formally shifted to penalize programs with service participation requirements and incentivize housing assistance with low barriers to entry and no service participation requirements. Speed of placement became the focal measuring stick supplanting robust holistic wraparound services combined with housing to optimize self-sufficiency and reduce returns to homelessness.[25]

Such shifts in priorities toward Housing First ultimately yielded a change in process. For instance, bureaucratic changes in federal funding between 2012 and 2019 caused more resources to be allocated toward the newly categorized rapid rehousing beds (a key component of Housing First) as opposed to transitional housing beds. Although each form of housing has a twenty-four-month limit, those in transitional housing are still considered to be homeless by the Department of Housing and Urban Development. Those in rapid rehousing are not. This was little more than bureaucratic sleight of hand. Unsurprisingly, the number of transitional housing beds dropped while the total number of rapid rehousing beds increased. The Interagency Council on Homelessness report goes on:

> In many, if not most cases, the same local agencies that were providing the transitional housing beds were now providing the rapid rehousing beds, most often within the same buildings for the same individuals. . . .
>
> "Reclassifying" 101,746 individuals that moved from transitional programs to rapid rehousing programs as no longer experiencing homelessness has been cited as evidence of the reduction of homelessness. This reclassification has also been used to support the effectiveness of housing first, thus this may not represent a true reduction.

Just as the Big Government Socialists declared success by moving the supply chain crisis farther away from the California shore, they recategorized what defines a homeless American to make a failed program appear successful. Before Housing First, the total number of unsheltered people in the United States decreased by 31.4 percent between 2007 and 2014.[26] (According to the Department of Housing and Urban Development, "Unsheltered homelessness refers to people whose primary nighttime location is a public or private place not designated for, or ordinarily used as, a regular sleeping accommodation for people. For example, the streets, vehicles, or parks.")[27]

Although federal funding for targeted homelessness is more than 200 percent higher than it was approximately ten years ago, homelessness has increased. Between 2014 and 2019, before the COVID-19 pandemic, those experiencing unsheltered homelessness increased across the country by 20.5 percent.[28] In January 2020—before the pandemic—580,466 were homeless on a given night in the United States, a 2.2 percent increase from 2019.[29] (This figure includes those experiencing unsheltered or sheltered homelessness. The latter refers to those residing in emergency shelters, transitional housing programs, or safe havens.)[30]

To see how disastrous the Housing First policy is in practice, we can look at California as a revealing case study. In 2016, statutory changes were put in place that mandated that all programs and funding for homelessness would be in line with the Housing First approach. This switch, coupled with California's increasing cost of housing, proved to be a catastrophe. Throughout the state of California, unsheltered homelessness rose by 47.1 percent between 2015 and 2019, whereas statewide homelessness increased by 30.7 percent.[31]

According to the most current figures available, more than one in four people who are homeless and more than half of all unsheltered people in the nation reside in California. Before the pandemic, in January 2020, there were an estimated 161,548 people who were homeless in California. The state had the highest increase in the number of people experiencing homelessness in the United States from 2019 to 2020.[32]

The "one-size-fits-all" approach of Housing First does not take into consideration the root causes of what leads an individual or family to being homeless in the first place. As Christopher Rufo wrote in a report for the Heritage Foundation, "Policymakers must understand that homelessness is primarily a human problem, not a housing problem."[33]

Mental health issues, substance abuse, and experiences of trauma or abuse are significant driving factors leading to homelessness. According to a 2019 national survey by the California Policy Lab, trauma or abuse conditions were the cause of homelessness for 46 percent of unsheltered people and 34 percent of sheltered people. For 50 percent of the unsheltered homeless population, mental health conditions contributed to a loss of housing, whereas for 51 percent of unsheltered homeless, substance abuse of drugs or alcohol was a contributing factor.[34]

In the aftermath of the pandemic, these health, addiction, and safety challenges are not likely to subside. As my wife, former U.S. ambassador to the Holy See Callista Gingrich, wrote, "It is clear that mental health struggles, substance abuse, and domestic violence have intensified since 2020."[35] Globally, domestic violence rose by 25–33 percent in 2020. A review of studies conducted in the United States found that after stay-at-home orders were put in place, reports of domestic violence rose nationally by an average 8.1 percent.[36]

Additionally, based on data from April 2020–2021, drug overdose deaths surpassed 100,000 in a twelve-month period for the first time.[37] Overdoses of fentanyl, a synthetic opioid, are now the leading cause of death for Americans ages 18–45.[38] Further, alcohol consumption increased; 31 percent of those who consume alcohol reported drinking more during the pandemic.[39]

Therapists have reported a surge in those seeking treatment for mental health issues. On December 17, 2021, Massachusetts licensed clinical social worker Tom Lachiusa told the *New York Times*, "All the therapists I know have experienced a demand for therapy that is like nothing they have experienced before."[40] This increase in mental health conditions has severely impacted young girls. A public advisory from the U.S. surgeon general wrote, "In early 2021, emergency room visits in the United States for suspected suicide attempts were 51 percent higher for adolescent girls . . . compared to the same time period in early 2019."[41]

The rise in all these trends in the wake of the pandemic raises concerns—particularly for women. As the California Policy Lab report found, "Health and behavioral health care needs and experiences of abuse and trauma, are major factors in loss of housing among unsheltered people, most especially for unsheltered women."[42]

Certainly, stable housing is a critical component of reducing homelessness in the United States. However, Housing First programs fail to simultaneously prioritize these driving causes of homelessness alongside securing shelter. Eliminating preconditions and participation requirements does not incentivize those who are homeless to seek treatments for various ailments. In New York's Pathways to Housing program—the Housing First "gold standard"—despite twenty-four-hour access to a team, including social workers, psychiatrists, and substance abuse specialists, the number of residents afflicted with substance abuse impairment increased over the course of a year. Moreover, no person experiencing a substance abuse disorder reached recovery.[43]

The overemphasis on shelter and "harm reduction" merely relocates the tragic health and trauma issues impacting so many homeless individuals from the street to the government-provided or subsidized housing. This doesn't empower the individual facing real challenges, nor encourage independence from government assistance. As former U.S. secretary of housing and urban development Dr. Ben Carson said, "Some people think compassion is: 'There, there you poor little thing I'm going to take care of you.' That's not compassion. Compassion is: 'How do I get this person to realize their potential?'"[44]

Big Government Socialism's Housing First policies are abject failures that ultimately harm the people they set out to help. Keeping vulnerable people dependent on the government and imprisoned by their afflictions is not compassionate; it is ultimately cruel and destructive.

THE DECLINE OF EDUCATION

It is overwhelmingly clear that Big Government Socialists are failing yet another group of vulnerable Americans: our children. To be sure, the COVID-19 pandemic severely disrupted learning progress among America's youth, leaving K–12 students across America an average of five months behind in math and four months behind in reading at the end of the 2020–21 school year.[45]

School districts across the United States saw an unprecedented rise in failing grades among students during the pandemic. Near Houston, Texas, almost half of middle and high school students in some districts were failing in at least one class in the first period of the 2020–21 academic year. In North Carolina's Wilson County Schools, the percentage of students earning at least one failing grade in fall 2020 (46 percent in grades 3 through 12) more than doubled from the year prior.[46] In the first three-quarters of the 2020–21 academic year, 41 percent of high school students in Baltimore City had a grade point average below 1.0.[47]

An assessment from the United Nations estimated that due to the widespread school closures and learning loss during the pandemic, today's students could lose a total of $17 trillion in lifetime earnings.[48] While these trends and figures are concerning, it is important to recognize that the failure of schools to educate students predates mandated remote learning and the COVID-19 pandemic shutdowns.

According to data collected by the National Assessment of Educational Progress's (NAEP) long-term trend study *before* the start of the pandemic, math and reading scores for thirteen-year-olds dropped for the first time in the fifty years that the test has been administered. The test, taken between October 2019 and December 2019, found a 5-point average drop in math scores and a 3-point average drop in reading scores across the country.

The commissioner of the National Center for Education Statistics, which oversees the test and data collection, was so shocked by the results that she told *Politico* she asked her staff to double-check the figures. "None of these results are impressive," she said. "They're all concerning. The math results were particularly daunting."[49]

When looking at state and local-level data, the findings are equally troubling. Take New York City, Baltimore, and Chicago, for example. For context, the NAEP scores are divided into a four-part scale: below basic, basic, proficient, and advanced.

In New York City, 27 percent of fourth-grade students scored at or higher than the NAEP proficient level during the reading exam in 2019.[50] In Chicago, just 25 percent of fourth graders earned a score at or above the NAEP proficient level in reading.[51] In Baltimore City, the percentage was much lower, with only 13 percent of fourth graders reading at proficient or above levels.[52] Such low reading scores early in a child's education will have long-term effects on their long-term academic achievement. A report from the Annie E. Casey Foundation described why reading proficiency is so important for young students:

Reading proficiently by the end of third grade (as measured by NAEP at the beginning of fourth grade) can be a make-or-break benchmark in a child's educational development. Up until the end of third grade, most children are *learning to read*. Beginning in fourth grade, however, they are *reading to learn*, using their skills to gain more information in subjects such as math and science, to solve problems, to think critically about what they are learning, and to act upon and share that knowledge in the world around them. Up to half of the printed fourth-grade curriculum is incomprehensible to students who read below that grade level, according to the Children's Reading Foundation. And three quarters of students who are poor readers in third grade will remain poor readers in high school, according to researchers at Yale University. Not surprisingly, students with relatively low literacy achievement tend to have more behavioral and social problems in subsequent grades and higher rates of retention in grade. The National Research Council asserts that "academic success, as defined by high school graduation, can be predicted with reasonable accuracy by knowing someone's reading skill at the end of third grade. A person who is not at least a modestly skilled reader by that time is unlikely to graduate from high school."[53]

The easy solution (and the go-to for Big Government Socialists) is to throw money at these underperforming schools and districts. But the problem isn't funding. For the 2018–19 academic year, the state of New York spent $25,139 per student at its public elementary and secondary schools, a whopping

91 percent more per student than the national average. Out of the one hundred largest school systems in the United States, New York City came in first for the highest amount of spending per student, at $28,004. (For context, Montgomery County, Maryland, spent the second-highest amount among large school systems, with a price tag of $16,490 per student.)[54] Additionally, according to *U.S. News & World Report*, Chicago Public Schools spends $15,201 per pupil annually and Baltimore County Public Schools spends $13,907.[55, 56]

In short, school systems across the country have been serving the adults (teachers and bureaucrats) instead of students.[57] Consider that woke ideologues are implementing divisive, radical curriculum that rewrites American history. Unionized teachers have refused to go back to school, forcing school closures.[58] Students across America have been forced to comply with confusing, excessive COVID-19 protective mandates, making learning and socialization difficult. To "combat racism" the grading systems have been totally overhauled.[59] New math curriculum has been proposed that claims so-called "Western Math" is a tool wielded for power and oppression.[60] To get more money, schools have issued fake grades to "ghost students" who were no longer attending school.[61] Incompetent school administrators and teachers who should be fired remain on the employment rolls.

The list goes on. But this is just a sampling of some of the events, ideas, and policies throughout the United States that are failing the next generation of Americans. These approaches do not encourage students to achieve success; rather they redefine what success is and give too much power to bad teachers by eliminating the potential to fail. Similarly, underperforming schools, incompetent teachers, and corrupt school administrators are getting rewarded while not doing their jobs.

When looking at the rising prices, rising homelessness, and the continuous failures of school systems, it's no wonder Americans are frustrated. Without a good education, how are young Americans going to get a good-paying job to support themselves? How will the homeless population get back on their feet when Big Government Socialists keep investing in policies and programs that don't work? How are Americans supposed to pay for bills, housing, food, gas, and necessities when they can't get what they need—or can no longer afford it?

It is overwhelmingly clear that Big Government Socialist policies do not focus on outcomes that empower Americans to reach their full potential and stand on their own two feet. They only bring poverty and despair.

CHAPTER SEVEN

OPPORTUNITY AND HOPE

B ig Government Socialism is a rejection of classic American exceptionalism.

At its core, American exceptionalism is based on the belief that regardless of background, gender, status, class, or race, your only limits to success and advancement are your own self-doubt and effort.

This is as true today as it was at America's Founding. Take Alexander Hamilton, for example. Hamilton was born out of wedlock in the 1750s on Nevis, an island in the Caribbean. His father abandoned him, and his mother died when he was still in his youth. In 1772, orphaned Hamilton came to New York after locals helped raise money for his education in America. He studied at King's College in New York and while there, at approximately seventeen years old, he took up the colonial cause and wrote anonymous pamphlets that were so discerning they were thought to be written by John Jay. During the Revolutionary War, Hamilton rose through the ranks and became Washington's aide-de-camp. After America's victory over the British, Hamilton studied law and passed the New York bar.

Hamilton was later selected as a delegate from New York to the Constitutional Convention in Philadelphia in 1787 and played an important role in ratifying the Constitution by authoring more than fifty of the eighty-five Federalist Papers. He became the first secretary of the Treasury and established the first Bank of the United States.

Although the story of Hamilton ended in tragedy in a duel with former vice president Aaron Burr (as brilliantly recounted in the musical *Hamilton*), his rise from humble beginnings to become one of our nation's most consequential historic figures embodies the spirit, drive, and achievement that define Americanism. Our nation's history has been shaped by opportunity and hope. Americans across generations have blazed new trails to unexplored lands in the West, taken flight in the world's first airplane, and landed on the moon.

For centuries America has been the shining city on a hill, the place where millions from around the world have flocked in search of their own American dreams. It is a country that got its start as an underdog but, through the grit, intelligence, vision, and courage of the American people, emerged as the world's leading technological, economic, and military power.

The achievement of the American experiment has been remarkable. But despite our nation's success in its youth (America is still a young nation compared to other countries), continued prosperity, freedom, and security is by no means guaranteed. As President Ronald Reagan warned, "Freedom is a fragile thing and it's never more than one generation away from extinction."[1]

For America to successfully face the threat from Communist China, Russia, and any other challenge that may emerge in the future, Americans must first be free, empowered, and encouraged to succeed in their own lives and on their own merit.

WORK IS THE BEGINNING OF EVERYTHING

Work is at the heart of a healthy life and healthy society. As Reagan also said, "The best social program is a job." Benjamin Franklin asserted, "It is the working man who is the happy man. It is the idle man who is the miserable man." Again Franklin: "Work while it is called today, for you know not how much you may be hindered tomorrow."

Every government program must be rethought to return to the principle that people must work—except for the severely disadvantaged—and that dependence, passivity, and avoiding work are destructive of the individual and society.

In early America, the European settlers found themselves in a wilderness that required hard work and constant effort to survive. For example, winters in the North required serious vigilance and preparedness. Because virtually everyone worked, there was little sympathy for anyone who was able-bodied and did not work. Because farming often took the entire family to succeed, everyone had to work for the entire family to survive and possibly flourish.

This bias in favor of work continued despite the best efforts of intellectuals to disparage middle-class behavior and undermine the work ethic. As Thomas Jefferson wrote, happiness "does not depend on the condition of life in which chance has placed them, but is always the result of a good conscience, good health, occupation, and freedom in all just pursuits."[2] Even in the middle of the Great Depression, President Franklin Delano Roosevelt insisted on the importance of work. Consider his emphasis on work in his 1935 State of the Union address:

> The lessons of history, confirmed by the evidence immediately before me, show conclusively that continued dependence upon relief induces a spiritual disintegration fundamentally destructive to the national fiber. To dole our relief in this way is to administer a narcotic, a subtle destroyer of the human spirit. It is inimical to the dictates of a sound policy. It is in violation of the traditions of America. Work must be found for able-bodied but destitute workers.
>
> The Federal Government must and shall quit this business of relief.
>
> I am not willing that the vitality of our people be further sapped by the giving of cash, of market baskets, of a few hours of weekly work cutting grass, raking leaves, or picking up papers in the public parks. We must preserve not only the bodies of the unemployed from destitution but also their self-respect, their self-reliance, and courage and determination.[3]

Consider the extraordinary work FDR put into recovering from polio and living a full life. He could have gone along with his relatives' and friends' efforts to have him slow down and accept a limited life as an invalid—but he didn't. It is little wonder FDR continued to advocate for work to build character and as an essential aspect to a satisfying life. The idealized attitude of the Depression era was exhibited when world heavyweight champion James J. Braddock used part of his championship winnings to pay back the relief money he had accepted when he broke his hand and was out of work.[4]

While Presidents Roosevelt, Harry Truman (whose store had once gone bankrupt), and Dwight Eisenhower all personified the work ethic, the intellectual left was increasingly anti-work. Beginning in 1965, the Great Society of Lyndon Johnson began to develop a structure of income without effort, indolence without guilt, and the passive accepting of money and goods from others.

If you work for what you have, you appreciate its value and you respect that others have also worked for what they have. If you are given money and goods without effort, they lose their value. There is no natural limit to unearned incomes. The result is a rise of crime as a source of revenue. The $20 billion stolen from the California unemployment compensation fund since the start of the pandemic is an example of the degree to which casual criminality has penetrated and distorted American society.[5] When 10 percent of our national health care spending for Medicare and Medicaid may be stolen every year (or more than $300 billion), the same question of corrupt citizenship becomes vital.[6]

For nearly sixty years, we have been growing a dependency class that receives money for the act of existing. It makes no effort and imputes no value to getting the money. A significant share of that dependency class is now becoming a criminal class as they apply the same absence of earned value to getting whatever they can get. Reasserting the work ethic, the value of money, and the importance of honesty are essential if America is to become a healthy, productive, safe society again. President Reagan said in a 1983 radio address, "you must earn the rewards of the future with plain hard work. The harder you work today, the greater your rewards will be tomorrow."[7]

One year after Reagan's radio address, Peter Cove founded America Works. This innovative program was sponsored by New York governor Mario Cuomo and brought a whole new model of helping people get off welfare. As Cove outlined in his book, *Poor No More: Rethinking Dependency and the War on Poverty*, he was convinced that performance-based contracting in social services provides better results for the poor and yields greater value to the local community.[8] I visited America Works in the early 1990s. President Bill Clinton and I relied on them for advice on how to help the hard-core unemployed learn the skills and habits of work. Cove and CEO Dr. Lee Bowes advised us on the design of the 1996 welfare reform bill, which became extraordinarily successful because it encouraged the right changes and the right behaviors at a practical level.

The team at America Works believes that a work-based system fostering independence should replace virtually all the dependency-based models. Few people should get any aid without effort, because of the negative and destructive effects that FDR warned about in 1935.

Every government program and government policy should be evaluated to ensure that they are pro-work, pro-ownership of property, pro-achievement, and pro-advancement through honest effort. Every effort should be made to help the widest possible range of Americans lead productive, energetic, fulfilling, and independent lives. Since the ability to acquire property (both real and financial) increases the reward for the work ethic, every effort should be made to change the rules so people can work their way up from the bottom despite difficulties and— at the earliest opportunity—begin to acquire property. This will further increase their commitment to their work.

If we are serious about tackling the homelessness crisis, we need an approach that prioritizes work alongside affordable housing, treatment for substance and alcohol abuse, mental health and trauma-informed care, and reentry programs. We need to focus on outcomes. And the ultimate desired outcome should be that every able-bodied American is able to hold down a job with a sufficient paycheck. If you can keep a good-paying job, odds are you are able to pay your rent, you are not in jail, and any challenges with addiction or mental health have been resolved—or are being handled.

This is why work is so important to the prosperity of American society and the success and satisfaction of each individual.

EDUCATION: A NATION (STILL) AT RISK

Americans must acquire the skills and knowledge they need to succeed in the workplace, at home, and in their communities. This is why education is at the heart of a free society. Education is also at the heart of a safe society. Education is essential for people to learn to become good citizens. Education is essential for American workers to compete successfully with other countries in a time of rapid scientific and technological change.

For the last five decades, the American educational system has steadily declined. Now we are not capable of fully educating young citizens and preparing enough people with the tools to win the worldwide competition for new science and technology. Creating an effective education system for citizenship and economic competition is the most important single challenge on which America's future will rest.

This commitment to education has deep roots in the American experience. The colonists had a deep passion for learning. In 1635, the first public high school in America, the Boston Latin

School, was founded. A year later—and only sixteen years after the Pilgrims arrived in the New World—Harvard College was founded by a vote of the Great and General Court of the Massachusetts Bay Colony. In colony after colony, schools were established, and learning was valued.

America's Founding Fathers emphasized the importance of learning. Benjamin Franklin, who knew from his career as a printer the value of literacy and was a passionate supporter of libraries and schools, said, "The good Education of Youth has been esteemed by wise Men in all Ages, as the surest Foundation of the Happiness both of private Families and of Commonwealths. Almost all Governments have therefore made it a principal Object of their Attention, to establish and endow with proper Revenues, such Seminaries of Learning, as might supply the succeeding Age."[9]

Thomas Jefferson also understood the significance of education and was fascinated by the challenge of extending access to education to everyone. According to Jefferson in 1785, "the ultimate result of the whole scheme of education would be the teaching all the children of the State reading, writing, and common arithmetic; turning out [several] annually, of superior genius, well taught in Greek, Latin, Geography, and the higher branches of arithmetic; turning out . . . others annually, of still superior parts, who, to those branches of learning, shall have added such of the sciences as their genius shall have led them to."[10]

The Founding Fathers' commitment to education was turned into a practical investment with the passage of the Land Ordinance of 1785 (one of the Northwest Ordinances). This was two years before the Constitutional Convention and was the most important act of the Confederation Congress after the end of the Revolutionary War and before its replacement by the new government. In the Land Ordinance of 1785, the government dedicated one square mile of land in each township to be used for the maintenance of public schools.[11]

Over the years, the American commitment to education grew stronger and more widespread. *Ray's Arithmetic* series (first volume published in 1834) and the *McGuffey's Reader* (first volume published in 1836) sold in enormous numbers. For three generations they were the benchmark for American education and were much more difficult than any texts used in the same grades today.

But beginning in the 1960s, the American education system began decaying. Part of it was a desire by the World War II generation to have an easier life for their children. Another part of it was the rise of an educational philosophy that emphasized feelings and processes over hard work and substance. Yet another part of it was the combination of education bureaucrats and the teachers' unions dumbing down the learning requirements and dramatically lowering the incentive to learn.

By 1983, the decay in American education had become such a crisis that President Reagan created a blue-ribbon commission of prestigious educators to propose reforms. The commission, led by David P. Gardner, wrote *A Nation at Risk: The Imperative for Education Reform*. The report concluded:

> Our Nation is at risk. Our once unchallenged preeminence in commerce, industry, science, and technological innovation is being overtaken by competitors throughout the world. This report is concerned with only one of the many causes and dimensions of the problem, but it is the one that undergirds American prosperity, security, and civility. We report to the American people that while we

can take justifiable pride in what our schools and colleges have historically accomplished and contributed to the United States and the well-being of its people, the educational foundations of our society are presently being eroded by a rising tide of mediocrity that threatens our very future as a Nation and a people. What was unimaginable a generation ago has begun to occur—others are matching and surpassing our educational attainments.

If an unfriendly foreign power had attempted to impose on America the mediocre educational performance that exists today, we might well have viewed it as an act of war. As it stands, we have allowed this to happen to ourselves. We have even squandered the gains in student achievement made in the wake of the Sputnik challenge. Moreover, we have dismantled essential support systems which helped make those gains possible. We have, in effect, been committing an act of unthinking, unilateral educational disarmament.

Our society and its educational institutions seem to have lost sight of the basic purposes of schooling, and of the high expectations and disciplined effort needed to attain them.[12]

In a national radio address on April 30, 1983, President Reagan responded to the report's alarming findings:

Yet today, we're told in a tough report card on our commitment that the educational skills of today's students will not match those of their parents. About 13 percent of our

17-year-olds are functional illiterates and, among minority youth, the rate is closer to 40 percent. More than two-thirds of our high schoolers can't write a decent essay. . . .

The study indicates the quality of learning in our classrooms has been declining for the last two decades—a fact which won't surprise many parents or the students educated during that period. Those were years when the Federal presence in education grew and grew. Parental control over local schools shrank. Bureaucracy ballooned until accountability seemed lost. Parents were frustrated and didn't know where to turn.

Well, government seemed to forget that education begins in the home, where it's a parental right and responsibility. Both our private and our public schools exist to aid your families in the instruction of your children. For too many years, people here in Washington acted like your families' wishes were only getting in the way. We've seen what that "Washington knows best" attitude has wrought.

Our high standards of literacy and educational diversity have been slipping. Well-intentioned but misguided policymakers have stamped a uniform mediocrity on the rich variety and excellence that had been our heritage. . . .

Federal spending increased seventeenfold during the same 20 years that marked such a dramatic decline in quality. We will continue our firm commitment to support the education efforts of State and local governments, but the focus of our agenda is, as it must be, to restore parental choice and influence and to increase competition between schools.[13]

This report and Reagan's national address began the ongoing struggle between the education establishment and the demands of parents and reformers for better outcomes.

In Wisconsin, a breakthrough occurred when the former state chair of Jesse Jackson's presidential campaigns, state legislator Annette Polly Williams (known as the "mother of school choice"), teamed up with Governor Tommy Thompson to pass the nation's first school voucher program in 1990.[14]

We see this fight play out today between teachers' unions, who are universally opposed to parents having the right to choose which schools their children attend—or even to know what is being taught to their children—and a steadily growing movement of parents and interested citizens insisting on the right to know and to choose. The struggle between educational attainment adequate to prepare for citizenship and to compete successfully with Communist China, and the education bureaucracy and teachers' unions efforts to keep and grow power, continues to rage. There is growing popular support for accountability, parental involvement, and choice, but there is still massive power, strength, and resources defending the failures of the old order.

Rebuilding the effectiveness of America's schools is *the* key project for America's long-term survival. Students must acquire the knowledge and attain the skill levels necessary to be informed citizens and to undertake jobs as competent and sophisticated as the Chinese Communists who would like to replace our freedoms with a totalitarian system. Parents must be involved in their children's educations and have a right to know what is being taught in the classroom. In the Reagan tradition, American history must be taught accurately. The models being developed by 1776

Action are a good starting point for replacing the Marxist woke indoctrination that has become the norm in too many schools.

Whenever possible, students must be encouraged and challenged to do their best. Schools of excellence (magnet schools) and other centers of achievement must be nurtured. Parents should have the right to send their children to the schools that they think are best for them. Taxpayers' money should follow students, not the unions or the bureaucracies.

BUILDING A SUCCESSFUL AMERICA ON A BALANCED BUDGET

Continued reckless federal spending is a recipe for disaster for the American people. As I described in the preceding chapter, inflation has hit record highs and the supply chain has been significantly disrupted. Government spending was already high due to the COVID-19 pandemic, but the Biden administration and Big Government Socialists have prioritized spending even more of Americans' money. With the American Rescue Plan and the infrastructure bill, the Biden administration has already signed into law a combined total of $3.1 trillion.[15] Had the Build Back Better Act passed, this total would have climbed much higher.

President Biden has said that this multi-trillion-dollar new spending "will reduce inflation."[16] But with fewer goods to absorb the flagrant government spending, we have a textbook definition of what will make the already skyrocketing inflation worse. The size of the U.S. economy has not kept pace with the amount of government spending. Today the national debt is more than $30 trillion, while the gross domestic product of the United States is $20.95 trillion.[17, 18] In 1980 (during the Jimmy Carter administration, the last high-inflation Democrat president), the U.S.

economy was three times larger than the national debt. But today the roles have reversed. Now the debt is bigger than the economy.

This means today's Federal Reserve has much less room to raise interest rates to cool off the economy. Because the debt is so large, a high interest rate would eat into federal, state, and local budgets due to the crushing costs of servicing the debt. When the Carter administration raised interest rates, a recession ensued. But at the time of this writing, the *Wall Street Journal* reported that Americans should anticipate an oncoming hike in interest rates. According to the newspaper on February 10, 2022:

> The question facing Federal Reserve officials ahead of their policy meeting next month is no longer whether they will raise interest rates but rather by how much. . . . The debate still has weeks to play out but could lead officials to begin lifting interest rates from near zero next month, with a larger half-percentage-point increase rather than the standard quarter-percentage-point move. The Fed hasn't raised rates by a half percentage point since 2000.[19]

The American people are the ones who bear the brunt of this poor and irresponsible federal fiscal policy. Regardless of the result of the March meeting, the case for balancing the budget is urgent—and the American people agree. According to a recent poll we sponsored at the American Majority Project and conducted by McLaughlin & Associates, 70 percent of Americans support passing a constitutional amendment that would require that Congress pass a balanced federal budget annually.

Diving into this further during focus groups, we found: "Support for balancing the budget is driven by a belief that it will force Congress to set priorities, solve the root causes of problems, and that it is something that every family and business must do, therefore Congress should do it as well."[20]

Passing a balanced federal budget is challenging, but it's not impossible. When I was Speaker of the House, congressional Republicans passed the only four years of balanced budgets in our lifetime. As a team, we made balancing the budget a priority by finding savings and passing reforms. Our approach in the 1990s was not to be stingy with Americans' money, but to be smarter. We didn't carelessly slash budgets or mindlessly continue to do "what had always been done." We invested in Americans and the future of our country. This approach requires discipline and focusing on returns, outcomes, and metrics of success.

For example, we saw the benefit of the National Institutes of Health, so we set out to double its budget. This budgetary increase led to more lives saved, as well as more money earned in the world market, and secured American global leadership in a high salaried industry. We reformed welfare and the telecommunications industry, which resulted in more people working, more jobs, and more savings for taxpayers and consumers.[21] The results we saw from a collective and determined focus on balancing the budget were remarkable. In 1995, when the congressional Republican majority took office, the Congressional Budget Office's projection for the cumulative federal budget deficit over the next ten years was $2.7 trillion in total. But in January 1999, just four years later, the CBO projected a $2.3 trillion federal *surplus* over the next ten years. In just four years, we had turned around the financial outlook of the United States to the tune of $5 trillion.

While it is true that a lot has changed since the turn of the century, there is no reason why Congress cannot and should not balance the budget using the same approach congressional Republicans implemented when I was Speaker. We informed Americans in our American Majority Project and McLaughlin & Associates poll, "The successful formula in the 1990s was to control government spending, cut regulations, reform welfare so people had incentives to work, and cut taxes in order to increase economic growth and increase revenues as the economy got bigger." We then asked, "Would you approve or disapprove of Congress using the same economic policies now?"

An overwhelming, bipartisan majority supported this approach; a total of 73 percent of people approve of these economic policies, including 65 percent of Democrats, 71 percent of independents, and 83 percent of Republicans.[22] There is a strong moral case and political incentive for members of Congress to prioritize smarter spending. It's time Congress listens to its constituents and balances the federal budget.

MAKE AMERICA ENERGY INDEPENDENT AGAIN

Energy is the backbone of the American economy and oil is the lifeblood. Yet, in an attempt to appease radical climate activists, since day one of his administration, President Biden has been attacking U.S. energy security. As I mentioned previously, in 2019, under President Donald Trump, the United States was energy independent for the first time since 1952—meaning America produced more energy than it consumed. During the Trump administration, oil production increased by 28 percent and natural gas production increased by 26 percent—reaching record highs in 2020.[23]

President Trump's approach, which largely hinged on cutting red tape and supporting American energy suppliers, has been reversed by President Biden. To be fair, I must note that high gas prices are due in large part to the fact that three million barrels per day of oil production was lost in the spring of 2020 during the COVID-19 pandemic. Though production has not fully recovered, demand has.[24] According to the International Energy Agency, around the world, the supply shortfall is still at least one million barrels per day.[25] Despite this grim reality of the American energy sector, President Biden's strategy of prioritizing climate apologists over struggling Americans has failed to lower prices for consumers or encourage the resurrection of U.S. energy independence. This is especially concerning since rapidly rising oil prices have been a factor leading up to every recession since World War II.[26]

Canceling the Keystone XL pipeline and reversing America's support of the EastMed natural gas pipeline from Israel to Europe—while effectively green-lighting Russia's Nord Stream 2 pipeline (which has since been halted after the invasion of Ukraine)—is not smart policy from an energy, climate, or security perspective.[27] Indeed, by effectively pulling the United States out of the global oil and natural gas market, Russia is now a principal supplier. In a real way, Biden's anti-petroleum stance is funding Russia's invasion of Ukraine. Further, pausing new federal oil, gas, and coal leases, when federal lands supply 22 percent of U.S. oil and 13 percent of natural gas, could destroy a million jobs, raise costs for consumers, and force America to increase energy imports.[28] Big Government Socialists have tried to disguise Green New Deal policies within the disastrous COMPETES Act. They laugh when asked about rising gas prices and tell Americans to simply buy an electric car or get a new job. They are astonishingly out of touch with the American people.[29, 30]

This is evident in a recent Gallup poll that found that "of all the issues and societal aspects measured in the survey, satisfaction with energy policies has fallen the most this year." In 2021, 42 percent of Americans were very or somewhat satisfied with the nation's energy policies. But in 2022, that number dropped down to 27 percent.[31]

The choice between boosting support for American oil and gas and protecting the environment is not binary—though Big Government Socialists will have you believe the two are foils of one another to score political points. As House Minority Leader Kevin McCarthy said, "Here's the answer to [Biden's] energy crisis: let America produce what we have and need."[32] Republicans in Congress have set up a task force to develop an agenda that prioritizes American innovation, utilizes American resources, and promotes American competitiveness. Through this approach, based upon proven conservative principles, the agenda will reduce energy costs for consumers, lower global emissions, and protect American families' economic security.

It's easy to blame the United States—as Big Government Socialists often do—for the world's environmental challenges. But this would be wrong. In 2019, Dr. Fatih Birol, executive director of the International Energy Agency, said, "In the last 10 years, the emissions reduction in the United States has been the largest in the history of energy."[33] This was achieved, however, through a focus on American resources and innovation and the power of the free market. We need to embrace these same principles as we chart the course forward.

Ultimately, by implementing these approaches and changes, we can reinvigorate the promises of opportunity and hope for the future that have made America successful since our Founding and that will continue to ensure prosperity for generations.

CHAPTER EIGHT

CRISIS AND CHAOS

One of the biggest weaknesses of Big Government Socialism is that it is inherently incapable of dealing with crises and finding solutions.

This is partly due to the knowledge gap Big Government Socialism creates between reality and bureaucracy. When you centralize power into a bureaucracy, run by a small group of people relative to an entire population, there is simply not enough brainpower to find solutions that can work everywhere. Many times the solutions that are developed end up creating a host of unforeseen consequences, which then make more problems.

We see this play out on a smaller scale in everyday life when isolated bureaucrats or academics come up with regulations or guidance that look good on paper but then create chaos in practice. The cloistered experts cannot possibly have the breadth of experience required to make sweeping changes to the entire country and they don't account for unintended consequences.

There are grim examples in the so-called "three strikes, and you're out" and aggressive antidrug laws developed the 1990s.

Generally, the "three strikes" laws mandated that anyone convicted of a third felony automatically got twenty-five years in prison. This may seem like a rational way to be tough on criminals—and strongly encourage people to abide by the laws. But the consequences were devastating.

For starters, the war on drugs laws created a wave of mass incarceration of people convicted for nonviolent addiction-related crimes. Because virtually any crime involving a federally scheduled narcotic was automatically a felony, people found themselves imprisoned, sometimes for the rest of their lives, because they couldn't beat an addiction, had untreated mental health problems, or both. But the "three strikes" legislation had an even more violent result. As Robert P. Murphy wrote for the Foundation for Economic Education, the laws made life much more dangerous for police officers.

"An unintended consequence of the 'three strikes' rules is that someone with two prior felony convictions now has a serious incentive to evade arrest for a third. And in fact, empirical studies of Los Angeles data suggest that more police officers have been killed because of this effect," Murphy wrote.[1]

In an effort to make the streets safer for Americans, we put hundreds of thousands of struggling Americans in jail and made keeping the peace much more dangerous for police.

There are other less dramatic, but still critical examples. Government-mandated occupational licensing for trades and other jobs that don't normally require formal education make it harder and more expensive for those who don't have formal education to find work. Simply put, this means a poor person who wants to try to get a good job can't get one because he or she can't afford the licensing, classes, or government-imposed requirements. This creates a shortage of licensed employees. Due to the short supply, these employees can demand more pay, which means companies can't hire as many of them. This is a big driver in cost for child care, landscaping, construction, and a host of other everyday, vital industries.[2]

This knowledge problem becomes exponentially more destructive when the people making the rules are also driven by ideology. This is what we saw play out with Obamacare (or the Affordable Care Act). The framers of the bill were more interested in imposing an ideological model upon the American health insurance system than they were in making health care available and accessible to all Americans.

Before the law was passed, the Obama administration said health care premiums would drop by an average of $2,500 for families nationwide. Instead, according to a Department of Health and Human Services report from May 2017, "premiums have doubled for individual health insurance plans since 2013, the year before many of Obamacare's regulations and mandates took effect." Specifically, the report noted, "Average individual market premiums more than doubled from $2,784 per year in 2013 to $5,712 on Healthcare.gov in 2017—an increase of $2,928 or 105%."[3]

The bill's proponents also claimed it would provide insurance coverage to Americans who didn't have it or couldn't afford it. As of 2017, before the mandate requiring that Americans purchase health insurance was revoked, there were still nearly 30 million people in the United States without coverage, according to HHS data (which is still roughly the figure today).[4] Millions of Americans also lost access to the coverage they liked and were forced to find new doctors (contrary to what the experts had promised). And significant parts of the law were ultimately ruled unconstitutional. So, in many ways, Obamacare is a great example of what happens when a small group of ideologically driven people with a lot of power gets to impose new rules upon the rest of America. Obamacare is, in essence, the first great emergence of Big Government Socialism in health care in modern American society.

But enough history. It is particularly important that we defeat Big Government Socialism now, because Americans are presently experiencing a wide array of crises. After more than two years, we are still battling—and learning to cope with—the COVID-19 pandemic. A record number of people are illegally crossing our borders without serious scrutiny by law enforcement or health officials (and being secretly shipped to cities across the nation). And the policies and actions embraced by Big Government Socialists abroad have left us vulnerable.

Indeed, the Associated Press summarized President Joe Biden's specific inability to handle our various crises in a January 14, 2022, article:

> He was supposed to break through the congressional logjam. End the pandemic. Get the economy back on track.
>
> Days before he hits his one-year mark in office, a torrent of bad news is gnawing at the foundational rationale of President Joe Biden's presidency: that he could get the job done.
>
> In the space of a week, Biden has been confronted by record inflation, COVID-19 testing shortages and school disruptions, and the second big slap-down of his domestic agenda in as many months by members of his own

party. This time, it's his voting rights push that seems doomed.

Add to that the Supreme Court's rejection of a centerpiece of his coronavirus response, and Biden's argument—that his five decades in Washington uniquely positioned him to deliver on an immensely ambitious agenda—was at risk of crumbling this week.[5]

As of this writing, Biden and the Big Government Socialists are still failing to find solutions. Rather than doing the work of solving problems with legislators on the other side of the aisle, they seek to use crises to force through parts of their agenda or to gain more control. In some ways, Big Government Socialists have a passion for catastrophism, which they learned from the Vladimir Lenin–Mao Zedong tradition. Both leaders used crises as means to gain power and impose their agendas.

It's from this tradition that you get the Rahm Emanuel[6]— and later Hillary Clinton[7]—line that you must "never let a crisis go to waste." Of course, crises that aren't helpful to the Big Government Socialist agenda (or those created by Big Government Socialist policies) get downplayed, denied, or simply ignored through a series of social controls including a compliant news media.

THE COVID-19 CRISIS

America is presently enduring a series of crises. The most obvious and persistent crisis is the now more than two-year-old COVID-19 pandemic, which has been managed entirely by the Big Government Socialists since President Donald Trump left office in January 2021—and it is clear the Big Government Socialists in the bureaucracies were working against him while he was there.

As I'm writing in March 2022, nearly 950,000 Americans have died while infected with the COVID-19 virus. The Omicron, which quickly overtook the Delta variant for dominance, is hopefully flagging.

Bear in mind, the Big Government Socialists and their media allies excoriated the previous administration daily over the initial spread of COVID-19. The highest ever per-day case number during President Trump's administration was 300,777 on January 8, 2021. One may say these are not clean comparisons. The Omicron variant is reportedly the most transmissible version of the virus yet, but it also appears to be the least deadly. However, also keep in mind that during the initial spread, almost no one was vaccinated. As of late January 2022, 75 percent of Americans had at least one dose of a vaccine, almost 63 percent had two vaccine doses, and another 23 percent of them had booster shots. That we are still seeing record-breaking infection rates only makes Biden's failure to contain and defeat the virus clearer.

Recall that Biden largely campaigned (from his basement) in 2020 claiming that Trump was mishandling the crisis and didn't have the understanding or the ability to defeat the virus. Also keep in mind that this was the same Biden who, in a debate with Trump, said that it would be impossible to have a usable vaccine before Trump left office (in fact, we had two—Pfizer-BioNTech and Moderna). In July 2021, after previously trying and failing to take credit for the development of the COVID-19 vaccines, Biden triumphantly claimed we were "closer than ever to declaring our independence from this deadly virus." He continued, "So, today, while the virus hasn't been vanquished, we know this: It no longer controls our lives. It no longer paralyzes our nation. And it's within our power to make sure it never does again."[8]

Yet, a few months later, we are living through a massive uptick in caseloads and a dramatic shortage of testing supplies. Many businesses are, again, shuttering because they don't have enough healthy employees to operate. Schoolchildren are, once again, forced into online learning regimes that we know are crippling many of their futures—especially those who were already struggling in school. In response, the White House has pledged to build a website where people can go to request COVID-19 tests shipped to their homes. In December 2021, Biden promised 500,000 tests to the effort, and he doubled the figure in January.[9] But it has been clear to everyone—including many Biden allies—that this is too little, too late.

Gregg Gonsalves, an associate professor of epidemiology at the Yale School of Public Health and adjunct associate professor at Yale Law School, wrote in the *Washington Post* in December 2021:

> I've lived through two pandemics in my lifetime, first AIDS and now covid-19. From those experiences, I know no one roots for our leaders' failures in such crises. Their successes can be measured in lives saved.
>
> That's why it pains me to admit it: President Biden is failing on covid-19.
>
> After weeks of urging by public health and medical experts, Biden spoke to the public on Tuesday about his plan to address the omicron variant, which has swept the world in just a few weeks. Many of us have been asking for a policy "reset" to ramp up U.S. efforts as cases mount across the country. We hoped this would be the moment.

Sadly, what we saw this week was an administration floundering and a president not in command of facts or willing to shift course in any substantial way on the pandemic.[10]

Gonsalves is not alone.

In response to Biden's announcement to ramp up test availability, Lev Facher wrote for *PBS NewsHour*:

The first deliveries, however, won't begin until sometime in January, and it's not clear how many tests will be available immediately.

Even if people who feel sick do access a rapid test, and it comes back positive, they have limited options besides monoclonal antibody treatments, many of which appear to be less effective against cases of the omicron variant.

The same is true for COVID-19 antiviral treatments under development by a number of companies including Pfizer and Merck. Those two manufacturers' drugs finally received emergency use authorizations from the FDA in late December.[11]

CNN's Stephen Collinson pointed out in late December 2021 that defeating COVID-19 was a central pillar of Biden's 2020 campaign. He reminded us that the president had promised to make at-home testing more available back in March 2021:

More than nine months later, he is now admitting not enough has been done. Such comments make it hard to accept arguments that the White House was taken off guard by the Omicron variant. Many experts have said for months that rapid testing needs to be more available to the public. It's hardly a secret that new variants of the virus were inevitable. And a recent episode in which White House press secretary Jen Psaki mocked the idea of sending a test to all Americans—a goal Biden has now embraced—further muddled the administration's stance on this new phase of the pandemic.[12]

One of Biden's biggest COVID-19 efforts has also been one of his most controversial. In typical Big Government Socialist fashion, Biden announced in November 2021 that federal contractors, health care workers, and employees at big companies must either be vaccinated or submit to weekly testing at the start of 2022. The mandate for federal employees and contractors is arguably within his authority. And the mandate for health care workers makes sense in some case—although one questions whether federal bureaucrats know more about health risks that nurses or doctors face than the medical professionals themselves do. However, Biden also roped in workers at any U.S. company with more than one hundred employees. This was a clear overreach and an insidious power grab for the Occupational Safety and Health Administration (OSHA) that would have impacted up to 80 million Americans.

As the deadline approached, numerous states and companies sued the administration over the mandate. Millions of Americans worried they would lose their jobs if they didn't submit to the Biden administration's demand that they take the shot. Several states, such as Alaska, Florida, Iowa, Kansas, and Tennessee, passed laws to ensure that Americans who lost their jobs because they declined to get vaccinated could still get unemployment benefits. Ultimately, the administration suspended the requirement for companies, and on January 13, 2022, the U.S. Supreme Court ruled the OSHA rule on private businesses would not stand. The Court said that OSHA lacked the authority from Congress to enact such "a significant encroachment into the lives—and health—of a vast number of employees."[13] Separately, the Court partially curtailed Biden's imposition on health care workers by ruling the mandate only could apply to health facilities that received federal funding (which is still a significant number).

As I'm writing, the most egregious power-grabbing effort has been using the COVID-19 pandemic to impose woke ideology upon the American people—to a potentially deadly effect. The Food and Drug Administration's December 27, 2021, guidance informed doctors they should prioritize non-white and non-Hispanic patients to receive medicine to fight COVID-19. Specifically, the FDA listed "race or ethnicity" as a high-risk factor doctors should consider when they dole out the limited doses of the monoclonal antibody sotrovimab.[14] Administration officials later explained that people from non-white, non-Hispanic backgrounds were more likely to have health conditions that prevented them from successfully fighting off COVID-19 infections.

This meant if doctors had a group of COVID-19 patients with near identical health conditions, doctors should give medicine to the non-white and non-Hispanic patients first, then treat the rest if there was medicine left over. It was blatant, woke-think racial discrimination. Naturally, a few Big Government Socialist–run states, such as New York and Minnesota, cued off the FDA's move and pointed specifically to past disparities in health care as a reason to discriminate against white and Hispanic patients for other COVID-19 drugs.

Responding to the absurd guidance, Senator Marco Rubio, who is Hispanic, wrote a letter to Acting FDA Commissioner Dr. Janet Woodcock on January 11, 2021, calling on the agency to reverse the guidance. Rubio wrote:

> While our nation should seek to better understand and address real disparities that exist in health outcomes, that important work is a far cry from the rationing of vital medicines based on race and ethnicity. Rationing life-saving drug treatments based on race and ethnicity is racist and un-American. There is no other way to put it.
>
> Healthcare providers should focus on individual medical conditions that research shows puts patients at higher risk. Appropriate factors include individuals 65 years or older, those who are obese, pregnant, suffering from chronic kidney disease, cancer, diabetes, cardiovascular disease, respiratory disease, and other conditions. Medical research has long documented that many of these comorbidities disproportionately impact people of color. Therefore, by prioritizing an individual's medical history, healthcare providers would ensure racial minorities at highest risk of disease, including all other high-risk patients, can receive these life-saving drugs.
>
> This latest action illustrates how far woke Democrats are willing to go in their quest to further divide America based on the color of our skin. One's race or ethnicity should not be the driving factor that decides whether or

not you live. Everyone that is at high risk should have a fair shot at our nation's growing arsenal of COVID-19 therapeutics.[15]

Similar to Senator Rubio, former U.S. Department of Housing and Urban Development secretary Ben Carson, who is Black and a medical doctor, said on Fox News that the race-based guidance was clearly discriminatory and a profound step backward in the effort to ensure all Americans are treated equally.

> I remember the people, the millions of people of all races who worked so hard to get rid of discrimination. And here we are trying to bring it back. It's unbelievable. . . . [Minority communities] have those [conditions] anyway. You don't have to throw race into this. All you have to do is treat the people that need to be treated.[16]

Perhaps the most jarring thing about the FDA guidance was that it came just days before Rev. Martin Luther King Jr. Day. It was King who dreamed that his "four little children will one day live in a nation where they will not be judged by the color of their skin, but by the content of their character." As Callista and I wrote on the national holiday, "The COVID-19 pandemic is a national challenge. We will only defeat it by being a united nation. These discriminatory efforts will only divide us and keep us from fully achieving Reverend King's dream."[17]

It is my sincere hope that by the time this book is published in July 2022, the COVID-19 crisis will be behind us, Americans will be protected from the virus, and we can all get back to leading normal, happy lives. This would require a profound change in direction and leadership from the Biden administration and the Big Government Socialists in Congress.

BIDEN'S OPEN BORDER

Soon after President Biden took office, we began to see caravans of migrants begin to move through South and Central America. They were heading to the U.S. border, because they saw that the party of open borders had won control of Congress and the White House in 2020. When the migrants arrived, they found a border that was physically porous, since Biden had rescinded nearly all the previous efforts to secure it—including the wall itself and heightened U.S. Customs and Border Protection staffing levels. Caravanners also found border officials who had been stripped of any authority or ability to maintain control. Biden had also canceled the Remain in Mexico policy, which had been integral in establishing an orderly way to process asylum seekers (this was later reinstated by a federal court order). More importantly, the migrants found a complete lack of institutional will by the U.S. government to stop them from crossing over.

As a result, 2021 saw the largest number of illegal crossings at the U.S.-Mexico border since 1960, when the government first started tracking them.[18] As Alex J. Rouhandeh wrote for *Newsweek* in August 2021, the previous month had seen more than 210,000 people encountered by Border Patrol agents.

"That pushes the total number of encounters since January to over 1,111,000, surpassing the population of San Jose, California, which is the 10th-largest city in the nation. According to U.S. Customs and Border Protection's data, the number of people met at the border has increased each month since April of 2020," Rouhandeh wrote.[19]

And this story was written with nearly four months left in the year. By October 2021, Rouhandeh had reported that "the mother of all caravans" was assembling in Tapachula, Mexico. It included tens of thousands of migrants from Haiti and Central America.[20] A few days later, it came out that the Biden administration was considering paying up to $450,000 to any families who had been separated from their children while trying to illegally cross the border under the Trump administration. Tennessee senator Bill Hagerty captured the absurdity of this proposal when he tweeted:

> If you think Biden's policies were a magnet to illegal immigrants before, just wait until illegal immigrants are paid $450k EACH for coming here illegally. Offering free open borders apparently wasn't enough. Doing this in the middle of a record border crisis is jaw-dropping.[21]

According to final data from U.S. Customs and Border Protection, 1,734,686 people were caught trying to cross the border in 2021. This was up from 458,008 in 2020 and 977,509 in 2019.[22] At the time of this writing, so far in 2022, agents have encountered 338,373 people trying to illegally cross the border, a 42 percent increase from the same time period last year (144,042). So, we could potentially expect to exceed last year's all-time record by almost half.

But this isn't just about policing the border for the border's sake. Radically open borders are dangerous for everyone involved. In Biden's first year, more than 650 migrants died while trying to illegally immigrate to the United States. This was 24 percent higher than the deadliest year under President Trump (524 in 2019) and 58 percent higher than the deadliest year under President Barack Obama (412 in 2016).[23] From these grim numbers alone, you must wonder: Where is the righteous indignation and virtuous anger from the American left and the media? Where is the outrage over the border that was so impassioned from January 20, 2016, to January 19, 2020?

In fact, the U.S. southern border with Mexico is home to a series of related crises—almost all of which are caused by Big Government Socialist policies and ignored by Big Government Socialists and their allies. There is a humanitarian crisis as hundreds of thousands of people risk a perilous journey through the desert only to be housed under a bridge or in ramshackle dwellings without basic nutritional, hygienic, or medical needs met. There is a humanitarian crisis in the many thousands of immigrants who are paying dangerous criminals to smuggle them into the country. Tens of thousands of these are children. Often, they become deeply indebted to criminal cartels—or in some cases trapped into a system of enslavement and sex trafficking. In fact, Teresa Ulloa Ziaurriz, director of the Latin American branch of the Coalition Against Trafficking International, has estimated that 60 percent of Latin American children who are smuggled over the border are forced into child pornography, prostitution, or drug smuggling.[24]

There is a public health crisis as millions of immigrants are allowed into the country without being tested for COVID-19. Even as Big Government Socialists locked down cities and states across the country in the name of stopping COVID-19, the Biden administration allowed migrants to cross the border in droves with no systematic screening process. Further, the Biden administration reportedly began sending border crossers from

Texas to suburban New York,[25] Pennsylvania,[26] and other cities on so-called "ghost flights." These take off in the dead of night and operate without manifests. This makes it difficult to find out who was on the flights and where they went after the plane landed.

There is a public safety crisis in the record number of drugs being trafficked across our porous border, which are killing a record number of Americans. As ABC News reported, agents seized more fentanyl at the border in the first five months of Biden's administration than had been found in all of 2020.[27] This comes at a time when the Centers for Disease Control and Prevention reported more than 100,000 Americans died of drug overdose from May 2020 to April 2021—the most annual overdose deaths in history.[28] How can anyone justify allowing this to continue? Along with the narcotics come the dangerous, often violent people who deal in them—many of whom are being allowed in without serious scrutiny from overwhelmed, and undersupported, law enforcement.

There is an economic crisis for American cities along the border whose communities do not have the resources or infrastructure to support the influx of people coming over. Texas governor Greg Abbott has had to make border security—which is constitutionally the responsibility of the federal government—a major responsibility of the state of Texas. He is building a Texas border wall starting in Rio Grande City.[29] Finally, there's a national security crisis as those who want to harm large numbers of Americans see our sovereignty collapse and our border become easier to penetrate. At its core, border security *is* national security.

All of these crises are the direct result of Big Government Socialist policies that seek to make our border open to anyone who wants to come to the United States. People from all over the world are incentivized to come to America and avoid our legal immigration process. This is exactly how you end up with hundreds of thousands of people living under bridges, being packed into underequipped military facilities, or dying in the desert. The national news media has largely ignored these crises (after a brief, obligatory moment of holding the Biden White House to account for its failure in the early days of the administration). The administration itself has also largely ignored the border, with Vice President Kamala Harris, supposedly in charge of the border, visiting once in June. However, these issues have not gone away—nor will they. In fact, over the next few years they are going to get steadily worse.

THE AFGHANISTAN DISASTER

A final, but vital, example of a created crisis with no solutions is the disastrous evacuation of Afghanistan—and the terrible consequences that followed.

In July 2021, Biden ordered the abrupt withdrawal of all U.S. forces from Bagram Airfield. This was not the final evacuation that had been initiated by the previous administration. There were still thousands of Americans—soldiers, diplomats, and civilians—who were still in the country. Why Biden would elect to give up the largest, most secure, U.S.-controlled airfield and military base in the country before all Americans were safely evacuated is still a tragic and inexcusable mystery. This terrible decision made the final military retreat in August much more chaotic and deadly.

Without Bagram, which is northeast of Kabul and is more isolated, Americans—and Afghan allies who had helped us for decades—had to rely on Hamid Karzai International Airport in Kabul for their escape. The airport is in the middle of the city, surrounded by traffic, shops, and industrial buildings. Evacuating from there guaranteed that mobs of desperate people would gather around the airport, trying to get on flights to escape the inevitable Taliban oppression. It guaranteed that U.S. service members would have to divide their attention between safely evacuating Americans and keeping others from rushing the planes. It guaranteed that everyone involved would face greater risks.

This decision resulted in thirteen American soldiers and seamen being killed by an ISIS-K suicide attack while trying to safely execute their missions (the terrorist group had gained influence in the wake of America's announced withdrawal).[30] It was the deadliest day for American forces in nearly a decade in Afghanistan. Days later, due to the chaos created by Biden's chosen evacuation point, ten Afghan civilians—including seven children—were killed in a U.S. drone strike that was meant to target ISIS-K members.[31] In addition to being tragic for the Afghans who were killed, this failure was a clear signal to our enemies in the area that the United States had no practical control of or knowledge about the chaotic situation.

Within days of the withdrawal, the Afghanistan government's forces had completely collapsed, and the Taliban had taken over. Former Afghan president Ashraf Ghani reportedly fled the country in a helicopter filled with cash.[32] As a result, more than $82 billion of military equipment that the United States had given the Afghan government now belonged to the Taliban (a fact the Biden administration ham-fistedly tried to hide).[33] At the time, Biden and other officials claimed they had underestimated how quickly the Afghan government would fall.

We now know that the Department of Defense and the administration had been amply warned that the Afghan military had no ability to withstand the Taliban, months before the withdrawal. As the Associated Press reported in January 2022:

> The report by the Special Inspector General for Afghanistan Reconstruction John Sopko, submitted to the Department of Defense in January 2021, underscores that American authorities had been alerted that Afghanistan's air force did not have the capabilities to survive after a U.S. withdrawal. In particular, the report points to U.S. failure to train Afghan support staff, leaving the air force unable to maintain its aircraft without American contractors.[34]

So, from start to finish, the Afghanistan surrender was a complete failure. The thousands of American contractors and Afghan allies who were left in Afghanistan and told to find their own ways out are a signal that under President Biden the United States will leave its friends out to dry.

The Taliban's undisputed rule of the country is a signal to all radical Islamist terror groups that they can inflict medieval tyranny upon whomever they like without consequence. The United States under Biden will stand aside. This includes the millions of women and girls who had finally gained autonomy and freedom while the United States had influence in Afghanistan. As my wife, former ambassador Callista Gingrich, wrote on October 9, 2021:

> The Taliban has instituted measures to exclude women from public life. Working women have lost their jobs to

men, girls have been restricted from attending schools and universities, and females have been prohibited from participating in athletics. Additionally, the new Taliban cabinet has no female members, the Women's Ministry in Kabul has been closed, and officials have instructed women to stay at home for their own safety.

Brave Afghan women have tried to defend their rights by peacefully marching in the streets. During a march in early September, women demonstrators chanted, "we want equal rights, we want women in government." But when the Taliban arrived, these heroic women were beaten with whips and batons.[35]

More broadly, our adversaries across the globe have seen the limit of our willpower—and the current administration's inability to execute strategic goals. Specifically, I suspect Biden's incompetence in Afghanistan emboldened Vladimir Putin to invade Ukraine. And depending on how Biden ultimately handles Putin, Xi Jinping may be emboldened to invade Taiwan. Weakness creates a domino chain of catastrophe.

These are just a few examples of how a government committed to Big Government Socialism creates crises, chaos, and conflict. Since Biden took the White House and the Big Government Socialists took control of the Congress, almost no problems have been solved.

Of course, we should have seen all this coming. Remember former president Obama's warning during the 2020 Democrat presidential nomination campaign: "Don't underestimate Joe's ability to f*** things up."[36]

CHAPTER NINE

PRAGMATISM AND PROSPERITY

To solve the crises that we are facing and break out of the cycles of chaos and conflict into which Big Government Socialism has dragged our nation, we must get back to reason, logic, and an enthusiastic spirit of finding consensus.

This means we must refocus our efforts on finding solutions to our various troubles so they appeal to the widest possible number of Americans, can be practically implemented, and will actually work. All three steps are important. If people don't want a proposed solution, it will likely be skipped over or only given lip service. It will therefore never be put into effect, and you would have wasted all the time and energy developing the idea and trying to get people to do it.

One example of this could turn out to be President Joe Biden's dictate that half of all new vehicles sold in America by 2030 must be electric.[1] Most of the world's automakers predict demand for electric vehicles will be about two-thirds of the market by that time—which they pliantly announced shortly after

Biden's executive order and alongside debate over his $1 tril-lion infrastructure bill (from which automakers hope to benefit greatly). The trouble is, as of 2021, most Americans weren't inter-ested in buying electric vehicles. As the Associated Press reported on March 15, 2021, electric vehicles accounted for only 2 per-cent of all sales nationwide. Expecting a 3,200 percent increase in nine years (when Americans on average buy new cars every six years) doesn't seem likely.

If people want a solution, but it can't be practically imple-mented, it will similarly not get done. This is what happened with the $800 billion in stimulus for so-called shovel-ready infrastruc-ture jobs that passed under the Barack Obama administration. Everyone wanted to spend the money if it meant creating a lot of ready-to-go jobs. The trouble was, the jobs weren't shovel ready.[2] There were still years of approvals and studies that had to be made for most of the infrastructure projects Obama had touted. We spent the money, but it didn't ultimately create any jobs. Unfortunately, you can expect a repeat of this issue with President Joe Biden's $1 trillion infrastructure plan, which became law in November 2021. Watch to see how much of the $550 billion dedi-cated to new transportation, communications, and utility projects actually gets spent on putting jobless people to work.

Finally, an idea may have a lot of support, and be possible to put into place, but if it doesn't solve the problem, what's the point? Consider that since the passage of President Lyndon B. Johnson's Great Society legislation, the U.S. poverty rate has not reduced in a meaningful way. While it is slightly down from 19 percent in 1964, the percentage of Americans in poverty has remained largely flat since (roughly 13 percent on average). In fact, with population growth, this actually means that 10 million more Americans were impoverished in 2014 (46.7 million people at 14.8 percent poverty) than in 1964 (36.1 million at 19 percent poverty).[3]

So, making Americans prosperous again requires our leaders to get back to doing things that people want, can be done, and work.

PRAGMATISM (DOES IT WORK IN THE REAL WORLD?)

Pragmatism was a central pattern of the American system from the first day settlers landed in Jamestown, Virginia, to the rise of large theoretical philosophical academic and bureaucratic systems after World War II. Returning to an honest focus on what works and insisting on changing theories until the outcomes are acceptable would be a return to the pre-bureaucratic America that became the strongest, safest, and most prosperous nation in history.

The nature of opening up a new world forced the European colonists to constantly learn new things and measure expectations against results. In something as simple as growing crops, the wide variation in climate and soil led different groups of immigrants to stop in different places. They were looking for conditions that resembled the home country they had left behind. They knew how to grow crops and prosper within limited patterns, and it was those patterns that turned some areas into strongholds for people of different backgrounds.

In early America, practical outcomes clearly dominated theoretical inquiries. It was little wonder that President John Quincy Adams's desire to build an astronomical observatory struck Andrew Jackson's frontier and small farmer supporters as a weird idea. They could see the stars by just stepping out of the tavern.

The theoretical concept of a scientific exploration of the universe (while a good pursuit) was simply too abstract and distant for everyday Americans in the 1820s.

However, this focus on the practical was not the same as a rejection of useful knowledge. Lincoln is the only president to have patented an invention. He spent considerable time (first as a lawyer and then as president) studying technology and looking for better ways to do things. There was a constant American drive for improvements, but it was for practical improvements. George Washington as a farmer bred larger and stronger mules and introduced the new breed to American farmers. Thomas Jefferson was constantly seeking knowledge, including fossils from Kentucky, and sent the Lewis and Clark Expedition across the continent in a journey almost comparable to going to Mars today (their material is still at the Academy of Natural Sciences in Philadelphia and is amazing to examine). Jefferson saw knowledge as a practical step toward a better world.

As a case study in pragmatism (what works), Henry Cabot Lodge's introduction to Alexander Hamilton (in the first of the twelve volumes of Hamilton's papers) is a masterpiece:

> He had a powerful imagination for facts, if such an apparent contradiction in terms may be permitted. That is, he saw and felt the realities of every situation so strongly himself that he never failed to depict them vividly, and bring them home sharply to the minds of others.[4]

It is no accident that Hamilton was deeply impressed by Adam Smith's *An Inquiry into the Nature and Causes of the Wealth of Nations*. Smith was not a theoretician. His work is a series of observations of the emerging reality of the manufacturing-commercial system that would dominate the production of wealth for the next two centuries. Smith is not taking a theory and trying to select the facts that make it seem correct. He is describing facts and then seeking an explanation that would make sense of the facts.

Smith's impact on Americans was made easier by the fact that the world he was describing maximized freedom and he argued that free markets were the best system for creating wealth. It was symbolically helpful that *The Wealth of Nations* and the Declaration of Independence both were written in 1776 and each articulated the power of freedom to create a better future—one in economics and the other in politics and government.

This American passion for facts extends far beyond the political class. Successful inventors followed the facts. Thomas Edison patented 1,093 inventions including the lightbulb, the motion picture camera, and the forerunner of the X-ray machine. For the lightbulb alone, he said he tried more than one thousand materials. It was the focus on outcomes and deriving insights from facts that marked Edison's approach to invention. Similarly, Henry Ford invented the modern mass-produced automobile system by a relentless focus on solving one component at a time until the assembly line was finally working.

In modern management, the two most powerful influences, W. Edwards Deming and Peter Drucker, were both codifiers and explainers of what was really working. Their theories of effective management came from carefully observing the success they achieved. In Deming's case, he had developed his systematic problem solving while working for AT&T. When he taught it to the Japanese in the early 1950s, he was not sharing a theory, he was sharing a working system that could be applied by any corporation with the discipline to follow his principles. The award for the best-managed company in Japan today is the Deming Award, in honor of the profound impact he had on growing modern Japanese industrial and management capabilities.

Drucker was a finance reporter, a philosopher, and a college professor seeking a systematic alternative to fascism and communism. Alfred Sloan, the legendary genius who developed the modern General Motors, invited Drucker to come to Detroit and study the system Sloan had invented, which had enabled GM to replace the Ford Motor Company as the dominant American manufacturing system. Drucker, like Adam Smith in the eighteenth century, was a codifier of observations not a theoretician. His first great management work, *Concept of the Corporation*, came after two years of work inside General Motors and especially in the Chevrolet division, which was the most popular selling GM car in that era. The rest of Drucker's life he was a consultant to the best and most innovative CEOs. It was from that practical experience that he kept gaining insights into what worked and what failed. Drucker's most important book, *The Effective Executive*, was the product of this practical experience, which then led to insights rather than theories.

To the degree that American thinking started with the practical and learned from reality, it has been extraordinarily powerful. As theories of academics, who have done nothing but theorized everything, have become more dominant, the systems of business and government have grown more incompetent, ineffective, and self-deceiving.

So, if we are going to succeed as a nation, we must stay focused on what is really happening and what really works. We must observe what works and do more of it. Importantly, we must also observe what fails and wean America away from it—even if it is the current fad. Reinforce success, starve failure. We must let reality be the guide to creating a better future and be cautious about theoretical models that may have no basis in the real world.

THE ENTREPRENEURIAL SPIRIT

Another key to American success has been a widespread entrepreneurial spirit that operated within a remarkably free market. Enabling people to pursue happiness and work to fulfill their dreams (while allowing customers to define what works and what doesn't) has been the most powerful engine for economic success in world history. More people have come from more cultures and changed their effectiveness and productivity by learning to be American than with any other country in human experience. It is vital that America reward and sustain the entrepreneurial experience—and that the free market remain the central economic organizing system in America.

The nature of early America created a remarkable breeding ground for entrepreneurs of all types. The emerging British commercial system that Smith wrote about was a remarkable device for ambition and opportunity. The openness of the New World and the explosion of new technologies that began in the early eighteenth century created pathways for daring people willing to work hard to create a better future.

The entrepreneur is remarkably different from the corporate bureaucrat. In fact, one of the great challenges to American innovation and ingenuity has been the rise of the business school mentality, which overvalues academic knowledge and has no reward system for simply knowing and doing. Entrepreneurs are by definition risk takers. They also know that whatever their dream of success is, they must get the job done. Entrepreneurs learn to measure achievement, not activity. They learn to value success over clever explanations of failure. Entrepreneurs learn that achieving almost any goal means watching for the unexpected and the unplanned. They learn that doing and achieving is far more challenging than explaining and reporting.

Bureaucracies seek routine, predictability, time-tested norms, hierarchies that are stable and deferential, and a system in which the power of the rules trumps the requirements of success. In many bureaucracies, if the meeting was good and the report was readable, the outcome was acceptable even if it failed to meet the goals or standards that had been set.

The free market is central to this entire process because it puts power in the hands of the customer. It is the customer who defines value (as Deming pointed out, it takes an entrepreneur to create potential value but then the customer must decide if it is real). Customers' habits (what time do they shop, what fashions do they like, what food do they want, how long will they wait, etc.) set the terms for successful entrepreneurship.

Bureaucratic systems are virtually the opposite of entrepreneurial systems. Bureaucrats have clients. The client comes when the bureaucrat wants them to, fills out the forms the bureaucrat creates, and is offered only the choices the bureaucrat defines. Power is centered in the bureaucrat, and they often enjoy demonstrating that power. The bureaucrat-centered system has come to permeate American life from local, state, and federal government—and into the large corporations whose systems are as rule-ridden and bureaucratic as any government. This transition from entrepreneur-customer free market to bureaucrat-client limited choice has been gaining momentum for a little over a century and has reduced economic success and quality of life for most Americans.

Philip K. Howard has written a series of insightful books about how to take much of the bureaucracy, waste, time consumption, corruption, and arrogance out of the current bureaucratic systems. His reforms are an important start to moving back toward a more dynamic, customer-oriented, efficient, and productive America.

The importance of the free market was described by Smith as an invisible hand that used prices to signal where opportunities existed. It helped guide people to being more productive and doing things that improved the lives of customers. Smith's insights were expanded by the Austrian School of Economics, when its students studied the sale of fish in pre-refrigerator Vienna. They noticed that when fish arrived in the morning, they were freshest and sold for the highest price. Then, since refrigeration did not exist, they would lose their freshness as the day went on. What intrigued the Austrian students of economics was the dramatic differences in what the same person would buy and when they would shop. The same person, shortly after payday, might buy the most expensive fish. Then, at the end of the month, that person might buy older fish to put into soup or stew. The key insight was that no bureaucrat could imagine the values decision all day, every day, for every customer. Therefore, the bureaucracy could never have the quality, accuracy, and speed of the market.

Whenever possible, we must return to designing systems around customers, entrepreneurs, and markets. There is an enormous scale of change needed to move from bureaucratic controls,

bureaucratic attitudes, and the stifling power of red-tape regulations. Every time American leaders see someone being treated as
a client subservient to a bureaucrat, they should ask themselves
how to change that relationship into an entrepreneur-customer
market-oriented system.

In every part of government in which processes and activities define success rather than achievements, the system must be
redesigned.

TECHNOLOGY DRIVES PROGRESS AND OPPORTUNITY

Technology is a key factor in improving life, securing our safety,
and developing the best possible future for the maximum number of people. From the beginning, Americans have been deeply
committed to technology as a key to a better life. Part of this was
driven by the need to develop a huge wilderness spanning a continent. Part of it was driven by a perennial shortage of labor and
the higher price that free men and women could charge compared to peasants, serfs, and slaves. Part of it was inherent in
the core belief that the future could be better, that in President
Ronald Reagan's words, "you ain't seen nothing yet."

The Founding Fathers had an abiding faith in the promise
and power of technology. In fact, the Founders felt so deeply
about technological progress, they wrote it into the Constitution.

Article I, Section 8, Clause 8 calls on Congress "To promote
the Progress of Science and useful Arts, by securing for limited Times to Authors and Inventors the exclusive Right to their
respective Writings and Discoveries."[5]

This generational belief in the power of invention was captured by James Madison in Federalist 43 when he wrote, "The

utility of this power will scarcely be questioned. The copyright of authors has been solemnly adjudged, in Great Britain, to be a right of common law. The right to useful inventions seems with equal reason to belong to the inventors."[6]

The concept of "useful inventions" had been demonstrated by the oldest of the Founding Fathers, Benjamin Franklin. Franklin invented bifocal glasses, which we still use. His Franklin stove was so effective, it is still in use in wood-burning areas. Franklin not only discovered electricity in lightning through his famous experiment of flying a kite during thunderstorms, he went on to develop the lightning rod to protect buildings. This passion for constant tinkering and inventing produced wave after wave of innovations that increased productivity, improved the quality of life, and increased American economic and military power.

As early as the 1790s, Eli Whitney was developing both the cotton gin and through the use of standardized parts was revolutionizing the mass production of guns. His understanding of the power of interchangeable parts in lowering cost and increasing the speed of production would a century later be used by Henry Ford to develop the mass-produced automobile and an assembly line on a grand scale. By 1807, Robert Fulton was developing a commercially successful steamship. The increase in speed and decline in cost of shipping by water was revolutionary in its impact.

The momentum created by the early pioneering generations was expanded and deepened by following generations of industrial and scientific pioneers. Whether it was the easier use and greater carrying capacity of the Conestoga wagon, the practical impact of barbed wire, or the invention of a series of machines for planting and harvesting, virtually every time people turned around, something new was being developed to increase productivity or improve the quality of life.

As part of this pattern, then–Illinois lawyer Abraham Lincoln developed a device to help steamships get over shoals in the river. He became the only American president to hold a patent (the device was never commercially manufactured). As president during the Civil War, Lincoln spent a good bit of time looking at new technologies and new weapons and worked to apply technology to winning the war.

As previously mentioned, Edison's impact at the end of his life was estimated to be 6 percent of the gross domestic product (GDP) and a range of improvements and inventions that had affected the lives of every American. The tide of invention has continued to our day and expanded to include breakthroughs in health care, computing, artificial intelligence, communications, and an extraordinary range of new developments that continue to shape us.

However, the rise of giant bureaucracies and the attitudes of the Big Government Socialists have slowed down the rate of developing and applying new ideas. Where the news media once celebrated breakthroughs and were fascinated by a better future, the reporting of the last few decades has been so negative that a sobering number of young people fear the future, expect to die in a cataclysm, and have no faith that a better future could be truly achieved.

The bureaucracies have an enormous capacity to avoid new technologies and innovations. In areas such as education, the resistance to improvement has been enormous. Even in the U.S. Department of Defense, where the threat of losing a war or being killed on the battlefield provides enormous pressure to constantly modernize, the bureaucratic structures have enabled old systems and patterns of power to minimize what should be a dramatically more rapid pattern of new technologies changing the entire national security system.

We must start every day by looking widely for innovations and new methods, successes, and capabilities. We must define every major area in which a breakthrough would improve productivity—or dramatically extend the ability to get things done—and methodically look for people who are developing and implementing new ideas and new technologies.

We must seek out innovators, inventors, and system developers and build advisory groups of people who think differently and challenge the status quo method of getting things done. Our leaders in government and business must be willing to try new things, explore new approaches, and risk some failures to achieve breakthroughs. We must always ask, "Can it be done better?" and "Is someone somewhere already doing it better?" Remember that imitation is much cheaper than invention.

EVERYONE CAN BECOME AN AMERICAN

Despite the Big Government Socialist myths that conservatives want to stop all immigration and that the melting pot era is over, we must work to solve our immigration system—and this is much bigger than simply securing the border. Following the previously mentioned pattern of pragmatism, our immigration system needs to be popular, and practical, and it must work.

From the beginning, America has attracted a remarkable range of people and enabled them to pursue happiness and lead productive and fulfilling lives. People learn to be Americans. They decide to become Americans. They switch their loyalty from their country of origin to America. You can learn to be an

American and be accepted as an American in a way that is not true of any other civilization.

Remember, America was created in a New World in which there was an enormous amount of opportunity. Because the opportunities were so enormous (first in land and then in technologically driven progress), people were accepted from an astonishing range of backgrounds. There were limitations in that it was harder for Native Americans, Asians, and Africans to be accepted early on—but in every instance there were exceptions who were assimilated.

It was symbolically powerful that the first American killed on March 5, 1770, in the Boston protests against the British Empire was Crispus Attucks, an African American freedman. By the 1850s, Black abolitionists were using his memory and the date of his murder by British soldiers as a symbol in the fight to abolish slavery. There has been a constant process of expanding the definition of being an American and making it possible for millions of immigrants to learn to be American. Because being American is a learned and not an inherited system, there are both geographic migrants and temporal migrants (children). Both need to be able to learn to be American.

The decay in the certainty of teaching people how to become American is a major factor in weakening American civilization. The habits, rules, principles, and historic precedents that make it possible for 330 million people from across the planet to learn to be American are not formed overnight. They take time and effort. They also must be reinforced by the larger society.

Never forget that America is totally unique in its ability to accept people from across the planet—and allow them to prosper and participate in our society. Historically, most countries had rigid systems. European serfs were born serfs and were overwhelmingly likely to remain serfs. Western civilization in the Middle Ages was deeply hierarchical, and it was almost impossible for a peasant to become a noble. People had their places and often force was used to remind them not to try to get too far from the status into which they were born.

For most of history, people identified with their immediate neighborhood, local food, and the customs and habits of their area. Highland Scots had contempt for lowland Scots—let alone for the English and others. The Irish deeply resented (often hated) the English who had conquered them—and the English returned the attitude by viewing the Irish with contempt and disdain. In many countries, the term *foreigner* meant someone from the next valley.

In Asia, the combination of race, language, and religion set up barriers that conquest could overcome. But short of that, Chinese remained Chinese, Indian Buddhists remained Indian, etc. The Mongol Empire was the one exception in that it conquered an enormous area and a remarkable number of different populations. But in the end, it remained on top of the conquered people and did not acculturate them into a Mongol civilization.

The remarkable American experiment of creating a "learned civilization" open to everyone on the planet is a continuous struggle. As I mentioned before, Ronald Reagan asserted in his 1967 inaugural address as governor of California that "[f]reedom is never more than one generation away from extinction. We didn't pass it to our children in the bloodstream. It must be fought for, protected, and handed on for them to do the same."[7]

Because the 1960s included an enormous rebellion against the inherited American civilization that had won World War II but was unwilling to impose its values and principles on its children, the process of teaching American civilization has weakened dramatically. For the last sixty years, the academic world has grown more contemptuous of the concept of teaching the rules, principles, and history of American civilization. That attitude has spread into the K–12 school systems, which are increasingly hostile to American civilization. Often, it is first-generation immigrants who have a better understanding of why America is unique—and a deeper passion for the right to pursue happiness and the importance of the rule of law.

Ironically, the activists on the left who want open borders refuse to teach people to be Americans. So, they make the dangers of millions of immigrants who remain committed to and understanding of their native cultures while failing to learn to be Americans a much bigger and more difficult challenge. Of course, these activists also reject the melting pot concept of everyone becoming American.

They reject *E Pluribus Unum*, "out of many, one," the motto adopted by Congress in 1782 and reproduced on money, passports, and official documents as a symbol that the United States are truly united. Since the Big Government Socialists reject the concept of American civilization and reject the concept that its principles, habits, and policies should be learned, it is impossible for them to teach people to be American. Furthermore, they would regard learning to be American as a bad thing, implying cultural appropriation of everyone's past. Yet the unique concept of America as a learned culture is central to the survival of a society capable of absorbing people from everywhere and teaching them how to work together.

If we are going to survive, our schools, immigration process, and public ceremonial occasions must all have a powerful component of honoring and learning about America. If our remarkably diverse and inclusive country is to survive—with opportunities for everyone from every background to learn to be American—we must end the divisive rot of wokeness and identity politics. The alternative is the collapse of America into bitterly divided groups focused on fighting rather than respecting and cooperating.

SOLUTIONS THAT WORK

Fortunately, there are leaders across the federal and state systems who are developing positive solutions that are popular, practical, and that work in the real world.

U.S. House Leader Kevin McCarthy has been building on his Commitment to America plan since he helped lead Republicans to remarkably successful congressional gains in the 2020 election. Recall that virtually every so-called expert was calling for Republicans to lose up to 25 seats in the U.S. House, citing President Donald Trump's approval ratings at the time. Instead, McCarthy helped create a net gain of 15 seats and has set Republicans up to comfortably retake the House in 2022. McCarthy's plan calls for lowering drug prices by investing in research and innovation, cutting crime with increased funding for police, strengthening our economy by disentangling it from China and lowering taxes, helping all students succeed by supporting school choice and STEM (science, technology, engineering, and mathematics) programs, and a host of other popular, positive efforts.

Similarly, Senator Rick Scott of Florida released his "Plan to Rescue America," an inspired eleven-point document, which included 128 specific policy ideas. Scott's leadership in the U.S. Senate is complementing and helping to magnify McCarthy's in the U.S. House. In addition to many of the solutions McCarthy offered, Scott is calling to reinforce the teaching of American history in school (including the pledge of allegiance); eliminate identity politics by getting rid of questions related to race, ethnicity, or skin color from government forms; close government programs that do not work in a set amount of time; and stop paying Congress members when they fail to pass a budget.

But Congress is not the only source of solutions. Governors and state legislatures all over the country are developing ideas that could help improve the lives of millions of Americans if applied nationwide.

Texas has applied a deeply entrepreneurial system for education funding that promises to greatly improve education for its students. The state has begun allowing more funding flexibility to school systems that are successful (meaning they produce more higher-achieving graduates). According to the Foundation for Excellence in Education, "Thanks to recent policy changes, districts are receiving $3,000 for each student who graduates college, career or military ready. Success with an economically disadvantaged student means $2,000 more, and another $2,000 is added for students with disabilities."[8] The policy has reportedly allowed schools to move more quickly in making changes to programs and efforts that aren't working—or further support ones that do.

The foundation reported that Tennessee has similarly begun "making it easier for districts to invest in the evidence-based strategies they need most." The Volunteer State is using federal COVID-19 support money to bolster local and public-private funds to support programs that work for students.

Finally, civic organizations are working every day to develop good, pragmatic ideas that people want to try to implement for a better future. The Heritage Foundation is at the forefront of this kind of thinking. Its Solutions project has collected a vast array of positive policy ideas that span civil society, economic life, government, national security, and foreign policy.[9]

The ideas we need to defeat and replace Big Government Socialism are out there. Many of them are already being implemented. We just need the willingness to put them in place and lead America to a brighter future.

CHAPTER TEN

INHERENT HUBRIS

Any form of communism or Big Government Socialism requires the abandonment of religion. I do not mean simply that the government must be secular or (as in the United States) "respect no establishment of religion." I mean strict atheism must be enforced upon the people at personal and societal levels. Religious morality must be replaced by government-imposed morality. This has been true since the political theories of communism and socialism were developed by Karl Marx and Friedrich Engels. As Engels wrote in the 1847 *Draft of a Communist Confession of Faith*:

> All religions which have existed hitherto were expressions
> of historical stages of development of individual peoples
> or groups of peoples. But communism is that stage of
> historical development which makes all existing religions
> superfluous and supersedes them.[1]

Engels was a German philosopher and perhaps the closest confidant of Marx—who is more widely known as the father of modern communism and socialism. Together they drafted *The Communist Manifesto* and hundreds of other papers that laid the groundwork for Vladimir Lenin, Joseph Stalin, Mao Zedong, Bernie Sanders—and every communist-socialist leader in our history.

The purported necessity for this imposed atheism is that a perfect society must be guided by science, logic, and reason rather than religion or superstition. More importantly, Marx and Engels argued that religion was a lever of control used by the ruling, upper classes (the bourgeois) to keep the working classes (the proletariat) oppressed and under control. They cited the centuries of war and conflict that were predicated on religious disagreements.

But more practically, Marx and Engels knew that their ideas simply cannot coexist within a religious society. In the Marxist-Leninist model, for communism or socialism to work (spoiler: they can't and never have), the government must be the sole arbiter of what is right and wrong. More importantly, the central government must be held as a higher authority than God—and there must be no authority between the government and the people. You can see how religion simply can't be tolerated in this system.

This is why Lenin began a campaign to undercut and diminish the Russian Orthodox Church and other religious institutions when he became the first leader of Soviet Russia and later the Soviet Union. Lenin's campaign against the church included denying clergy the right to vote, seizing and selling church property, and ramping up atheist propaganda programs while outlawing proselytization.[2]

Stalin followed Lenin's lead to a much more violent end. Stalin sought to impose the idea of the "New Soviet Man"—as a play on the earlier "New Socialist Man." Stalin's ideal Soviet Man was deeply ideological but completely irreligious—devoted to the fundamentals of Marxism and Leninism and devoid of any religious ties. Stalin went so far as to insist that the ideal Soviet citizen dissolve his or her national ties as well. There were no more Russians, there were only Soviets. In 1928, Stalin announced a five-year plan that would render the Soviet Union entirely godless. More pointedly, the name of God was to be forgotten in the Soviet Union by 1937.[3] Religious leaders were rounded up, labeled enemies of the state, and either imprisoned or killed. Religious schools and civil institutions were forced closed. Stalin took an ancient church on Red Square and turned it into a men's room so people would be forced to desecrate the church every time they went to the bathroom. Today it is a church again. Stalin even released a new Soviet calendar that eliminated weekends and all religious holidays to make it harder for Jews, Christians, Muslims, and other religious people to practice their faiths.[4]

For the same reasons as Lenin and Stalin, the necessity of religious intolerance drove Mao to kill as many as 20 million of his own people in China during his historically brutal Cultural Revolution. Mao's goal was to abolish traditional Chinese religion and spiritual practices and replace them with a political religion. In the process he exhibited enduring hostility toward Christianity and other religions.

As Thomas F. Farr wrote for *First Things*, published by the Institute on Religion and Public Life in January 2020:

> Mao had overreached, attempting to eliminate all religion. He understood, as had Stalin and Hitler, that religion (some religions in particular) poses a threat to the totalitarian state by encouraging fidelity to a greater authority. Churches were desecrated, looted, and turned

into factories and storerooms. Priests, pastors, and nuns were tortured, raped, murdered (some were burned alive), and imprisoned in labor camps. Lay Christians were paraded through towns and villages with cylindrical hats detailing their "crimes." Millions died terrible deaths, including by starvation. Tens of millions were brutalized, their lives destroyed.[5]

This vigorous antireligious sentiment is not merely a vestige of a bygone form of Marxism. It remains central to the movement today. As Victims of Communism Memorial Foundation executive director Marion Smith wrote for the *Wall Street Journal* in August 2019, "No amount of hope or hermeneutic effort can cleanse communism's record of blood—especially the blood of religious adherents. Every communist regime has sought to purge the faith of its people. An atheistic ideology, communism is not only irreligious but antireligious."[6]

As Smith pointed out, the dictatorship in North Korea has banned the Holy Bible, and countless people have been imprisoned or killed for possessing one. Communist regimes in Cuba, Venezuela, and Nicaragua have also persecuted people of faith because of the inherent threat religious freedom poses to Marxist ideology.

But far more than any other contemporary example, the Chinese Communist dictatorship is aggressively executing the antireligious tenet of Marxism. As Smith wrote:

Communist China is today's worst offender. Since its founding, the People's Republic of China has tried to control or eradicate every religion within its borders.

Some, like Tibetan Buddhist monks, regularly face arrest, imprisonment or even death. Others, like Falun Gong practitioners, have their organs forcibly harvested for the benefit of party officials and foreign medical tourists. Christian churches are either shut down or forced to preach the party line. This includes the Catholic Church, which recently struck a deal with Beijing that allows the Chinese Communist Party to approve the selection of bishops and priests.

Modern communism's inherent hatred of religion has perhaps found its most brutal demonstration in China's treatment of the Muslim Uighurs. Since the time of Marx, the communist goal has always been the creation of a "new man." That is the sole purpose of the so-called re-education camps in the province of Xinjiang. As many as three million Uighurs—more than a quarter of the population—have undergone political brainwashing in these camps. The goal is to strip them of their faith and culture, making them "fit" for the Chinese socialist system. As investigative scholar Adrian Zenz notes, those who are released from the "re-education" camps are most likely to be put into forced labor camps, which also continue to maintain regular ideological training in Marxist thought.[7]

Similarly, Russian president Vladimir Putin is presently persecuting people of faith—although he is going about it in a different way. Putin outwardly champions the Russian Orthodox Church (having filled its leadership with those loyal to the Kremlin). But Putin has been deeply oppressive of other religious minorities, namely Muslims, Jehovah's Witnesses, and other non-Russian Orthodox Christians. According to Radio Free Europe, in occupied Crimea, Putin's forces have been imprisoning religious minorities on made-up charges of extremism and terrorism.[8] In October 2021, a Russian court sentenced three Jehovah's Witnesses to eight years in prison, and another to three and a half years, for gathering to worship. The court called the activity "extremism."[9] This case was only a recent example. According to the U.S. Department of State's 2020 Report on International Religious Freedom, there were 109 people of faith imprisoned for practicing their religion in occupied Crimea.

"Religious activists, human rights groups, and media reports said Russian authorities in occupied Crimea continued to persecute and intimidate minority religious congregations, including Muslim Crimean Tatars, Jehovah's Witnesses, and orthodox Church of Ukraine members and clergy," according to the report.[10]

While Putin's Russia is not overtly imposing atheism, it is promoting the state-approved (and essentially state-run) church while oppressing all others. This is Putin's way of achieving the Marxist goal of making the state the supreme moral authority. After all, Putin ultimately wants to remake Russia back into Lenin's Soviet Union.

In every other Marxist regime in the world, socialism and religion cannot coexist. There is plenty of evidence building that the same is true for Big Government Socialism in America. Wokeness is inherently antireligious by the nature of its totalitarian belief system.

SECULAR SUPREMACY

Even before the full rise of Big Government Socialism, which has been developing in the American left and corporate ecosystem for decades, there has been a prevailing effort to erase religion and symbols of faith from public life. This includes doing away with prayer in public schools (including simple moments of silence in some states), efforts to bar religious schools from receiving otherwise available public funding, and the erasure or removal of religious icons from public spaces. Specifically, it has included efforts to punish religious institutions, such as religious hospitals or charitable organizations, that do not provide health insurance or services for those seeking abortion, contraception, or other treatments and procedures that conflict with the institutions' deeply held religious beliefs. This antireligious effort has come almost entirely from the American left.

In fact, in 2019, the Pew Research Center found that both Republicans and Democrats in America agreed that religion was losing influence in our society—but there was huge disagreement between the two parties over whether that was a good thing. According to Pew, about 63 percent of Republican-leaners reported that religion was losing its prominence—and that was not good for the country. However, Democrat-leaning adults were completely divided (27 percent said religious decline was bad, 25 percent said it was good, and 24 percent said it didn't matter too much).[11]

The pressure for this erasure of religion can be found in the Big Government Socialists' inherent hostility toward it. Not only are federal government officials increasingly hostile to people of faith, but state and local government agencies are now following the federal lead.

Consider how churches and synagogues have been treated throughout the COVID-19 pandemic. In cities and states across the country, churches were forced to close, drastically limit the size of their congregations, and abstain from some sacraments or rituals. At the start of the pandemic, when we didn't really know how dangerous the virus could get, temporary restrictions made some sense while health officials accessed the specific risks—and people made their own decisions about accepting those risks.

However, city and state officials across the country quickly began making bizarrely discriminatory decisions about what activities were safe and what were too dangerous. In many cases, religious observances were made public enemy number one. New York was perhaps the most aggressive and public in its antireligious discrimination. Governor Andrew Cuomo—before he was forced to resign amid sexual harassment allegations—had put together a color-coded map that applied variously stringent COVID-19 restrictions across the state. It just so happened that churches and synagogues were almost always placed in "red" zones, which prohibited gatherings of more than ten people— and in some cases forced houses of worship to simply close. Meanwhile, bars, restaurants, and other businesses were arbitrarily assigned less restrictive zoning. As the *New York Times* reported, the Roman Catholic Diocese of Brooklyn and two synagogues challenged Cuomo's discriminatory rules—and won. The U.S. Supreme Court ultimately favored religious freedom over Cuomo's antireligious bigotry. As Justice Neil M. Gorsuch wrote in a concurring opinion:

> It is time—past time—to make plain that, while the pandemic poses many grave challenges, there is no world in which the Constitution tolerates color-coded executive edicts that reopen liquor stores and bike shops but shutter churches, synagogues and mosques.[12]

Of course, in the face of the pandemic, many churches got creative and sought safe ways to worship together and avoid breaking social distancing rules. Many churches began offering "drive-in" services, wherein congregants could drive their cars to church parking lots and hear services either on their car radios or through loudspeakers outside the churches.

However, as the Georgia Baptist Mission Board[13] reported, governments in Wilmington, North Carolina; Greenville, Mississippi;[14] Chattanooga, Tennessee;[15] and Kent County, Michigan, all sought to prevent even these gatherings—despite worshippers having zero contact with anyone outside their own cars. At the same time, in many of these jurisdictions, fast-food restaurants and other "drive-through" businesses were allowed to keep operating.

In more egregious examples (more in line with Cuomo's edicts in New York), religious institutions in Kansas, Massachusetts, Oregon, Indiana, Nevada, Washington, and other states were held to strict occupancy limits while other businesses faced fewer or no restrictions. In Nevada specifically, massive casinos that could hold thousands of people could reopen at 50 percent capacity, but churches of any size could have no more than fifty people in attendance, according to the Georgia Baptist Mission Board.[16]

But draconian, discriminatory COVID-19 social distancing restrictions were just the beginning. The Biden administration is also seeking to track federal employees who claim religious exemptions from taking the mandated COVID-19 vaccine and other intrusive rules. Sarah Parshall Perry reported for the *Daily Signal* in January 2022 that nineteen federal agencies were proposing to keep "personal religious information" lists of employees who request religious exemptions for various reasons. This includes the departments of defense, health and human services, transportation, the Treasury, and other major centers of bureaucratic power.

As Perry wrote:

> As the nation's largest employer, with over four million civilian and military employees, the federal government has received tens of thousands of religious exemption requests. It now appears that an increasing number of federal agencies are keeping and preserving those individuals' names, religious information, personally identifying information, and other data stored in lists across multiple government agencies.
> Why?[17]

Why indeed? At best, the various government agencies could be using the data to review or improve various rules they impose on their employees—although I find this unlikely. It's more probable that the Biden administration is seeking to use the lists to pressure or punish employees who don't follow orders that contradict their deeply held religious beliefs. After the *Daily Signal* broke the story, Republicans in the U.S. House of Representatives quickly introduced a bill to bar the government from collecting and keeping this information. South Carolina Republican representative Ralph Norman, who introduced the bill, told Fox News:

> The ability for individuals to openly practice their faith without fear of retribution is a precious right we must guard closely. As if overreaching government vaccine mandates aren't bad enough, it is highly inappropriate

for federal dollars to be used to collect information about someone's religious beliefs. The only way to prevent this information from being abused is to prevent its collection in the first place.[18]

Outside of government, these public, overt efforts to delegitimize First Amendment rights to the free exercise of religion have been accompanied by real threats and harm to people of faith throughout the United States. On January 15, 2022, an antisemitic gunman entered Congregation Beth Israel synagogue in Colleyville, Texas, and held four members of the clergy and congregation hostage for eleven hours. The offender was demanding the release of an imprisoned terrorist in exchange for the hostages' safe release. Ultimately, the gunman was shot and killed by police, and the hostages escaped safely. The FBI announced it was investigating the attack as an act of terrorism.[19]

Two days later, according to CNN, the FBI reported in January 2022 that people of faith and religious institutions should expect to continue to face threats and attacks. The federal agency urged states and local governments to review and update their plans to protect churches, synagogues, and other large gathering places.[20]

This message doesn't inspire a great deal of confidence that the federal government is vigorously defending religious communities from violence and persecution.

IDENTITY POLITICS, CRITICAL THEORY, AND WOKENESS: THE NEW STATE MORALITY

Like the Marxist regimes that came before, the Big Government Socialists are seeking to erase traditional morality and impose a new morality upon the American people that is approved and dictated by the state. The movement that started as political correctness in the late 1980s and early '90s has been fully codified today into identity politics, Critical Theory, and the pervasive woke-think that is being absorbed by our government, corporate, academic, entertainment, and media institutions.

Make no mistake, all three of these concepts are rooted in Marxism. In particular, identity politics and Critical Theory (including Critical Race Theory, Critical Social Theory, Critical Gender Theory, etc.) accept and further the Marx-Engels belief that all of society is based on the bourgeois oppressing the proletariat. Instead of applying this notion to socioeconomic class, identity politics and Critical Theory apply the model to race, gender, sexuality, or other "identity" traits. In the new interpretation, non-white Americans become the victimized proletariat, and white Americans (regardless of their own beliefs or actions) become the oppressive bourgeois. In other cases, transgender people are the oppressed proletariat, while everyone else is the cruel bourgeois. Gay and lesbian Americans—proletariat. Heterosexual Americans—bourgeois. You get the model. Creating these divisions is imperative to Marxist theory, because without division and conflict, you can't have a revolution—and that's the ultimate goal of Marxism.

Wokeness, wokeism, or woke-think is the modern expression of the Marxist method of using language and propaganda to drown previous cultural notions of morality and replace them with the new, state-defined notions of morality.

In this case, the goal of American wokeness is in part to erase the American belief laid out in the Declaration of Independence:

"We hold these truths to be self-evident, that all men are created equal, that they are endowed by their Creator with certain unalienable Rights, that among these are Life, Liberty and the pursuit of Happiness."[21]

The woke doctrine says Americans can't be created equal, because all non-white Americans are born into a systemically racist system that prevents such equality. Even further, they say that because non-white Americans cannot have been created equal under this system, equality itself must be wrong (or a tool of systemic oppression invented by the white bourgeois). So, instead of God-given equality as a goal of society, adherents of wokeness say equity (or government-imposed equal outcomes) should instead be the goal. In other words, Americans aren't created equal by a Creator. They are made equal by the state.

As I wrote in my book *Beyond Biden*, the problem is not that Critical Race Theory (the college-level course) is being taught to young students as curriculum—it's being taught to them by example. In school systems across the country, administrations have applied Critical Race Theory to lessons, school rules, and the most mundane activities.

Second graders in a Connecticut school were made to verbally identify characters in books by race as they read aloud in class. A teacher in the system ultimately resigned in protest.[22] At a school in Virginia, a class was made to play "privilege bingo" to identify aspects of their classmates' lives that gave them "unearned advantages" over their others. One such point of privilege was being the child of a member of the military.[23]

These are just a few. As the *Washington Examiner* reported on July 12, 2021:

There are plenty of other examples that prove racial essentialism and collective guilt are being taught to young students. In Cupertino, California, an elementary school required third graders to rank themselves according to the "power and privilege" associated with their ethnicities. Schools in Buffalo, New York, taught students that "all white people" perpetuate "systemic racism" and had kindergarteners watch a video of dead black children, warning them about "racist police and state-sanctioned violence." And in Arizona, the state's education department sent out an "equity toolkit" to schools that claimed infants as young as 3 months old can start to show signs of racism and "remain strongly biased in favor of whiteness" by age 5.[24]

It should come as no surprise that school systems across the country are suddenly adopting these policies. The Biden administration, which controls a trove of grant money for state and local systems, has been explicit about supporting them, and the academic left is passionately and aggressively in support of imposing these radical policies.

After Congress passed nearly $200 billion to help reopen schools that had been closed during the worst of the COVID-19 pandemic, Biden's Department of Education released guidance urging (read: coercing) those schools to spend the money on various woke programs. As reported by the *New York Post*, some of these included, among other things, the removal of punishments that "spirit-murder black, brown and indigenous children," "learning from students, families and educators who disrupt Whiteness and other forms of oppression," and "'antiracist therapy for White educators and support staff,' and 'free, radical self/collective care and therapy for educators and support staff of color.'"[25]

Unfortunately, schools are just the start. The leadership of our military has begun implementing woke curricula at our top military colleges. Books such as *How to Be an Antiracist*, *The New Jim Crow: Mass Incarceration in the Age of Colorblindness*, and *Sexual Minorities and Politics* have been added to mandatory reading lists alongside essential texts on military history, tactics, and combat.

In June 2020, a U.S. Navy task force set up to help find and stop discrimination in the service proposed that its members should have to take a new pledge that was rife with language taken straight from Critical Theory:

> I pledge to advocate for and acknowledge all lived experiences and intersectional identities of every Sailor in the Navy. I pledge to engage in ongoing self-reflection, education and knowledge sharing to better myself and my communities. I pledge to be an example in establishing healthy, inclusive, and team-oriented environments. I pledge to constructively share all experiences and information gained from activities above to inform the development of Navy-wide reforms.[26]

At a time when we face serious threats from China, and potential NATO-involved conflict over Russian aggression toward Ukraine, does this seem like something on which warfighters should be focused? Especially considering the complete catastrophe of the evacuation of Afghanistan (which was entirely the fault of leadership—not service members), do we want our top brass spending time defending the implementation of the woke agenda on Capitol Hill or thinking deeply about how to start winning wars again?

Further, the infection of woke doctrine on the military has potentially devastating political implications. As the *Wall Street Journal* editorial board wrote on June 25, 2021, of General Mark Milley's defense of the military's curriculum to Congress, "The military is a rare American institution that commands bipartisan confidence. If that trust is torpedoed over the next few years, Gen. Milley and his colleagues will share responsibility for the long-term damage."

With this level of woke activity coming from government, it is no wonder that many American corporations have read the tea leaves and adopted woke-think into their company standards. As Fox Business reported in December 2021, whistleblower employees at several major U.S. companies had reported being forced to take trainings that were clearly guided by wokeness.

Coca-Cola employees were reportedly made to sit through a seminar to help them "be less white." White workers at Walt Disney Company were told they needed to "work through feelings of guilt, shame, and defensiveness to understand what is beneath them and what needs to be healed." Similar stories were shared with Fox Business by employees of Bank of America, Lowe's, and Truist Financial Corporation.[27]

Ironically, the aggressive movement of woke-think should be the clue that wakes up the world to what is going on. Anyone who has read George Orwell's dystopian, anti-totalitarian classic *1984* should immediately be able to identify woke-speak as Newspeak, the new language that the fictitious socialist British regime developed to better control its populous. Just as the Party did in Orwell's novel, the Big Government Socialists are seeking to replace our language, so they can more easily replace objective truth—which is, according to woke-think, an entirely racist, white construct of control.

All this effort also comes back to the inherent hubris of attempting to destroy religion and replace it with a man-made version of morality. I'm not arguing that a person who is atheist cannot also be moral. But I would argue that a group of people with a great deal of power—who actively reject and persecute the religious freedom of others—cannot possibly be moral.

CHAPTER ELEVEN

CIVILITY AND GRACE

Big Government Socialism undermines civility, cancels anyone with different viewpoints, and denies understanding or grace to its opponents.

It may seem anachronistic in this age of atheism, satanism, Aztec gods of death, moral relativism, and sixty different pronouns to ensure sensitivity, but the fact is that the Founding Fathers believed deeply in honesty, morality, and faith. Their policies were designed to reinforce those virtues and they would have been appalled by Senator Daniel Patrick Moynihan's essay on "Defining Deviancy Down," which I discussed earlier. They would have seen tolerance for massive theft, widespread crime, and open dissolution as totally destructive to a healthy free society.

If this challenge is not met, nothing else will save America in the long run. The evidence that America was founded by people who believed deeply in the core principles of honesty, morality, and faith is simply overwhelming.

As a young man, George Washington copied a book on *Civility and Decent Behavior in Company and Conversation*. These

110 rules had been compiled by French Jesuits in 1595 and translated into English. While Washington apparently copied them originally as an exercise in penmanship, he took them to heart. By every report, he tried to live by them for his entire life. The dignity and sense of honor that Washington embodied became the bedrock on which America would be created between 1775 and 1796. We all stand on Washington's shoulders, and he was truly the father of this country.

In his Farewell Address at the end of his second term as our first president, Washington said, "I hold the maxim no less applicable to public than to private affairs, that honesty is always the best policy."

The enormity of Washington's impact on his fellow countrymen was captured at his death by his close friend, Henry Lee, who had served under Washington during the Revolutionary War. Lee later served as a member of the Continental Congress and governor of Virginia. He was also the father of Robert E. Lee, who went on to lead the Confederate Army. Lee's eulogy said, "first in war, first in peace, and first in the hearts of his countrymen."[1] And Lee was right: No one has ever unified and personified the American Republic to the degree Washington did. His leadership was based on honesty, morality, and faith.

Washington himself recognized his debt to these larger values. As he said in his first inaugural address: "No People can be bound to acknowledge and adore the invisible hand, which conducts the Affairs of men more than the People of the United States. Every step, by which they have advanced to the character of an independent nation, seems to have been distinguished by some token of providential agency."[2]

Furthermore, Washington thought God was essential in a society to block evil. As he wrote in an earlier draft of the inaugural: "The blessed Religion revealed in the word of God will remain an eternal and awful monument to prove that the best Institutions may be abused by human depravity; and that they may even, in some instances be made subservient to the vilest of purposes."[3]

Washington felt that he personally had been saved by God's intervention. In 1778, in explaining the miraculous survival of the American army, Washington wrote: "The hand of Providence has been so conspicuous in all of this, that he must be worse than an infidel that lacks faith, and more than wicked, that has not gratitude enough to acknowledge his obligations."

The other Founding Fathers shared Washington's belief in the importance of honesty, faith, and morality.

In Federalist 55, Madison wrote that our Constitution requires "sufficient virtue among men for self-government," otherwise, "nothing less than the chains of despotism can restrain them from destroying and devouring one another."[4] John Adams wrote: "Our Constitution was made only for a moral and religious People. It is wholly inadequate to the government of any other."[5]

Thomas Jefferson shared the belief that God and America were inextricably intertwined. In reflecting on slavery in a letter he wrote to Washington: "God who gave us life gave us liberty. And can the liberties of a nation be thought secure when we have removed their only firm basis, a conviction in the minds of the people that these liberties are of the Gift of God? That they are not to be violated but with His wrath? Indeed, I tremble for my country when I reflect that God is just; that His justice cannot sleep forever. Commerce between master and slave is despotism."[6]

President Abraham Lincoln continued this belief in an intervening Providence: "If it were not for my firm belief in an overruling Providence, it would be difficult for me, in the midst of such complications of affairs, to keep my reason on its seat. But I am confident that the Almighty has His plans, and will work them out; and, whether we see it or not, they will be the best for us."

After the Civil War, Lincoln's second inaugural is only 701 words long and yet references God six times, the Almighty and Lord once each. That is one divine reference for every 88 words. In trying to understand the agony of civil conflict, Lincoln had turned to the Bible and to prayer.

For two generations the elites have been working to drive God out of public life. From outlawing school prayer, to tearing down crosses and historic monuments, to defunding religious schools, to restricting voluntary religious activities, the American left has worked to erase religion in America. Contrary to the Washington and Lincoln experience, support for military chaplains has been steadily reduced. Restrictions on their religious activities have grown more cumbersome and celebrated in entertainment, news media, and academia.

Since human nature requires a passionate embrace of something larger than the mundane, Marxist secular revolutionary impulses tend to become religious. The 1949 collection of six essays called *The God That Failed* expose the inability of communism to replace God. Theodore White's 1972 description of the liberal ideology being converted into a liberal theology was a landmark on the emergence of the woke religious impulse that now dominates the American left and Big Government

Socialism. The disastrous nature of false, secular religions is captured in the second of the Ten Commandments when God says, "Thou shall have no other God before me." Whether that false god is wealth, drugs, sexuality, power, or ideological zealousness, they are clearly false.

In the eighteenth century, the Wesley Brothers launched Methodism. Its life-changing impact reshaped life for the working class and directed toward salvation the energies that in France went into a revolution. Furthermore, Methodism inspired William Wilberforce to spend his lifetime abolishing slavery. The Wesleys helped inspire a religious revival in America called the Great Awakening, which created an emotional certainty and fervor that helped launch the American Revolution.

America today needs a spirit of revival and recommittal to overcome a decaying secular culture of despair that has produced drug addiction, mental illness, homelessness, and suicide on a scale no previous American generation could have imagined.

In practical terms, decisions need to be made from a basis of favoring honesty, morality, and faith. Where Moynihan described secular society as coping with decay by defining deviancy down, maybe it is time to rebalance. The real cultural clash may not be between right and left but rather between faith and honesty on one side and antireligious hostility and toleration for drugs, decay, and destruction on the other.

One effect of the collapse of honesty as a core principle has been a rise in criminal activity on a scale that would have been unthinkable for virtually all American history. We have witnessed eighty-five people as a gang running through a Nordstrom store stealing everything they can carry. We have watched an explosion of carjackings, many of them violent. We have seen murder rates

225

skyrocket in our biggest cities. However, the greatest increase in criminal behavior has been nonviolent, white-collar crime. When we are told the total stolen from the various government stimulus programs may be as much as $400 billion, how many Americans have crossed the line to being thieves? Newspapers and TV channels report things they know are untrue. Senior FBI officials break the law. A clear commitment to reasserting honesty as a fundamental value is a key building block to getting back to a healthy America.

Furthermore, despite the disasters of drug addiction and overdoses, suicide, mental illness, and homelessness, it has been impossible to have a passionate debate about saving the lives of the afflicted because the secular world simply refuses to confront the price of driving God out of our lives. It is time to have that debate head-on. Millions of Americans will be better off if we can recapture the classic American belief that Providence, honesty, and morality matter.

THE AUTHORITY OF RELIGION IN OUR NATION

Religious freedom in America is part of a long tradition that has been upheld by our history and solidified by our Founding Fathers and national documents. Yet the ideas of Marx and Engels seem to be permeating our nation, disassembling the morality and civility instilled in our communities. This national amorality rejects our history of supporting religious freedom. It also fails to acknowledge the impact that religious charities, schools, and rehabilitation programs have on the nation.

There is a deep national morality in America that dates to the arrival of the first European settlers in the 1600s. The Puritans were devout Protestants who journeyed to the New World for economic prosperity and religious freedom. The Puritans modeled modesty, a strong work ethic, and a Christ-centered lifestyle. The early colonial people were not subject to the authority of government, but rather the authority of God.

John Winthrop was a Puritan leader of the Massachusetts Bay Colony for twelve years. Despite his power and leadership, he conveyed to his fellow Puritans that their primitive government was not the source of all authority. Winthrop taught that God was the leader of this new nation in his 1630 lecture titled "A Model of Christian Charity." This speech went on to define how morality and the authority of religion would prevail in America.

Winthrop's speech created a covenant among Puritans, not a law. This covenant acknowledged God's authority and granted lesser authority to government. It gave the Puritans the opportunity for political establishment with a brotherly reciprocity and support for those in need. This new community became God's new promised land—a place of future prosperity and success.

Winthrop proclaimed:

> We shall find that the God of Israel is among us, when ten of us shall be able to resist a thousand of our enemies; when He shall make us a praise and glory that men shall say of succeeding plantations, "may the Lord make it like that of New England." For we must consider that we shall be as a city upon a hill. The eyes of all people are upon us. So that if we shall deal falsely with our God in this work we have undertaken, and so cause Him to withdraw His present help from us, we shall be made a story and a by-word through the world.[7]

A city upon a hill? Indeed, this phrase became a symbol of American exceptionalism—a chosen nation selected by God to become the leader of the free world. This important phrase is taken from the gospel of Matthew's "Ye are the light of the World. A city on a hill cannot be hidden."[8] This phrase has been repeated throughout our history by Republican and Democratic presidents alike. Presidents John F. Kennedy, Lyndon B. Johnson, Ronald Reagan, and George H. W. Bush are just a few who have called upon this divine message to inspire the nation. The authority of our nation is not grounded in government; it has always been grounded by the grace and freedoms endowed to each one of us by our Creator.

America's national morality was made stronger by our Founders, who consciously chose to not implement a national religion. This separation was not to deny the legitimacy or importance of religion. It was to ensure religious freedom by acknowledging that no religion was more respected than another. It is often misunderstood that our Founders were faithless figures who denied the role of religion in the country. The Founders, however, were deeply moved by Enlightenment ideals and the principles of natural law. Natural rights are not dependent on the laws or customs of a government. They are universal, inherent, and unalienable rights that each person has. Our most treasured national documents—the Declaration of Independence, Constitution, and Bill of Rights—are each based on these fundamental natural rights.

The First Amendment reads:

Congress shall make no law respecting an establishment of religion or prohibiting the free exercise thereof; or abridging the freedom of speech, or of the press; or the right of the people peaceably to assemble, and to petition the government for a redress of grievances.[9]

Madison championed the Bill of Rights through the first Congress in 1789.[10] Madison's fellow Virginians and constituents were predominantly Baptists who encouraged Madison to create a provision that would protect religion.[11] America has remained committed to religious freedom by protecting people of all faiths. The First Amendment is not a statement against religion. It is a statement freeing people from oppression against religious persecution or the implementation of a national religion.

Just because the Constitution does not nationalize religion, does not mean that it was not a vital part of our Founding. In the most contentious days of the Constitutional Convention, Benjamin Franklin moved to convene the remaining sessions with a prayer. He said, "the longer I live, the more convincing proofs I see of this Truth—that God governs in the Affairs of Men."[12] He continued: "without his concurring aid, we shall succeed in this political building no better than the Builders of Babel."[13]

Franklin's message still holds true. Religion invokes selflessness and sacrifice in times of conflict and hatred. The contentious moments of the convention could have been the breaking point of our nation, yet in persisting through these challenges our Founders thought to invoke the guidance of God. The day of prayer and fasting turned out to be the turning point in the deliberations of the convention.

Limited government and a strong national morality have helped our system to endure time and challenge. Communism and socialism attempt to make the government the sole arbiter of what is right and what is wrong. Through an expansive network of rules, regulation, and oppression, socialist and communist nations purport to *give* rights to the people. The critical misunderstanding here is that rights are not given to us by the government; they are given to us by God.

The Constitution itself does not grant us freedom. It prevents the government from taking it away. Our inalienable, God-given rights cannot be infringed upon by the government. Take a look at the language in our Constitution. It is filled with phrases proclaiming that "Congress shall make no law . . ." What the Big Government Socialists (and the historic American left) misunderstand is that our founding documents are intended to protect us from the oppression of government, not to establish the authority or prestige of the government.

Communism and socialism seek to remove faith from everyday life. While America remains a nation with no endorsed religion—our country is certainly not irreligious. This is supported by our founding documents, which protect us from the rule of a tyrannical and oppressive regime. Our Creator has endowed us with life and liberty—our government must recognize the importance of faith and freedom in our nation if we are to remain true to the American tradition.

A NATIONAL MORALITY AND ITS REINFORCERS

As I wrote in the previous chapter, communist and socialist regimes actively try to weaken moral systems and venerate the government. This same behavior has been shown through hateful and arbitrary actions toward churches, religious schools, and even faith-based and nonprofit organizations. Like other Marxist movements, Big Government Socialism is threatened by the strength of faith and moral institutions. The principles of love, kindness, respect, and forgiveness are not useful in propagating the hateful and destructive means needed to implement a socialist government.

Right now, America is facing a moral crisis. The shift in the moral climate of the country is instigating dangerous changes that destroy the values upon which our country was founded. These attacks on religion and the family separate the glue that binds our nation together. America was built to last—but the burden to maintain the nation's freedom falls on us to support and defend our natural rights.

As I mentioned, President Washington recognized the importance of upholding a strong, national morality. In his Farewell Address he said:

> Of all the dispositions and habits which lead to political prosperity, religion and morality are indispensable supports. In vain would that man claim the tribute of patriotism, who should labor to subvert these great pillars of human happiness, these firmest props of the duties of men and citizens.[14]

Instead of trying to destroy the impact of religious institutions, we should understand the good that they do in communities across the nation. Christianity, and all Abrahamic religions, teach that human beings are valuable because they are created in the image and likeness of God. Like God, the human person is endowed with reason. Our ability to engage in long-term and complex thought processes is what distinguishes us from other forms of life.

Recognizing the preciousness of our will and intellect elicits respect for all creation and human beings. Socialism and communism reject our inherent equality by sowing discord throughout the nation, facilitating a system in which those who work hard are punished, and those who don't work hard enough are celebrated.

Our God-given ability to understand right and wrong guides us to make informed decisions and understand the repercussions. The irreligious left attacks the church to take authority away from God and give power to the government. In doing this they redefine right and wrong. Without a boundary between what is right and what is wrong, socialist groups eliminate national morality and civility, facilitating harmful divisions in the nation. When Americans fail to see one another as equally created, equally valuable human beings, the government becomes the source of moral authority.

The impact of religion has long been denied by members of the left. Yet in 2021, more than 75 percent of Americans said they identified with a religious faith.[15] Of that group, 69 percent of Americans identified with Christianity and 7 percent identified as non-Christian, including Muslim or Jewish.[16]

The left has painted religion as archaic and obsolete. But there is a strong American majority that identifies as religious and recognizes its importance in our everyday lives. A Gallup poll found that 76 percent of Americans say religion is either "very" or "fairly" important in their lives.

A 2021 Pew study reported that the pandemic strengthened religious faith and tightened familial bonds in many families.[17] According to Pew, many Americans reported a stronger personal faith in light of the pandemic and 35 percent of Americans said that the pandemic carries one or more lessons from God.[18]

In the face of illness, economic lockdowns, and national instability, more people have turned to their church communities for morally informed guidance during this challenging time. As federal, state, and local guidelines became convoluted and misinformed, many people became frustrated and confused by the direction of the government.

This ushered in the opportunity to reestablish the necessity and reliability of religion to inform and unite the nation. Longitudinal studies have shown increased religious observance after people experience crisis.[19] Despite the restrictions on in-person religious services, Americans still found comfort in their church. Religious practice can be a tool used to address some of our gravest social and political challenges of today—if only we let it.

America is home to a broad range of congregations and religious communities. Aside from enhancing spirituality and community, churches also facilitate economic growth and individual rehabilitation. In 2016, it was estimated that religious organizations contributed $1.2 trillion each year to America's economy and society.[20] A National Congregations Study survey from 2018 found that there were an estimated 380,000 religious congregations across the United States.[21] Churches across the nation employ hundreds of thousands of staff members who oversee facility and buildings operations, ministry, and charitable operations, making them a source of both moral direction and community enrichment.[22]

Religious congregations have helped establish and strengthen communities in ways that the United States government cannot. In the absence of a bloated bureaucratic system, religious congregations effectively aid individuals and families in varying forms of need. Religious congregations coordinate 7.5 million volunteers to run 1.5 million social programs each year.[23] These programs provide individualized and effective treatment for people suffering from alcohol or drug abuse, mental illness, or HIV/AIDS, and veterans suffering from injury, PTSD, or homelessness.

The charitable work of religious institutions provides more than just short-term relief for problems facing communities. The services offered by religious groups provide opportunities for communities to repair themselves over time. Take, for example, Mount Lebanon Baptist Church in Maryland. Situated in a community with one of the highest HIV/AIDS diagnosis rates in the United States, Mount Lebanon Baptist Church offers free and confidential testing and support for those impacted.[24]

An African Methodist Episcopal church in Queens, New York, addresses unemployment in its community by helping the unemployed search for local jobs.[25] The Greater Allen African Methodist Episcopal Church provides employment training opportunities and workshops for resume building and interview training.[26] The Greater Allen AME Church is currently providing workshops on financial empowerment and relationship building via Zoom.[27] This church is creating a lasting impact on the community by facilitating changes that will help people to overcome the adversities of their circumstances.

Church-based programs are helping families to rise above challenges. Right now, there are religious-run programs focusing on parenting assistance and other programs focusing on marriage improvement.[28] While socialist and communist groups attempt to destroy the power of religious organizations, these groups are thriving within their communities and supporting individuals and families in need of guidance and counseling.

STRENGTHENING BONDS

Americans need moral systems such as church communities to reinforce the values of our nation. Respect, rights, freedom, and equality are all major teachings of the church. As Big Government Socialists attack religion, they also attack family. America is a nation built on brotherly love, yet more and more people see themselves as individuals, not as members of a family, community, culture, or country.

The growing singleness of American society is downplaying the fundamental importance of family in our country. Families are an essential building block for society, as they educate and instill civic engagement in the next generation of Americans. Democracy begins around the dinner table, which makes family a necessary part of the functionality of our country. Strong relationships and communities help individuals succeed and provide the tools for future generations to succeed. Yet recent trends in American relationships are preventing this pattern from carrying on.

A Pew Research study found that nearly 40 percent of adults were not married or living with a partner.[29] The decline in marriage among adults is impacting the health of our nation altogether. Many studies have shown that children raised by married parents are more likely to do better in school and develop stronger skills that are useful later in life.[30] Family helps strengthen and stabilize society, yet without any connection to family, tradition, or culture, socialist and communist ideologies thrive.

Pew reported that "unpartnered" people (meaning unmarried and not living with a partner) have lower earnings than partnered adults, are less likely to be employed, and have lower education attainment.[31] These factors prevent Americans from realizing their dreams—mired in deprivation and despair, people will stop fighting and give up.

Marriage and family are foundational in a free society. The breakdown or delaying of marriage and family threatens freedom. The Institute for Faith, Work & Economics wrote: "Family is the primary institution of moral and character development, and society must protect the family as the smallest unit of political order."[32]

This small unit of political order is the first step in protecting and preserving the nation. Americans must recognize the importance of family as a means of continuing to live free, full, and happy lives.

CIVILITY AND GRACE

The American system requires civility and grace from its people. Yet a culture of hubris and amorality has damaged our national character. The deep and splintered factions curated by the left have promoted a culture in which our differences are not used as tools for unity but as tools for division. Brotherhood begins with recognizing that every human being is created equally and in the image and likeness of God. Failing to recognize the humanity in each person allows for a culture of hatred and division to spread throughout our nation.

Civility encompasses so much of what America stands for. The Institute for Civility in Government writes:

Civility is about more than just politeness, although politeness is a necessary first step. It is about disagreeing without disrespect, seeking common ground as a starting point for dialogue about differences, listening past one's preconceptions, and teaching others to do the same. Civility is the hard work of staying present even with those with whom we have deep-rooted and fierce disagreements. It is political in the sense that it is a necessary prerequisite for civic action. But it is political, too, in the sense that it is about negotiating interpersonal power such that everyone's voice is heard, and nobody's ignored.[33]

Civility makes America an exceptional nation that embodies respect for others, proper public behavior, and self-regulation.[34] Civility starts with our friends and family and extends to strangers on the street. President Washington's *110 Rules of Civility and Decent Behavior in Company and Conversation* asserts: "every action done in company ought to be with some sign of respect to those that are present."[35] Civility as public behavior is how we manage our attitudes toward those we do not know. Right now, we live in a society in which people judge others instantly (based on race, politics, profile pictures, etc.) and civility toward strangers has nearly disappeared. These instantaneous judgments make our nation feel more divided than it truly is.

Civility means regulating your self-interests for the sake of the community. We cannot forget that we have a civic obligation to care for our community and country at large. Civility can look different in each of our interactions. But what is most important is that we all embody care and respect for people. Civility is a virtue that each American is called to enact for social cooperation, even in the most polarized of times.[36] Civility promotes compromise and respect in a society in which Big Government Socialists promote repression and cancel culture.[37] It is time to see that there is more in our nation that can unite us than divide us.

Importantly, civility begins with the individual—not with the government. How can we expect our nation to look unified if our own communities are divided at home? America cannot achieve civility if we do not begin with mutual respect.

The culture that we live in today rejects a key principle of civility: disagreeing without disrespect. America's Framers wrote our founding documents during one of the most contentious times in our history. While the Founders created a nation, they faced setbacks and concerns raised by opposition, yet they learned to disagree without crippling the progress of the nation. The bitter rivalry between John Adams and Thomas Jefferson could have resulted in chaos for our young nation; however, they learned to disagree without crippling the progress of the country. Throughout history there have been many bipartisan friendships that have strengthened our nation. Yet, so many politicians forget that their friends across the aisle are just that—friends. The culture on Capitol Hill under the reign of Nancy Pelosi is toxic. The environment that Pelosi created instigates gridlock and disfunction among members instead of seeking common-ground resolutions. Her secretive and self-serving deals do not help everyday Americans. They only seek to serve the agenda of Big Government Socialism.

When I was serving as Speaker, we routinely passed bills with bipartisan support. This showed that no matter which party we were tied to—we ultimately cared about the American people. Under Pelosi this would simply be impossible. The Contract with America showed the great progress that can be achieved with civility. In working with Democratic president Bill Clinton, we convinced many House Democrats to vote with us, and to vote for American solutions, not just partisan proposals. Civility means looking past that which divides you to achieve a greater good.

Bipartisan friendships show the importance of civility in our nation—even in contentious times. President Ronald Reagan and House Speaker Tip O'Neill consistently opposed one another's political views. Yet the two forged a friendship based on respect and their commitment to serve the country.[38] The late Supreme Court justices Antonin Scalia and Ruth Bader Ginsburg shared a close friendship while on the Court. Ginsburg's and Scalia's judicial philosophies could not have been more different—yet they disagreed without disrespect, and continued to interpret the law without impairing the judicial system. Day after day, the two had supremely different philosophies but found respect in one another's brilliance.[39]

A 2021 American Enterprise Institute study found that 15 percent of adults ended friendships over politics.[40] America was never meant to be a nation in which everyone agrees. Taking part in dialogue is imperative for a healthy democracy, but right now, Americans are choosing to cut off relations with political opposition, rather than working to communicate past those differences.

Right now, if you disagree with another person, all it takes is a few snarky posts to cancel them. This is not disagreement, this is suppression. We need to relearn what it means to be civil. We must resurrect common ground before we invoke hateful or untrue comments about others.

The problem is that Big Government Socialists refuse to acknowledge that there is indeed a common ground among Americans. An angry and loud minority group is misrepresenting the vast American majority that can come together to achieve progress. Americans need to be able to debate issues without suppressing the thoughts and freedoms of those who have the courage to speak out against the common thought.

The whole nation was never meant to be convinced to agree and believe the same thing, yet socialist thinkers aim to impose one viewpoint on all members of the society. America was founded on principles of civility and grace. These ideals are supposed to be upheld in individuals and localities. Communities can be the catalyst for change in a world in which cancel culture rules.

America is a nation that is reinforced by religion, family, society, and law. It is a country where we are all meant to share in the blessings of our God-given freedom from government oppression and thrive in the resilient system that was created by our Framers.

America supports civil debate, free speech, and grace. Yet these things seem like they have been eliminated as time presses on. The only solution to overcoming these differences is to recognize the humanity and grace in others. Combatting a culture of hubris and amorality means that we acknowledge that everyone is made in the image and likeness of God—our free speech and imperative as Americans depend on it.

THE PATRIOTISM OF PERSISTENCE

Defeating Big Government Socialism will be a daunting task. It has been developing and gaining power as a political theology within the American left since the 1960s. At this point its disciples make up the majority of our elite, media, and academic classes. They are accustomed to power, and they won't give it up quietly.

However, the American experience has been one of endless persistence. Opening up the wilderness was a constant process of learning by trial and error. Creating the wealthiest, most technologically advanced country in history was the result of constant persistence. Without persistence, nothing important can be achieved.

I may be biased about the importance of persistence because I had to run three times for Congress before I got elected. I lost in 1974 during Watergate and in 1976 when Georgia governor Jimmy Carter headed the Democratic ticket. I finally won in 1978. That was a five-year project (about the same length of time it took me to earn a PhD in European history from Tulane University).

When I got to Congress, I suggested to the House GOP leadership that since House Republicans had been in the minority for twenty-four years, it would be good to have a plan to become a majority. They thought that was a good idea and created a planning committee for a majority as part of the National Republican Congressional Committee. Then they asked me to chair the committee even though I had not yet been sworn in (it was December 1978). Little did I know that we would wage seven losing campaigns from 1980 to 1992 before finally winning in 1994 with the Contract with America.

That sixteen-year effort led us to teach all our activist members the concept of cheerful persistence—which we still uphold as an operating principle at Gingrich 360. We asserted that winning the majority was going to take a long, persistent effort—and that being cheerful during the persistence was the only way to attract more people to the party and minimize anger and conflict during periods of defeat or frustration.

Persistence is not a new trait for Americans. To win their independence, Americans persisted in an eight-year war against the most powerful empire in the world. When you consider that as many as one-third of the colonists were loyalists favoring the British government, and that another one-third tried to remain neutral and avoid involvement, the determination and force of will of the one-third who rebelled and fought for independence and freedom becomes even more impressive.

Lincoln had to endure a terrible civil war with more dead than all other American wars combined up through Korea. He initially had weak (or even bad) generals—some of whom did not want the Union to win. He had to keep the North unified and determined to save the union even though every town and village was losing young men in horrifying numbers.

Lincoln had to endure hostile, sometimes vicious newspaper attacks, congressional attacks on his wife's spending for furniture for the White House, and days of anti-draft riots in New York City (troops who had just won the Battle of Gettysburg were sent into our largest city to suppress the riots).

Through all this, he not only persisted but he retained a spirit of reconciliation strong enough to lead to the amazingly generous and spiritual second inaugural address. And then he was assassinated.

No persistence, no free America. No persistence, no saved American Union. The same principle of persistence applies to other aspects of American life.

As I previously mentioned, Thomas Edison had more than one thousand efforts to find the right material for the electric lightbulb. He once said to an assistant, "We have not had failures. We have successfully eliminated thousands of potential materials."

Henry Ford labored for years to build a mass-produced car that could lower the price and make automobiles available to virtually every American—a full generation before the same opportunity was developed in Europe.

The Wright Brothers kept going back to Kitty Hawk, North Carolina, year after year and undertook five hundred attempts to fly (at about one dollar per experiment). Then, on December 17, 1903, they flew for the first time. They had tinkered with and modified the plane repeatedly. They had studied birds. They went to Kitty Hawk because it had the most consistent updraft coming off the ocean of any place in the United States (courtesy of information from the U.S. Weather Service, which was the government's only contribution to their success).

The Wright Brothers' first flight was shorter than the wingspan of a Boeing 747. It was downhill and slow enough that one brother ran alongside the plane to make sure it did not flip over and kill the pilot. Four years later, the Wright Brothers flew around the island of Manhattan and more than a million people saw an airplane for the first time. That was how fast the technology was progressing once the initial flight had proven that the concept worked.

Whether you want to be a professional golfer, a great ballerina, a first-class surgeon, a first-generation success at business, or a full-time writer, persistence is necessary and unavoidable. It is also necessary to save our country from Big Government Socialism.

No matter what you do for a living, remind yourself and your team every day that anything worth accomplishing requires persistence. Teach your team to think of challenges and opportunities rather than problems. Grow an acceptance in your team and yourself that work and persistence are the heart of success. Teach everyone to respond to suggestions with "yes, we could do that if" rather than "no, we can't do that because." The difference in creativity and productivity will be amazing. Recognize, encourage, and reward those who persist.

The second vital constant in the American experience is patriotism.

Surviving in a dangerous world requires a strong sense of identity and a willingness to support the group whose success and safety is the necessary requirement for your success and safety. Since America is an invented country—with opportunities for everyone from every culture to become an American—the need to develop a patriotic spirit is especially strong.

The Founding Fathers knew that the new country on the edge of the Atlantic seaboard had to build a strong sense of identity and patriotism if it was going to survive in a dangerous world. Countries such as Britain, France, and Spain were much richer and more powerful than the new American republic.

Furthermore, the powerful European countries all worried about the danger a successful American republic of freedom posed to their own aristocratic systems of power. Even when the French revolutionaries overthrew their king, they saw America as a pawn in the struggle for power in Europe.

Benjamin Franklin captured this spirit of the importance of patriotism when he said, "We must all hang together, or assuredly we shall all hang separately." Throughout America's first decades, there were constant efforts to manipulate the new republic and subvert its government so it would be an ally to one side or the other. It was in response to these constant efforts at subversion that President George Washington in his Farewell Address warned against foreign entanglements. He knew that the new nation had to be careful not to get caught up in European wars.

The need to identify as Americans was made even greater by history and geography. Historically, Americans had thought of themselves as colonists. When they began to think about independence, they tended to identify with their states. Westerners were not sure they had any great common interest with the East. That led early in Washington's first term to the Whiskey Rebellion, as farmers in western Pennsylvania refused to pay the new tax on whiskey. Washington imposed national unity by calling out a large army of militia and planning to lead it himself until the farmers backed down.

The third vice president of the United States, Aaron Burr, was engaged in treason that would have dismembered the western part of the then United States (the western part being the Mississippi River valley, since Jefferson had not yet bought the Louisiana Purchase from Napoleon). Westerners worried about British backing for Native Americans engaged in constant warfare against the encroaching settlers. New Englanders worried about trade with England and the Caribbean. Southerners worried about protecting slavery and ensuring that their cotton could be sold overseas. The middle states worried about manufacturing and banking. There were a lot of good reasons to be concerned about national unity and making sure America was not pulled apart by various competing interests.

In our three major wars (the Civil War, World War I, and World War II) there was a deep, determined effort by each of the respective presidents (Lincoln, Woodrow Wilson, and Franklin Delano Roosevelt) to ensure that the American people (in Lincoln's case the Union) were unified and behind the war. In all three cases, the presidents moved slowly and cautiously until opponents made the war unavoidable and convinced the large majority of Americans we had to fight.

The depth of patriotism in the North growing out of the crucible of bloodletting that was the Civil War was captured in the December 1863 short story by Edward Everett Hale, "The Man Without a Country." It is the story of a man who was tried for treason along with former vice president Burr. In a moment of self-righteous anger, the man shouts in court, "I wish I may never hear of the United States again!" When he is convicted, the judge sentences him to spend the rest of his life on American naval vessels, with everyone instructed to never mention the United States to him. Over the course of a long life aboard a variety of ships, he becomes a total patriot and gathers up all the news he can about America. "The Man Without a Country" hit the mood of the moment and became wildly popular. Given the brutal human cost of preserving the Union, millions wanted to believe in patriotism and to condemn those who were not patriotic.

In the 1930s, the House Un-American Activities Committee was created to stop the Nazi effort to undermine American unity. It would become famous after World War II for its concern about communism, but the committee originated to deal with the real subversive efforts that came from Nazi Germany. During the Cold War, there was a continuous effort to maximize American patriotism and make it difficult for the Soviet Union and its communist allies to penetrate and undermine American patriotism.

One of the most worrying things about the current era is the eruption against patriotism (taking a knee rather than standing during the playing of the national anthem, refusing to say the pledge of allegiance, and athletes refusing to carry the American flag at the Olympics). Perhaps more distressing is the open preference of many big businesses and billionaires for Chinese profits over American patriotism.

If the United States loses its patriotic commitment to being one nation, there is a real danger our enemies will manipulate and subsidize the radical Marxist factions to tear our country apart and leave us helpless to defend ourselves.

President Reagan had been in the last U.S. Army Reserve cavalry unit in the 1930s, and then served in World War II. He was deeply involved in fighting against communism and the

Soviet Union from 1947 until the Soviet Union collapsed and disappeared. He felt deeply the importance of informed, educated patriotism.

In Reagan's 1989 Farewell Address, he focused on patriotic education:

> Finally, there is a great tradition of warnings in Presidential farewells, and I've got one that's been on my mind for some time. But oddly enough it starts with one of the things I'm proudest of in the past eight years: the resurgence of national pride that I called the new patriotism. This national feeling is good, but it won't count for much, and it won't last unless it's grounded in thoughtfulness and knowledge.
>
> An informed patriotism is what we want. And are we doing a good enough job teaching our children what America is and what she represents in the long history of the world? Those of us who are over 35 or so years of age grew up in a different America. We were taught, very directly, what it means to be an American. And we absorbed, almost in the air, a love of country and an appreciation of its institutions. If you didn't get these things from your family, you got them from the neighborhood, from the father down the street who fought in Korea, or the family who lost someone at Anzio. Or you could get a sense of patriotism from school. And if all else failed you could get a sense of patriotism from the popular culture. The movies celebrated democratic values and implicitly reinforced the idea that America was special. TV was like that, too, through the mid-sixties.

But now, we're about to enter the nineties, and some things have changed. Younger parents aren't sure that an unambivalent appreciation of America is the right thing to teach modern children. And as for those who create the popular culture, well-grounded patriotism is no longer the style. Our spirit is back, but we haven't reinstitutionalized it. We've got to do a better job of getting across that America is freedom—freedom of speech, freedom of religion, freedom of enterprise. And freedom is special and rare. It's fragile; it needs production [protection].

So, we've got to teach history based not on what's in fashion but what's important—why the Pilgrims came here, who Jimmy Doolittle was, and what those 30 seconds over Tokyo meant. You know, 4 years ago on the 40th anniversary of D-day, I read a letter from a young woman writing to her late father, who'd fought on Omaha Beach. Her name was Lisa Zanatta Henn, and she said, "We will always remember, we will never forget what the boys of Normandy did." Well, let's help her keep her word. If we forget what we did, we won't know who we are. I'm warning of an eradication of the American memory that could result, ultimately, in an erosion of the American spirit. Let's start with some basics: more attention to American history and a greater emphasis on civic ritual.[1]

Reagan was right, and a generation later the challenge of sustaining an informed and wise patriotism is greater than ever.

In our daily life we have an absolute obligation to nourish and foster patriotism. We should stand for the national anthem, and we should encourage it being played at every symbolic moment. We should encourage saying the pledge of allegiance. We should insist that schools teach American history accurately, without editorializing political motives. We should honor and encourage those who risk their lives to protect our country from abroad and here at home. We should encourage a spirit of patriotic community from the family and neighborhood through the school board and the local government to the state and federal government.

We should take on those in the news media and academia who denigrate, undermine, and repudiate patriotism. We should hold government to account at all levels and eliminate rules and regulations that are unpatriotic. When necessary, we should remove government officials—appointed and elected—who are determined to undermine and weaken patriotism.

In this book, I tried to illustrate that Big Government Socialism is a threat to our future as a country that must be defeated for our survival. I tried to give the examples we can take from history and apply them to this effort. But before any of these ideas can be put into place, we must commit to remaining persistent and patriotic.

If we do not love our country and lack the commitment to nurture and strengthen it, there will be no American future worth saving.

ACKNOWLEDGMENTS

Writing *Defeating Big Government Socialism* required a great deal of thought and assistance. It was not enough to describe what was wrong with Big Government Socialism as a model. To help get America back on track, we had to develop a policy framework and a solid foundation of principles that could be applied to solving the extraordinary range of problems that have been allowed to fester and undermine the American system.

We also had to think about the application of those principles in a world in which the United States is faced with a rising peer competitor in China and a series of secondary foreign challenges from Russia, Iran, North Korea, Venezuela, and Cuba.

We had to develop the case for American solutions based on American principles to get us back in the game—and give America a chance to again become the most dynamic, entrepreneurial, prosperous, free, and safe country in the world.

It would not have been possible for me to overcome the challenges this book posed without an exceptional group of people supporting the project every step of the way. This book would simply not have been possible without their advice, research, and analysis, for which I am deeply grateful.

ACKNOWLEDGMENTS

I thank Callista, who supported and encouraged me throughout this endeavor—both in her role as president and chief executive officer of Gingrich 360 and as my wife.

Thank you to my daughters, Kathy Lubbers and Jackie
Cushman; Kathy for being an incredible book agent and representative, and Jackie for all the ideas and concepts she helped
shape in her weekly columns.

Thanks to the team at Gingrich 360, without whom the
extensive research and ideas that created this book could not
have been compiled. Louie Brogdon took the lead in coordi-
nating and developing this project. With him were Claire
Christensen, who brought her expertise on foreign affairs, and
Joe DeSantis, who brought his knowledge on health care in
America. I must also thank Rachel Peterson for her tireless and
unmatched research.

Thanks to Bess Kelly for directing our team's efforts, and
Woody Hales for managing and organizing our many commit-
ments. To Taylor Swindle for keeping our financial focus and priorities straight. And to Rebekah Howell for her leadership and
support in virtually every aspect of Gingrich 360.

Thank you to Garnsey Sloan, the producer of my podcast, *Newt's World*. Through her work, our reach and impact
have increased.

Thanks to Allen Silkin for his expert management of the
Gingrich 360 website and our social media. Also, thank you to
our intrepid team of interns—Jessica Jacobs for her countless
contributions, and Faith Novak and Hazik Azam for their thor-
ough research.

Thanks to Randy Evans, my close friend since 1976, who
offered invaluable insights and advice, as well as to Stefan

Passantino, our friend and attorney, who contributed greatly to this project.

Another major group of contributors to *Defeating Big Government Socialism* includes all those working on the American Majority Project, which strives to understand the demographics of the nation and prove that most Americans trust conservative values and ideals. Joe Gaylord, who in 1994 worked with me to create the Contract with America, provided his unparalleled understanding of politics and public opinion to making this project successful.

I would also like to thank John McLaughlin, Stuart Polk, and Brian Larkin at McLaughlin & Associates, who impeccably coordinated and executed the American Majority Project's polling and surveys. Much of the early work on health and health care was developed by Dave Winston and Myra Miller at the Winston Group.

I owe a deep debt of gratitude to Bernie Marcus and Steve Hantler, who first approached me in 2017 about the concept of trying to find large enough majorities among the American people that we could break out of the current gridlock and begin to grow a stable governing majority capable of developing and implementing the strategic changes necessary for America to survive.

Among the many friends and observers who helped shape my thinking, I must specifically mention Ben Domenech, Vince Haley, Ross Worthington, Lynda McLaughlin, Sean Hannity, Herman Pirchner, Cliff May, Brooke Rollins, Scooter Libby, Chris DeMuth, and Ed Feulner (whose development of the *Mandate for Leadership* at the Heritage Foundation in 1980 was historic and the model for much of what I am doing).

For their openness to new ideas while trying to create a majority, I must also single out Ronna Romney McDaniel, Senator Rick Scott, and House GOP Leader Kevin McCarthy.

Lastly, my thanks go to our publisher, Daisy Hutton, and our editor, Alex Pappas, at Hachette Book Group, who worked tirelessly on this project.

This remarkable team made *Defeating Big Government Socialism* possible.

NOTES

CHAPTER 1: BIG GOVERNMENT SOCIALISM ISN'T WORKING—AND IT CAN'T

1. Twitter, accessed March 4, 2022, https://twitter.com/VP.

2. Amanda Holpuch, Derrick Bryson Taylor, and Neil Vigdor, "Stranded Drivers Are Freed after 24-Hour Snowy Ordeal on I-95 in Virginia," *New York Times*, January 4, 2022, https://www.nytimes.com/2022/01/04/us/i-95-closed -snowstorm-winter.html.

3. Raynor de Best, "Covid-19 Deaths per Capita by Country," Statista, March 3, 2022, https://www.statista.com/statistics/1104709/coronavirus-deaths -worldwide-per-million-inhabitants/.

4. Chris Papst, "6 Baltimore Schools, No Students Proficient in State Tests," WBFF, May 22, 2017, https://foxbaltimore.com/news/project-baltimore/6 -baltimore-schools-no-students-proficient-in-state-tests.

5. Chris Papst, "13 Baltimore City High Schools, Zero Students Proficient in Math," WBFF, December 17, 2018, https://foxbaltimore.com/news/project -baltimore/13-baltimore-city-high-schools-zero-students-proficient-in-math.

6. Chris Papst, "Explosive Report: City Schools Finds Grade Changing and Overreporting of Students," WBFF, September 5, 2021, https://foxbaltimore .com/news/project-baltimore/report-augusta-fells-administrators-scammed -taxpayers-changed-grades.

7. Andy Puzder and Will Coggin, "Meatpackers Are Biden's Latest Inflation Scapegoat," *Wall Street Journal*, January 9, 2022, https://www.wsj.com/articles /meatpackers-are-biden-latest-inflation-scapegoat-beef-pork-chicken-labor -fertilizer-fuel-bottleneck-work-force-participation-agriculture-11641759774.

8. "Lord Acton Writes to Bishop Creighton That the Same Moral Standards Should Be Applied to All Men, Political and Religious Leaders Included, Especially since 'Power Tends to Corrupt and Absolute Power Corrupts Absolutely' (1887)," Online Library of Liberty, accessed March 4, 2022, https:// oll.libertyfund.org/quote/lord-acton-writes-to-bishop-creighton-that-the-same -moral-standards-should-be-applied-to-all-men-political-and-religious-leaders -included-especially-since-power-tends-to-corrupt-and-absolute-power-corrupts -absolutely-1887.

9. Gordon Wood, *The Creation of the American Republic, 1776–1787*, accessed March 4, 2022, http://www.cameronblevins.org/cblevins/Quals /BookSummaries/Wood_TheCreationofthe%20AmericanRepublic .html#:~:text=Wood%2C%20The%20Creation%20of%20the%20 American%20Republic%2C%201776%2D1787&text=Gordon%20Wood%20 charts%20a%20transformation,1787%20based%20on%20social%20conflict.

10. Person, "CA Edd Admits Paying as Much as $31 Billion in Unemployment Funds to Criminals," ABC7 San Francisco, KGO-TV, January 26, 2021, https://abc7news.com/california-edd-unemployment-fraud-ca-scam -insurance/10011810/.

11. "Smash-and-Grab Thefts at L.A. Nordstrom Trigger Police Chase," NBCNews .com, November 24, 2021, https://www.nbcnews.com/news/us-news/smash -grab-robbery-nordstrom-los-angeles-triggers-police-chase-rcna6440.

12. "Drug Overdose Deaths in the U.S. Top 100,000 Annually," Centers for Disease Control and Prevention, November 17, 2021, https://www.cdc.gov /nchs/pressroom/nchs_press_releases/2021/20211117.htm.

13. "Defining Deviancy Down—JSTOR," accessed March 4, 2022, https://www .jstor.org/stable/41212064.

14. "Defining Deviancy Up," *Baltimore Sun*, March 3, 2022, https://www .baltimoresun.com/news/bs-xpm-1993-11-26-1993330030-story.html.

15. George L. Kelling and James Q. Wilson, "Broken Windows," *The Atlantic*, July 20, 2020, https://www.theatlantic.com/magazine/archive/1982/03/broken -windows/304465/.

16. *A Nation at Risk: The Imperative for Educational Reform*, accessed March 4, 2022, https://edreform.com/wp-content/uploads/2013/02/A_Nation_At _Risk_1983.pdf.

17. Tamar Jacoby, Jason L. Riley, Naomi Schaefer Riley, Josh B. McGee, and Jay P. Greene, "'Losing Ground' in Education Reform," Manhattan Institute, December 18, 2015, https://www.manhattan-institute.org/html/losing-ground -education-reform-1229.html.

CHAPTER 2: DANGER AND OPPORTUNITY

1. "Federal 1794 Government Spending," Government Spending in United States: Federal State Local for 1794—Charts Tables History, accessed March 4, 2022, https://www.usgovernmentspending.com/total_spending_1792USrn.

2. Ibid.

3. Jason Kelly, "Octopotus?" *University of Chicago Magazine*, accessed March 4, 2022, https://mag.uchicago.edu/law-policy-society/octopotus.

4. "Parkinson's Law," *The Economist*, accessed March 4, 2022, https://www .economist.com/news/1955/11/19/parkinsons-law.

5. "The 'Law' That Explains Why You Can't Get Anything Done," BBC, accessed March 4, 2022, https://www.bbc.com/worklife/article/20191107-the-law-that -explains-why-you-cant-get-anything-done?source=techstories.org.

6. https://www.axios.com/pandemic-unemployment-fraud-benefits-stolen -a937ad9d-0973-4aad-814f-4ca47b72f67f.html.

7. "California's Unemployment Fraud Reaches at Least $20 Billion," *Los Angeles Times*, October 25, 2021, https://www.latimes.com/california/story/2021-10 -25/californias-unemployment-fraud-20-billion.

8. "Washington Auditor Says State Unemployment Fraud Likely Much Higher than $647 Million," Northwest Public Broadcasting, April 14, 2021, https:// www.nwpb.org/2021/04/14/washington-auditor-says-state-unemployment -fraud-likely-much-higher-than-647-million/.

9. "Former Employment Security Department Employee Indicted for Filing False Unemployment Claims and Demanding Kickbacks," United States Department of Justice, September 24, 2021, https://www.justice.gov/usao -wdwa/pr/former-employment-security-department-employee-indicted-filing -false-unemployment.

10. "Newt's World—Episode 56: China's Coronavirus," Gingrich 360, December 31, 2021, https://www.gingrich360.com/2020/02/09/newts-world-episode-56 -chinas-coronavirus/.

11. "A Time for Choosing Speech, October 27, 1964," Ronald Reagan Library, accessed March 4, 2022, https://www.reaganlibrary.gov/reagans/ronald-reagan /time-choosing-speech-october-27-1964.

CHAPTER 3: WHAT WORKS: HISTORY, STABILITY, AND STRENGTH

1. "Founders Online: The Federalist No. 55, [13 February 1788]," National Archives and Records Administration, accessed March 4, 2022, https:// founders.archives.gov/documents/Hamilton/01-04-02-0204.

2. "How George Soros Funded Progressive DAs behind US Crime Surge," accessed March 4, 2022, http://billboard.io/cars-https-nypost.com/2021/12/16 /how-george-soros-funded-progressive-das-behind-us-crime-surge/.

3. "Sir Edward Coke Declares That Your House Is Your 'Castle and Fortress' (1604)," Online Library of Liberty, accessed March 4, 2022, https://oll4 .libertyfund.org/quote/sir-edward-coke-declares-that-your-house-is-your-castle -and-fortress-1604.

4. "Article VI," Legal Information Institute, accessed March 4, 2022, https:// www.law.cornell.edu/constitution/articlevi.

5. "Fourteenth Amendment Section 4 | Constitution . . . - Congress," accessed March 4, 2022, https://constitution.congress.gov/browse/amendment-14 /section-4/.

6. "The Federalist Papers No. 10," Avalon Project—Documents in Law, History, and Diplomacy, accessed March 4, 2022, https://avalon.law.yale.edu/18th _century/fed10.asp.

7. "Thomas Jefferson to William Plumer, July 21, 1816," Library of Congress, accessed March 4, 2022, https://www.loc.gov/resource/mtj1.049_0298_0298/.

8. Thomas Jefferson, extract from First Inaugural Address, March 4, 1801, Jefferson Quotes & Family Letters, March 4, 1801, https://tjrs.monticello.org /letter/1330.

9. CNN, accessed March 4, 2022, https://www.cnn.com/ALLPOLITICS/1996 /candidates/republican/withdrawn/gramm.announcement.shtml.

10. "George Washington's Farewell Address 1796," Constitution Facts—Official U.S. Constitution Website, accessed March 4, 2022, https://www.constitutionfacts.com /us-founding-fathers/george-washingtons-farewell-address/.

CHAPTER 4: THE ROT AT THE TOP

1. Eran Shalev, *Rome Reborn on Western Shores: Historical Imagination and the Creation of the American Republic* (Charlottesville: University of Virginia Press, 2009), https://www.amazon.com/Creation-American-Republic-1776-1787 /dp/0807847232.

2. Deborah D'Souza, "What Is Stakeholder Capitalism?" Investopedia, February 8, 2022, https://www.investopedia.com/stakeholder-capitalism-4774323.

3. Ariel Cohen, "Europe's Self-Inflicted Energy Crisis," *Forbes*, December 10, 2021, https://www.forbes.com/sites/arielcohen/2021/10/14/europes-self -inflicted-energy-crisis/.

4. Katherine Blunt, "California Blackouts a Warning for States Ramping up Green Power," *Wall Street Journal*, August 17, 2020, https://www.wsj.com/articles /california-blackouts-a-warning-for-states-ramping-up-green-power-11597706934.

5. Norman Doidge, "Why Is There So Much Vaccine Hesitancy?" *Tablet Magazine*, October 28, 2021, https://www.tabletmag.com/sections/science /articles/needle-points-vaccinations-chapter-one.

6. John Stuart Mill, *On Liberty* (Cambridge: Cambridge University Press, 2011).

7. Rowan Jacobsen, "Exclusive: How Amateur Sleuths Broke the Wuhan Lab Story and Embarrassed the Media," *Newsweek*, June 18, 2021, https://www .newsweek.com/exclusive-how-amateur-sleuths-broke-wuhan-lab-story -embarrassed-media-1596958.

8. Ibid.

9. Ibid.

10. Ibid.

11. Ian Birrell, "Did Scientists Stifle the Lab-Leak Theory?" UnHerd, August 1, 2021, https://unherd.com/2021/07/how-scientists-stifled-the-lab-leak-theory/.

12. Sainath Suryanarayanan, "EcoHealth Alliance Orchestrated Key Scientists' Statement on 'Natural Origin' of SARS-COV-2," U.S. Right to Know, March 2, 2021, https://usrtk.org/biohazards-blog/ecohealth-alliance-orchestrated-key -scientists-statement-on-natural-origin-of-sars-cov-2/.

13. Matt Ridley, "Why Did Scientists Suppress the Lab-Leak Theory?" spiked, January 12, 2022, https://www.spiked-online.com/2022/01/12/why-did -scientists-suppress-the-lab-leak-theory/.

14. Sarah Knapton, "Scientists Believed Covid Leaked from Wuhan Lab—but Feared Debate Could Hurt 'International Harmony,'" *Telegraph*, January 11, 2022, https://www.telegraph.co.uk/news/2022/01/11/scientists-believed-covid -leaked-wuhan-lab-feared-debate-could/?fr=operanews.

15. Mallory Simon, "Over 1,000 Health Professionals Sign a Letter Saying, Don't Shut down Protests Using Coronavirus Concerns as an Excuse," CNN, June 5, 2020, https://www.cnn.com/2020/06/05/health/health-care-open-letter -protests-coronavirus-trnd/index.html.

16. Tom Frieden, "When Will It Be Safe to Go out Again?" *Washington Post*, March 25, 2020, https://www.washingtonpost.com/opinions/when-will-it-be -safe-to-go-out-again/2020/03/24/7cb2e488-6de1-11ea-aa80-c2470c6b2034 _story.html.

17. Dr. Tom F. Frieden (@DrTomFrieden), "The Threat to Covid Control from Protesting Outside Is Tiny Compared to the Threat to Covid Control Created When Governments Act in Ways That Lose Community Trust. People Can Protest Peacefully and Work Together to Stop Covid. Violence Harms Public Health," Twitter, June 2, 2020, https://twitter.com/DrTomFrieden /status/1267796218496901121.

18. Jane Coaston and Aaron Rupar, "Thousands of Michiganders Took to the Streets to Protest the Governor's Stay-at-Home Order," Vox, April 16, 2020, https://www.vox.com/2020/4/16/21222471/michigan-protests-coronavirus -stay-at-home-extension.

19. Justin P. Hicks, "Gov. Whitmer Responds to Lack of Social Distancing at Protests against Police Brutality," mlive, June 5, 2020, https://www.mlive.com /public-interest/2020/06/gov-whitmer-responds-to-lack-of-social-distancing-at -protests-against-police-brutality.html.

20. Isabella Redjai, "Coronavirus: Churches Are Essential. If Protesters Can Assemble, so Should People of Faith," *USA Today*, August 8, 2020, https:// www.usatoday.com/story/opinion/voices/2020/08/08/coronavirus-pandemic -churches-essential-businesses-open-religious-freedom-column/3323082001/.

21. April Ryan (@AprilDRyan), "Should #StayAtHome protestors who endanger other Americans by not following @CDCgovguidelines about physical distancing be required to sign a waiver refusing medical attention at a hospital and not take up a ventilator if they contract coronavirus? #COVID19

#StayHome," Twitter, April 20, 2020, https://twitter.com/AprilDRyan /status/1252306443497353218.

22. Drew Holden (@Drew Holden), "@AprilDRyan doesn't seem to be asking this question anymore. Wonder why," Twitter, June 3, 2020, https://twitter.com /DrewHolden360/status/1268294879140106245.

23. Katie Camero, "Why Did CDC Change Definition for 'Vaccine'? Agency Explains," *Miami Herald*, September 27, 2021, https://www.miamiherald.com /news/coronavirus/article254111268.html.

24. Katie Rogers and Sheryl Gay Stolberg, "Biden Mandates Vaccines for Workers, Saying 'Our Patience Is Wearing Thin,'" *New York Times*, September 9, 2021, https://www.nytimes.com/2021/09/09/us/politics/biden-mandates-vaccines .html.

25. Abishek Chandrashekar, Lisa H. Tostanoski, Lauren Peter, Noe B. Mercado, Katherine McMahan, Amanda J Martinot, Jinyan Liu, et al, "SARS-COV-2 Infection Protects against Rechallenge in Rhesus Macaques," *Science*, May 20, 2020, https://www.science.org/doi/10.1126/science.abc4776.

26. Sivan Gazit, Roei Shlezinger, Galit Perez, Roni Lotan, Asaf Peretz, Amir Ben-Tov, Dani Cohen, Khitam Muhsen, Gabriel Chodick, and Tal Patalon, "Comparing Sars-COV-2 Natural Immunity to Vaccine-Induced Immunity: Reinfections versus Breakthrough Infections," medRxiv, Cold Spring Harbor Laboratory Press, January 1, 2021, https://www.medrxiv.org/content/10.1101/2 021,08.24.21262415v1.

27. Marty Makary, "The High Cost of Disparaging Natural Immunity to Covid," *Wall Street Journal*, January 26, 2022, https://www.wsj.com/articles/the-high -cost-of-disparaging-natural-immunity-to-covid-vaccine-mandates-protests-fire -rehire-employment-11643214336.

28. Ashley Collman, "2 Top FDA Officials Resigned over the Biden Administration's Booster-Shot Plan, Saying It Insisted on the Policy before the Agency Approved It, Reports Say," Business Insider, September 1, 2021, https:// www.businessinsider.com/2-top-fda-officials-resigned-biden-booster-plan -reports-2021-9.

CHAPTER 5: HUMAN NATURE, GOVERNMENT, AND THE RULE OF LAW

1. James Madison, "Federalist Papers No. 51 (1788)," Bill of Rights Institute, accessed March 7, 2022, https://billofrightsinstitute.org/primary-sources /federalist-no-51.

2. Stephen Soarce, "Shawn Laval Smith: Suspected Killer of Brianna Kupfer Has a Long History of Arrests," FOX 11 Los Angeles, January 19, 2022, https://www .foxla.com/news/brianna-kupfer-murder-shawn-laval-smith-arrest-record.

3. James Madison, "The Federalist Papers: No. 46," Avalon Project, Yale Law School, 2008, https://avalon.law.yale.edu/18th_century/fed46.asp.

4. John Locke, "Chapter 18. Of Tyranny," American History: From Revolution to Reconstruction and Beyond, 2012, accessed March 7, 2022, http://www.let .rug.nl/usa/documents/1651-1700/john-locke-essay-on-government/chapter-18 -of-tyranny.php.

5. John Adams, "John Adams," American History from Revolution to Reconstruction and Beyond, 2012, accessed March 7, 2022, http://www.let .rug.nl/usa/presidents/john-adams/thoughts-on-government.php.

6. Samuel Adams, "Benjamin Franklin's Preface to the English Edition of the Report," *Rights of Colonists*, 1772, Hanover Historical Texts Project, 2018, accessed March 7, 2022, https://history.hanover.edu/texts/adamss.html.

7. Abraham Lincoln, "Lyceum Address," Abraham Lincoln Online, 2018, http:// www.abrahamlincolnonline.org/lincoln/speeches/lyceum.htm.

CHAPTER 6: POVERTY AND DESPAIR

1. Karl Rove, "Jen Psaki Tries to 'Fake' Out the CBO's Build Back Better Score," *Wall Street Journal*, December 15, 2021, https://www.wsj.com/articles /jen-psaki-tries-to-fake-out-congressional-budget-office-cbo-build-back-better -cost-biden-11639603930.

2. Dani Romero, "Gas Prices Reach $6.00 a Gallon in Some Southern California Areas," Yahoo! News, February 28, 2022, https://news.yahoo.com/gas-prices -reach-6-00-182527994.html.

3. Ibid.

4. Peter Santilli and Ryan Dezember, "Why High Gasoline Prices Could Stick around for a While," *Wall Street Journal*, February 10, 2022, https:// www.wsj.com/articles/why-high-gasoline-prices-could-stick-around-for-a -while-11644489001.

5. Peter Hasson, "Biden Energy Sec. Granholm Laughs at Question about Boosting Oil Production: 'That Is Hilarious,'" Fox Business, November 5, 2021, https:// www.foxbusiness.com/politics/biden-energy-sec-granholm-laughs-boosting-oil -hilarious.

6. Anthony Salvanto, Jennifer De Pinto, Fred Backus, and Kabir Khanna, "Biden at Year One: Not Enough Focus on Inflation Leaves Many Frustrated," CBS News, January 16, 2022, https://www.cbsnews.com/news/biden-inflation-first -year-opinion-poll/.

7. Gwynn Guilford, "U.S. Inflation Hit 7% in December, Fastest Pace since 1982," *Wall Street Journal*, January 12, 2022, https://www.wsj.com/articles /us-inflation-consumer-price-index-december-2021-11641940760?mod=series _inflation.

8. Greg Ip, "Why 7% Inflation Today Is Far Different than in 1982," *Wall Street Journal*, January 12, 2022, https://www.wsj.com/articles/why-7-inflation-today -is-far-different-than-in-1982-11642012166.

9. Will Weissert and Hannah Fingerhut, "Inflation up, Virus down as Priorities in US: AP-Norc Poll," Associated Press, January 10, 2022, https://apnews .com/article/coronavirus-pandemic-joe-biden-business-health-elections -bb16c5c52e2bf719ec8a0c5415aaf66c.

10. Economics Daily, "Consumer Price Index: 2021 in Review," U.S. Bureau of Labor Statistics, January 14, 2022, https://www.bls.gov/opub/ted/2022 /consumer-price-index-2021-in-review.htm.

11. "Databases, Tables & Calculators by Subject," U.S. Bureau of Labor Statistics, accessed March 9, 2022, https://data.bls.gov/timeseries /APU000074714amp%253bdata_tool=XGtable&output _view=data&include_graphs=true.

12. "Databases, Tables & Calculators by Subject," U.S. Bureau of Labor Statistics, accessed March 9, 2022, https://data.bls.gov/timeseries /APU000072610?amp%253bdata_tool=XGtable&output_view=data&include _graphs=true.

13. Paul Wiseman, "Explainer: Why US Inflation Is So High, and When It May Ease," Associated Press, January 12, 2022, https://apnews.com/article/why-is -inflation-so-high-5f69bed77f98221f9936ae99f96fd361.

14. Greg Iacurci, "Despite Higher Wages, Inflation Gave the Average Worker a 2.4% Pay Cut Last Year," CNBC, January 12, 2022, https://www.cnbc .com/2022/01/12/higher-pay-eclipses-inflation-bite-for-some-.html.

15. "The People's Republic of China," Office of the United States Trade Representative, Executive Office of the President, 2020, https://ustr.gov /countries-regions/china-mongolia-taiwan/peoples-republic-china.

16. Vanessa Yurkevich, "Port of Los Angeles Traffic Sets Record in 2021," CNN, January 4, 2022, https://www.cnn.com/2022/01/04/business/traffic-los -angeles-port-record/index.html.

17. Aaron Kliegman, "Biden Tries to Define Away Ongoing Supply Chain Crisis, Declare Victory," *Just the News*, December 3, 2021, https://justthenews .com/nation/economy/biden-declares-victory-supply-chain-crisis-despite-no -improvement-cargo-logjam.

18. Pacific Merchant Association, "New Queuing Process for Container Vessels Bound for Ports of LA/Long Beach to Improve Safety and Air Quality Off California Coast," Pacific Merchant Shipping Association, November 11, 2021, https://www .pmsaship.com/wp-content/uploads/2021/11/Container-Vessel-Queuing-Release -FINAL.pdf.

19. Aaron Kliegman, "Biden Tries to Define Away Ongoing Supply Chain Crisis, Declare Victory," *Just the News*, December 3, 2021, https://justthenews

.com/nation/economy/biden-declares-victory-supply-chain-crisis-despite-no
-improvement-cargo-logjam.

20. Marine Exchange of Southern California, Facebook, February 23, 2015.
https://www.facebook.com/Mxsocal/.

21. David J. Lynch, "As Supply Chain Troubles Mount, Biden Touts Longer
Hours for L.A. Port," *Washington Post*, October 13, 2021, https://www
.washingtonpost.com/business/2021/10/13/biden-port-los-angeles-supply
-chain/.

22. Paul Berger, "Truckers Steer Clear of 24-Hour Operations at Southern
California Ports," *Wall Street Journal*, November 17, 2021, https://www.wsj
.com/articles/truckers-steer-clear-of-24-hour-operations-at-southern-california
-ports-11637173872.

23. Bethany Blankley, "Groups Warn of Supply Chain System Collapse, as
California Ports Face Record Backlogs," *Just The News*, September 31, 2021,
https://justthenews.com/politics-policy/transportation/frigroups-warn-supply
-chain-system-collapse-california-ports-see.

24. Jonathan Ponciano, "Biden Invests $14 Billion in U.S. Ports and Waterways
in Bid to Combat Climate Change and Ease Supply Chain Constraints—
Here's Where the Funds Will Go," *Forbes*, January 20, 2022, https://www
.forbes.com/sites/jonathanponciano/2022/01/19/biden-invests-14-billion-in-us
-ports-and-waterways-in-bid-to-combat-climate-change-and-ease-supply-chain
-constraints-heres-where-the-funds-will-go/?sh=4d425d444206.

25. United States Interagency Council on Homelessness, "Expanding the Toolbox:
The Whole-of-Government Response to Homelessness," Texas Policy, 2020,
https://www.texaspolicy.com/wp-content/uploads/2021/09/USICH-2020
-report401.pdf.

26. Ibid.

27. U.S. Department of Housing and Urban Development, 2020 Annual Homeless
Assessment Report (AHAR) to Congress, 2021, https://www.huduser.gov
/portal/sites/default/files/pdf/2020-AHAR-Part-1.pdf.

28. United States Interagency Council on Homelessness, "Expanding the Toolbox:
The Whole-of-Government Response to Homelessness," Texas Policy, 2020,
https://www.texaspolicy.com/wp-content/uploads/2021/09/USICH-2020
-report401.pdf.

29. HUD Public Affairs, "HUD Releases 2020 Annual Homeless Assessment
Report Part 1," U.S. Department of Housing and Urban Development (HUD),
May 21, 2021, https://www.hud.gov/press/press_releases_media_advisories
/hud_no_21_041.

30. U.S. Department of Housing and Urban Development, 2020 Annual Homeless
Assessment Report (AHAR) to Congress, 2021, https://www.huduser.gov
/portal/sites/default/files/pdf/2020-AHAR-Part-1.pdf.

31. United States Interagency Council on Homelessness, "Expanding the Toolbox: The Whole-of-Government Response to Homelessness," Texas Policy, 2020, https://www.texaspolicy.com/wp-content/uploads/2021/09/USICH-2020 -report401.pdf.

32. U.S. Department of Housing and Urban Development, 2020 Annual Homeless Assessment Report (AHAR) to Congress, 2021, https://www.huduser.gov /portal/sites/default/files/pdf/2020-AHAR-Part-1.pdf.

33. Christopher Rufo, "Homelessness in America: An Overview," Heritage Foundation, February 16, 2021, https://www.heritage.org/poverty-and -inequality/report/homelessness-america-overview.

34. Janey Rountree, Nathan Hess, and Austin Lyke, "Health Conditions among Unsheltered Adults in the U.S.," California Policy Lab, October 6, 2019, https://www.capolicylab.org/wp-content/uploads/2019/10/Health-Conditions -Among-Unsheltered-Adults-in-the-U.S.pdf.

35. Callista L. Gingrich, "Addressing the Aftermath of Covid-19," Gingrich 360, January 15, 2022, https://www.gingrich360.com/2022/01/15/addressing-the -aftermath-of-covid-19/.

36. Alex Piquero, Wesley Jennings, Erin Jemison, Catherine Kaukinen, and Felicia Knaul, "Domestic Violence during Covid-19," National Commission on COVID-19 and Criminal Justice, February 2021, https://build.neoninspire .com/counciloncj/wp-content/uploads/sites/96/2021/07/Domestic-Violence -During-COVID-19-February-2021,pdf.

37. Kaitlin Sullivan and Reynolds Lewis, "Yearly Drug Overdose Deaths Top 100,000 for First Time," NBCNews.com, November 17, 2021, https://www .nbcnews.com/health/health-news/yearly-drug-overdose-deaths-top-100000 -first-time-rcna5656.

38. Audrey Conklin, "Fentanyl Overdoses Become No. 1 Cause of Death among US Adults, Ages 18–45: 'A National Emergency,'" Fox News, December 16, 2021, https://www.foxnews.com/us/fentanyl-overdoses-leading-cause-death -adults.

39. "Americans Increasing Substance Use to Cope with Mental Strain; Parents at Highest Risk," Hazelden Betty Ford Foundation, June 24, 2021, https://www .hazeldenbettyford.org/about-us/news-media/press-release/mental-health-index -report.

40. Tara Parker-Pope, Christina Caron, and Mónica Cordero Sancho, "Why 1,320 Therapists Are Worried about Mental Health in America Right Now," New York Times, December 16, 2021, https://www.nytimes.com /interactive/2021/12/16/well/mental-health-crisis-america-covid.html.

41. Vivek H. Murthy, "Protecting Youth Mental Health," U.S. Department of Health and Human Services, December 2021, https://www.hhs.gov/sites /default/files/surgeon-general-youth-mental-health-advisory.pdf.

42. Janey Rountree, Nathan Hess, and Austin Lyke, "Health Conditions among Unsheltered Adults in the U.S.," California Policy Lab, October 6, 2019, https://www.capolicylab.org/wp-content/uploads/2019/10/Health-Conditions -Among-Unsheltered-Adults-in-the-U.S.pdf.

43. Christopher Rufo, "'Housing First': Homing in on the Problem," Heritage Foundation, August 24, 2020, https://www.heritage.org/housing/commentary /housing-first-homing-the-problem.

44. Rudy Koski, "Hud Secy Ben Carson Pitches New Homelessness Strategy," FOX 7 Austin, October 22, 2020, https://www.fox7austin.com/news/hud-secy-ben -carson-pitches-new-homelessness-strategy.

45. Emma Dorn, Bryan Hancock, Jimmy Sarakatsannis, and Ellen Viruleg, "Covid-19 and Education: The Lingering Effects of Unfinished Learning," McKinsey & Company, November 11, 2021, https://www.mckinsey.com /industries/education/our-insights/covid-19-and-education-the-lingering-effects -of-unfinished-learning.

46. Valerie Strauss, "Analysis | More Students than Ever Got F's in First Term of 2020–21 School Year—but Are A–F Grades Fair in a Pandemic?" *Washington Post*, December 6, 2020, https://www.washingtonpost.com /education/2020/12/06/more-students-than-ever-got-fs-first-term-2020-21 -school-year-are-a-f-grades-fair-pandemic/.

47. Chris Papst, "Covid Costs—Students Stand to Lose $17 Trillion in Lifetime Earnings," Fox 45 Baltimore (WBFF), January 13, 2022, https://foxbaltimore .com/news/project-baltimore/covid-costs-students-stand-to-lose-17-trillion-in -lifetime-earnings.

48. "Covid-19: Students Face $17 Trillion Loss in Lifetime Earnings," UN News, December 6, 2021, https://news.un.org/en/story/2021/12/1107282.

49. Jessica Calefati, "National Teen Test Scores Slip for the First Time—and It's Not Due to Covid," *Politico*, October 14, 2021, https://www.politico.com /news/2021/10/14/national-teen-test-scores-515996.

50. "The Nation's Report Card: 2019 Reading New York City Grade 4 Public Schools," Institute for Education Statistics, National Center for Education Statistics, 2019, https://nces.ed.gov/nationsreportcard/subject/publications /dst2019/pdf/2020016xn4.pdf.

51. Ibid.

52. Ibid.

53. "Early Warning! Why Learning to Read by the End of Third Grade Matters," Annie E. Casey Foundation, New York State Council on Children and Families, 2010, https://www.ccf.ny.gov/files/9013/8262/2751 /AECFReporReadingGrade3.pdf.

54. E. J. McMahon, "NY per-Pupil School Spending Topped $25K in 2018–19," Empire Center for Public Policy, May 18, 2021, https://www.empirecenter.org /publications/ny-per-pupil-school-spending-topped-25k-in-2018-19/.

55. "Chicago Public Schools—U.S. News Education," *U.S. News & World Report*, 2021, https://www.usnews.com/education/k12/illinois/districts/city-of -chicago-sd-299-110570.

56. "Baltimore County Public Schools—U.S. News Education," *U.S. News & World Report*, 2021, https://www.usnews.com/education/k12/maryland /districts/baltimore-county-public-schools-108287.

57. Editorial, "Black Parents' Righteous Fury at NYC Public School Failure," *New York Post*, June 16, 2021, https://nypost.com/2021/06/15/black-parents -righteous-fury-at-nyc-public-school-failure/.

58. Mitch Smith and Dana Goldstein, "In a Clash with the Teachers' Union, Chicago Cancels Classes for a Day," *New York Times*, January 5, 2022, https:// www.nytimes.com/2022/01/04/us/chicago-teachers-union-remote-learning .html.

59. Alexis Rivas, "San Diego Unified School District Changes Grading System to 'Combat Racism,'" NBC 7 San Diego, October 15, 2020, https://www .nbcsandiego.com/news/local/san-diego-unified-school-district-changes -grading-system-to-combat-racism/2425346/.

60. Lee Ohanian, "Seattle Schools Propose to Teach That Math Education Is Racist—Will California Be Far Behind?" Hoover Institution, Stanford University, October 29, 2019, https://www.hoover.org/research/seattle-schools -propose-teach-math-education-racist-will-california-be-far-behindseattle.

61. Newt Gingrich, "Newt's World—Episode 287: Baltimore's Failing Schools," Gingrich 360, August 5, 2021, https://www.gingrich360.com/2021/08/04 /newts-world-episode-287-baltimores-failing-schools/.

CHAPTER 7: OPPORTUNITY AND HOPE

1. "January 5, 1967: Inaugural Address (Public Ceremony)," Ronald Reagan Presidential Library and Museum, National Archives, accessed March 10, 2022, https://www.reaganlibrary.gov/archives/speech/january-5-1967 -inaugural-address-public-ceremony.

2. Thomas Jefferson, "Notes on the State of Virginia," Monticello Digital Classroom, 2022, https://classroom.monticello.org/view/72773/.

3. Franklin D. Roosevelt, "Franklin D. Roosevelt State of the Union Address of 1935," https://www.albany.edu/faculty/gz580/his101/su35fdr.html.

4. "Russell Crowe Plays Hardball," NBCNews.com, June 10, 2005. https://www .nbcnews.com/id/wbna8170650#.XXB1PShKiUk.

5. Associated Press, "California's Unemployment Fraud Reaches at Least $20 Billion," KXTV, October 25, 2021, https://www.abc10.com/article/news/local /california/californias-unemployment-fraud-at-least-20-billion/103-7385477d -6199-47e9-aed7-949ea89e7107.

6. "The Challenge of Healthcare Fraud," National Health Care Anti-Fraud Association, accessed March 10, 2022, https://www.nhcaa.org/tools-insights /about-health-care-fraud/the-challenge-of-health-care-fraud/.

7. Ronald Reagan, "Radio Address to the Nation on Education," Ronald Reagan Presidential Library and Museum, April 30, 1983, https://www.reaganlibrary .gov/archives/speech/radio-address-nation-education-0.

8. Peter Cove, *Poor No More: Rethinking Dependency and the War on Poverty* (Abingdon, Oxon: Routledge, 2017).

9. "Proposals Relating to the Education of Youth in Pennsylvania, [October 1749]," *Founders Online,* National Archives, https://founders.archives.gov /documents/Franklin/01-03-02-0166.

10. James B. Conant, *Thomas Jefferson and the Development of American Public Education* (Berkeley: University of California Press, 2021).

11. "Northwest Land Ordinance for Ohio River Territories, July 13, 1787," Iowa Department of Cultural Affairs, 2022, https://iowaculture.gov/sites/default /files/history-education-pss-shapes-nwordinance-transcription.pdf.

12. *A Nation at Risk: The Imperative for Educational Reform: A Report to the Nation and the Secretary of Education,* United States Department of Education (Washington, DC: U.S. Government Printing Office, 1983).

13. Ronald Reagan, "Radio Address to the Nation on Education," Ronald Reagan Presidential Library and Museum, accessed March 10, 2022, https://www .reaganlibrary.gov/archives/speech/radio-address-nation-education-0.

14. "School Choice History," School Choice Wisconsin, October 1, 2021, https:// schoolchoicewi.org/school-choice-history-timeline/.

15. Kyle Morris, "How Biden 'Spent' 2021: Over $3T Signed into Law, but He Wanted Trillions More," Fox Business, December 28, 2021, https://www .foxbusiness.com/politics/bidens-big-spending-in-review-2021.

16. Caroline Downey, "Biden Claims His Multi-Trillion Dollar Spending Packages Will 'Reduce Inflation,'" *National Review,* July 22, 2021, https://www .nationalreview.com/news/biden-claims-his-multi-trillion-dollar-spending -packages-will-reduce-inflation/.

17. U.S. National Debt Clock: Real Time, accessed March 10, 2022, https://www .usdebtclock.org/.

18. "GDP (Current US$)—United States," World Bank, 2022, https://data .worldbank.org/indicator/NY.GDP.MKTP.CD?locations=US.

19. Nick Timiraos, "Surging Inflation Heightens Fed Debate Over How Fast to Raise Rates," *Wall Street Journal,* February 11, 2022, https://www .wsj.com/articles/rising-inflation-keeps-pressure-on-fed-to-frontload-rate -increases-11644509103.

20. "Analysis: Americans Want a Return to Balanced Budgets," American Majority Project, Gingrich 360, February 25, 2022, https://americanmajorityproject .com/analysis-americans-want-a-return-to-balanced-budgets/#more-1442.

21. Newt Gingrich, "It Is Time to Balance the Federal Budget Again," Gingrich 360, February 7, 2022, https://www.gingrich360.com/2022/02/04/it-is-time -to-balance-the-federal-budget-again/.

22. "Analysis: Americans Want a Return to Balanced Budgets," American Majority Project, Gingrich 360, February 25, 2022, https://americanmajorityproject .com/analysis-americans-want-a-return-to-balanced-budgets/#more-1442.

23. John Barrasso, "ICYMI: Barrasso Op-Ed: US Energy Independence Is Vital— Biden's Policies Could Destroy It," U.S. Senate Committee on Energy and Natural Resources, July 9, 2021, https://www.energy.senate.gov/2021/7 /icymi-barrasso-op-ed-us-energy-independence-is-vital-biden-s-policies-could -destroy-it.

24. Robert Rapier, "Is the U.S. Energy Independent?" *Forbes*, December 10, 2021, https://www.forbes.com/sites/rrapier/2021/11/14/is-the-us-energy -independent/?sh=59f67f841387.

25. Jessica Resnick-Ault, "Explainer: Oil Price Spike Leaves Limited Options for Biden," Reuters, January 13, 2022, https://www.reuters.com/business/energy /oil-price-spike-leaves-limited-options-biden-2022-01-13/.

26. Tim Mullaney, "Risks Are Rising That Oil Prices Will Cause Next Recession," CNBC, July 23, 2018, https://www.cnbc.com/2018/07/13/risks-rising-that-oil -prices-will-cause-next-recession.html.

27. Lahov Harkov, "US Informs Israel It No Longer Supports EastMed Pipeline to Europe," *Jerusalem Post*, January 18, 2022, https://www.jpost.com /international/article-693866.

28. John Barrasso, "ICYMI: Barrasso Op-Ed: US Energy Independence Is Vital— Biden's Policies Could Destroy It," U.S. Senate Committee on Energy and Natural Resources, July 9, 2021, https://www.energy.senate.gov/2021/7 /icymi-barrasso-op-ed-us-energy-independence-is-vital-biden-s-policies-could -destroy-it.

29. Larry Kudlow, "Kudlow: Competes Act Has Nothing to Do with Competing with China," Fox Business, February 8, 2022, https://www.foxbusiness.com /media/kudlow-competes-act-china.

30. Senate Republican Policy Committee, "Democrats Fuel High Gas Prices," December 7, 2021, https://www.rpc.senate.gov/policy-papers/democrats-fuel -high-gas-prices.

31. Jeffrey M. Jones, "Americans Offer Gloomy State of the Nation Report," Gallup, February 2, 2022, https://news.gallup.com/poll/389309/americans -offer-gloomy-state-nation-report.aspx.

32. Kevin McCarthy, House Republican Leader, "McCarthy Calls on Biden to Increase Domestic Energy Production," February 7, 2022, https://www

.republicanleader.gov/mccarthy-calls-on-biden-to-increase-domestic-energy
-production/.

33. U.S. Department of Energy, "Global Energy Markets Update," YouTube, 32:18,
February 28, 2019, https://www.youtube.com/watch?v=ZtrG5zhPrAE.

CHAPTER 8: CRISIS AND CHAOS

1. Robert P. Murphy, "5 Unintended Consequences of Regulation and
Government Meddling," Foundation for Economic Education, July 15,
2015, https://fee.org/articles/5-unintended-consequences-of-regulation-and
-government-meddling/.

2. Patrick McLaughlin, "Policy Spotlight: Regulation's Unintended Consequences
Can Hurt Everyone—the Poor Most of All," Mercatus Center, George
Washington University, April 26, 2018, https://www.mercatus.org
/publications/regulation/policy-spotlight-regulation%E2%80%99s-unintended
-consequences-can-hurt-everyone%E2%80%94.

3. U.S. Department of Health and Human Services, "HHS REPORT: Average
Health Insurance Premiums Doubled Since 2013," May 23, 2017, https://
www.hhs.gov/about/news/2017/05/23/hhs-report-average-health-insurance
-premiums-doubled-2013.html.

4. Kenneth Finegold, Ann Conmy, Rose C. Chu, Arielle Bosworth, and Benjamin
D. Sommers, "Trends in the U.S. Uninsured Population, 2010–2020," Office of
the Assistant Secretary for Planning and Evaluation, U.S. Department of Health
and Human Services, February 11, 2021, https://aspe.hhs.gov/sites/default/files
/private/pdf/265041/trends-in-the-us-uninsured.pdf.

5. Zeke Miller and Colleen Long, "Analysis: Biden Overshoots on What's
Possible in Divided DC," Associated Press, January 14, 2022, https://apnews
.com/article/coronavirus-pandemic-voting-rights-joe-biden-business-health
-b7089af38364236f727cf45bd13a4c9c.

6. Rahm Emanuel, "Let's Make Sure This Crisis Doesn't Go to Waste,"
Washington Post, March 25, 2020, https://www.washingtonpost.com
/opinions/2020/03/25/lets-make-sure-this-crisis-doesnt-go-waste/.

7. "Hillary Clinton: 'This Would Be a Terrible Crisis to Waste,'" RealClear
Politics, accessed March 10, 2022, https://www.realclearpolitics.com
/video/2020/04/28/hillary_clinton_this_would_be_a_terrible_crisis_to_waste
_to_not_push_for_universal_healthcare.html#!.

8. "Page 104—The White House," accessed March 10, 2022, https://www
.whitehouse.gov/briefing-room/speeches-remarks/2021/0/page/104/.

9. ABC News, accessed March 10, 2022, https://abcnews.go.com/Politics/bidens
-plan-ship-americans-billion-free-covid-tests/story?id=82245949.

10. Gregg Gonsalves, "President Biden Is Failing on Covid-19," *Washington Post*, December 22, 2021, https://www.washingtonpost.com/opinions/2021/12/22/president-biden-is-failing-covid-19/.

11. Lev Facher, "3 Big Questions about the Biden Administration's Covid Response in 2022," PBS, December 30, 2021, https://www.pbs.org/newshour/health/3-big-questions-about-the-biden-administrations-covid-response-in-2022.

12. Stephen Collinson, "Analysis: Biden Grapples with a COVID-19 Testing Failure That Could Have Been Foreseen," CNN, December 28, 2021, https://www.cnn.com/2021/12/28/politics/joe-biden-covid-19-testing-failure/index.html.

13. Adam Liptak, "Supreme Court Blocks Biden's Virus Mandate for Large Employers," *New York Times*, January 13, 2022, https://www.nytimes.com/2022/01/13/us/politics/supreme-court-biden-vccine-mandate.html.

14. "Fact Sheet for Healthcare Providers Emergency," Food and Drug Administration, 2022, https://www.fda.gov/media/149534/download?ACSTrackingID=USCDC_511-DM72818&ACSTrackingLabel=HAN%20461-%20COCA%20Subscribers&deliveryName=USCDC_511-DM72818.

15. U.S. senator for Florida Marco Rubio, accessed March 10, 2022, https://www.rubio.senate.gov/public/index.cfm/%20%20.

16. Charles Creitz, "Dr. Ben Carson, in Response to Biden Covid Treatment Policy, Recalls Racial Discrimination of His Youth," Fox News, January 10, 2022, https://www.foxnews.com/media/dr-ben-carson-recalls-racial-discrimination-of-his-youth-in-response-to-biden-covid-treatment-policy.

17. Admin, "Commentary: What Reverend Martin Luther King, Jr. Would Say about Biden's New COVID-19 Policy," *Virginia Star*, January 17, 2022, https://thevirginiastar.com/2022/01/17/commentary-what-reverend-martin-luther-king-jr-would-say-about-bidens-new-covid-19-policy/.

18. Eileen Sullivan and Miriam Jordan, "Illegal Border Crossings, Driven by Pandemic and Natural Disasters, Soar to Record High," *New York Times*, October 22, 2021, https://www.nytimes.com/2021/10/22/us/politics/border-crossings-immigration-record-high.html.

19. Alex J. Rouhandeh, "Enough People Crossed the Border in 2021 to Create the 10th-Largest City in the U.S.," *Newsweek*, August 3, 2021, https://www.newsweek.com/enough-people-crossed-border-2021-create-10th-largest-city-us-1615776.

20. Alex J. Rouhandeh, "Border Officials Brace for Potential 'Mother of All Caravans' Assembling in Mexico," *Newsweek*, October 12, 2021, https://www.newsweek.com/border-officials-brace-potential-mother-all-caravans-assembling-mexico-1638211.

21. Twitter, accessed March 10, 2022, https://twitter.com/SenatorHagerty.

22. "Southwest Land Border Encounters," U.S. Customs and Border Protection, accessed March 10, 2022, https://www.cbp.gov/newsroom/stats/southwest -land-border-encounters.

23. Alex J. Rouhandeh, "650 Die at Border in First Year of Biden, 24 Percent More than Peak under Trump, Obama," *Newsweek*, December 10, 2021, https:// www.newsweek.com/650-die-border-first-year-biden-24-percent-more-peak -under-trump-obama-1658242.

24. Heather Robinson, "How Biden's Border Policies Will Increase Sex Trafficking of Children to US," *New York Post*, April 17, 2021, https://nypost .com/2021/04/17/how-bidens-border-policy-will-increase-child-sex-trafficking -to-us/.

25. Miranda Devine, Jack Morphet, Kevin Sheehan, Christopher Sadowski, and Bruce Golding, "Biden Secretly Flying Underage Migrants into NY in Dead of Night," *New York Post*, October 19, 2021, https://nypost.com/2021/10/18 /biden-secretly-flying-underage-migrants-into-ny-in-dead-of-night/.

26. *Express-Times* guest columnist, "'Ghost' Flights near Lehigh Valley Show Pa. Isn't Immune to Border Crisis Issues: Opinion," lehighvalleylive, January 2, 2022, https://www.lehighvalleylive.com/opinion/2022/01/ghost-flights-near -lehigh-valley-show-pa-isnt-immune-from-affects-of-border-crisis-opinion.html.

27. ABC News, accessed March 10, 2022, https://abcnews.go.com/Politics /fentanyl-seized-cbp-2021-2020/story?id=77744071.

28. "Drug Overdose Deaths Hit Record High," News, Harvard School of Public Health, November 19, 2021, https://www.hsph.harvard.edu/news/hsph-in-the -news/drug-overdose-deaths-hit-record-high/.

29. "Governor Abbott Debuts Texas Border Wall in Rio Grande City," Office of the Governor, Texas, accessed March 10, 2022, https://gov.texas.gov/news/post /governor-abbott-debuts-texas-border-wall-in-rio-grande-city.

30. Andrea Scott, "Here Are the Names of the 13 U.S. Service Members Killed in Afghanistan Attack," *Military Times*, August 28, 2021, https://www .militarytimes.com/news/your-marine-corps/2021/08/28/here-are-the-names -of-the-13-service-members-who-died-in-afghanistan-attack/.

31. Anna Coren, Julia Hollingsworth, Sandi Sidhu, and Zachary Cohen, "US Military Admits It Killed 10 Civilians and Targeted Wrong Vehicle in Kabul Airstrike," CNN, September 17, 2021, https://www.cnn.com/2021/09/17/politics/kabul -drone-strike-us-military-intl-hnk/index.html.

32. Yaron Steinbuch, "Russia Says Afghan President Fled with 4 Cars, Chopper Full of Money," *New York Post*, August 16, 2021, https://nypost.com/2021/08/16 /afghan-president-fled-with-cars-helicopter-full-of-money-russia/.

33. Adam Andrzejewski, "Biden Administration Erased Afghan Weapons Reports from Federal Websites," *Forbes*, September 1, 2021, https://www.forbes.com /sites/adamandrzejewski/2021/08/31/biden-administration-erased-afghan -weapons-reports-from-federal-websites/.

34. Kathy Gannon, "Before Pullout, Watchdog Warned of Afghan Air Force Collapse," Associated Press, January 18, 2022, https://apnews.com/article /afghanistan-joe-biden-kabul-taliban-air-force-e9fb454b7e9bebac58477e13d6 03fc06.

35. "Callista L. Gingrich: Defending the Women and Girls of Afghanistan," Gingrich 360, October 8, 2021, https://www.gingrich360.com/2021/10/09 /defending-the-women-and-girls-of-afghanistan/.

36. "Barack Obama Reportedly Said: 'Don't Underestimate Joe's Ability to (Expletive) Things up,'" KAKE, accessed March 10, 2022, https://www.kake .com/story/42501205/barack-obama-reportedly-said-dont-underestimate-joes -ability-to-expletive-things-up.

CHAPTER 9: PRAGMATISM AND PROSPERITY

1. Alexander Stoklosa, "40 to 50 Percent of New Vehicles Will Be Electric by 2030, per President Biden Executive Order," *Motor Trend*, August 5, 2021, https://www.motortrend.com/news/president-biden-ev-executive-order/.

2. Tim Worstall, "The Reason That Shovel Ready Stimulus Didn't Work Is That There Wasn't Any Stimulus," *Forbes*, November 1, 2013, https://www.forbes .com/sites/timworstall/2013/11/01/the-reason-that-shovel-ready-stimulus-didnt -work-is-that-there-wasnt-any-stimulus/.

3. "Poverty in the United States: 50-Year Trends and Safety Net Impacts," Office of the Assistant Secretary for Planning and Evaluation, Department of Health and Human Services, 2016, https://aspe.hhs.gov/sites/default/files/private /pdf/154286/50YearTrends.pdf.

4. Alexander Hamilton, "The Works of Alexander Hamilton: Volume 1 by Alexander Hamilton—Ebook," Scribd, Krill Press, 2015, https://www.scribd .com/book/372476966/The-Works-of-Alexander-Hamilton-Volume-1.

5. "Intellectual Property Clause," Legal Information Institute, Cornell Law School, accessed March 10, 2022, https://www.law.cornell.edu/wex /intellectual_property_clause.

6. James Madison, "The Federalist Number 43," Avalon Project, accessed March 10, 2022, https://avalon.law.yale.edu/18th_century/fed43.asp.

7. Reagan Library, "January 5, 1967: Inaugural Address (Public Ceremony)," Ronald Reagan Presidential Library and Museum, National Archives, accessed March 10, 2022, https://www.reaganlibrary.gov/archives/speech/january-5 -1967-inaugural-address-public-ceremony.

8. Matthew Joseph, "Texas, Tennessee Demonstrate New Ways to Leverage Education Resources," ExcelinEd, February 9, 2022, https://excelined .org/2022/02/09/texas-tennessee-lead-the-way-on-effective-use-of-education -resources/.

9. Heritage Foundation, "Solutions: The Heritage Foundation," 2021, https://www.heritage.org/solutions/.

CHAPTER 10: INHERENT HUBRIS

1. Frederick Engels, *Draft of a Communist Confession of Faith*, *Works of Frederick Engels*, 1971, https://www.marxists.org/archive/marx/works/1847/06/09.htm.

2. Oleg Yegorov, "How Did the Russian Orthodox Church Survive 70 Years of Atheism in the USSR? (Photos)," Russia Beyond, October 25, 2018. https://www.rbth.com/history/329361-russian-orthodox-church-ussr-communism.

3. Johannes Jacobse, "'Atheistic Five-Year Plan' Was Announced in the USSR 80 Years Ago [Video]," American Orthodox Institute USA, 2012, https://www.aoiusa.org/atheistic-five-year-plan-was-announced-in-the-ussr-80-years-ago-video/.

4. Natasha Frost, "Why Stalin Tried to Stamp Out Religion in the Soviet Union," History.com, April 23, 2021, https://www.history.com/news/joseph-stalin-religion-atheism-ussr.

5. Thomas F. Farr, "China's Second Cultural Revolution," First Things, Institute on Religion and Public Life, January 15, 2020, https://www.firstthings.com/web-exclusives/2020/01/chinas-second-cultural-revolution.

6. Marion Smith, "Communism and Religion Can't Coexist," *Wall Street Journal*, August 29, 2019, https://www.wsj.com/articles/communism-and-religion-cant-coexist-11567120938.

7. Ibid.

8. "U.S. Report Says Russia among 'Worst Violators' of Religious Freedom," Radio Free Europe/Radio Liberty, April 21, 2021, https://www.rferl.org/a/russia-worst-violators-religious-freedom-report-iran-turkmenistan/31215737.html.

9. Editorial Board, "The Absurd 'Crime' of Religious Worship in Putin's Russia," *Washington Post*, October 28, 2021, https://www.washingtonpost.com/opinions/2021/10/28/absurd-crime-religious-worship-putins-russia/.

10. "Crimea," U.S. Department of State, May 12, 2021, https://www.state.gov/reports/2020-report-on-international-religious-freedom/ukraine/crimea/.

11. Michael Lipka, "Republicans and Democrats Agree Religion's Influence Is Waning, but Differ in Their Reactions," Pew Research Center, May 30, 2020, https://www.pewresearch.org/fact-tank/2019/11/15/republicans-and-democrats-agree-religions-influence-is-waning-but-differ-in-their-reactions/.

12. Adam Liptak, "Splitting 5 to 4, Supreme Court Backs Religious Challenge to Cuomo's Virus Shutdown Order," *New York Times*, November 26, 2020, https://www.nytimes.com/2020/11/26/us/supreme-court-coronavirus-religion-new-york.html.

13. "A Look at the Treatment of Churches during COVID-19 Shutdowns," Georgia Baptist Mission Board, July 30, 2020, https://gabaptist.org/a-look-at-the-treatment-of-churches-during-covid-19-shutdowns/.

14. "Temple Baptist Church v. City of Greenville," Alliance Defending Freedom, accessed March 11, 2022, https://adflegal.org/case/temple-baptist-church-v-city-greenville.

15. "Metropolitan Tabernacle Church v. City of Chattanooga," Alliance Defending Freedom, accessed March 11, 2022, https://adflegal.org/case/metropolitan-tabernacle-church-v-city-chattanooga.

16. "A Look at the Treatment of Churches during COVID-19 Shutdowns," Georgia Baptist Mission Board, July 30, 2020, https://gabaptist.org/a-look-at-the-treatment-of-churches-during-covid-19-shutdowns/.

17. Sarah Parshall Perry and GianCarlo Canaparo, "18 More Federal Agencies Eye Making Vaccine Religious-Objector Lists," *Daily Signal*, January 21, 2022, https://www.dailysignal.com/2022/01/15/18-more-federal-agencies-eye-making-vaccine-religious-objector-lists/.

18. Sam Dorman, "House Republicans Introduce Bill to Block Tracking Religious Accommodations to COVID Vaccine," Fox News, January 26, 2022, https://www.foxnews.com/politics/norman-bill-religious-exemptions-covid-vaccine.

19. ABC News, accessed March 11, 2022, https://abcnews.go.com/US/hostage-incident-texas-synagogue-terrorist-act-hate-crime/story?id=82404960.

20. Geneva Sands, "FBI and DHS Warn Faith-Based Communities 'Will Likely Continue' to Be Targets of Violence," CNN, January 18, 2022, https://www.cnn.com/2022/01/17/politics/fbi-dhs-warn-faith-based-targets-violence-letter/index.html.

21. "Declaration of Independence: A Transcription," National Archives and Records Administration, accessed March 11, 2022, https://www.archives.gov/founding-docs/declaration-transcript.

22. Sam Dorman, "Connecticut Teacher Resigns over Racial Curriculum, Says It Was Stealing Kids' 'Innocence,'" Fox News, August 31, 2021, https://www.foxnews.com/us/jennifer-tafuto-connecticut-teacher-crt.

23. Aimee Cho, "'Privilege Bingo' in Fairfax Co. Class Meets Controversy for Including Being a Military Kid," NBC4 Washington, January 21, 2022, https://www.nbcwashington.com/news/local/northern-virginia/privilege-bingo-in-fairfax-co-class-meets-controversy-after-it-includes-being-a-military-kid/2942443/.

24. "Yes, Critical Race Theory Is Being Taught in Public Schools," *Washington Examiner*, July 12, 2021, https://www.washingtonexaminer.com/opinion/yes-critical-race-theory-is-being-taught-in-public-schools?_amp=true.

25. Max Eden, "Team Biden Wants White Teachers to Undergo Anti-Racist 'Therapy,'" *New York Post*, May 26, 2021, https://nypost.com/2021/05/26/team-biden-wants-white-teachers-to-undergo-anti-racist-therapy/.

26. Media.defense.gov, accessed March 11, 2022, https://media.defense.gov/2021
/Jan/26/2002570959/-1/-1/1/TASK%20FORCE%20ONE%20NAVY%20
FINAL%20REPORT.PDF?aff_id=1262.

27. Tyler O'Neil, "Major Corporations Had 'Woke' Trainings Exposed in 2021,"
Fox Business, December 24, 2021, https://www.foxbusiness.com/politics/major
-corporations-woke-trainings-exposed-in-2021.

CHAPTER 11: CIVILITY AND GRACE

1. "First in War, First in Peace, and First in the Hearts of His Countrymen,"
George Washington's Mount Vernon, accessed March 11, 2022, https://www
.mountvernon.org/library/digitalhistory/digital-encyclopedia/article/first-in
-war-first-in-peace-and-first-in-the-hearts-of-his-countrymen/.

2. "Founders Online: First Inaugural Address: Final Version, 30 April 1789,"
National Archives and Records Administration, accessed March 11, 2022,
https://founders.archives.gov/documents/Washington/05-02-02-0130-0003.

3. "Founders Online: Undelivered First Inaugural Address: Fragments,
30 April 1789," National Archives and Records Administration,
accessed March 11, 2022, https://founders.archives.gov/documents
/Washington/05-02-02-0130-0002.

4. "The Federalist Papers: No. 55," Alexander Hamilton or James Madison,
February 15, 1788, Yale Law School Lillian Goldman Law Library, accessed
April 4, 2022, https://avalon.law.yale.edu/18th_century/fed55.asp.

5. "Founders Online: From John Adams to Massachusetts Militia, 11 October
1798," National Archives and Records Administration, accessed March 11,
2022, https://founders.archives.gov/documents/Adams/99-02-02-3102.

6. "Founders Online: To George Washington from Thomas Jefferson, 4 January
1786," National Archives and Records Administration, accessed March 11,
2022, https://founders.archives.gov/documents/Washington/04-03-02-0419.

7. The Winthrop Society: Descendants of the Great Migration, accessed March
11, 2022, https://www.winthropsociety.com/doc_charity.php.

8. Matthew 5:14: "You are the light of the world. A city on a hill cannot be
hidden," accessed March 11, 2022, https://biblehub.com/matthew/5-14.htm.

9. "First Amendment," Legal Information Institute, accessed March 11, 2022,
https://www.law.cornell.edu/constitution/first_amendment.

10. Benjamin Franklin, James Madison, George Washington, John Adams, John
Leland, and Alexander Hamilton, "Religion and the Founding of the American
Republic Religion and the Federal Government, Part 1," Library of Congress,
June 4, 1998, https://www.loc.gov/exhibits/religion/rel06.

11. Ibid.

12. Ibid.

13. Ibid.

14. George Washington, "Farewell Address 1796," accessed April 4, 2022, https://avalon.law.yale.edu/18th_century/washing.asp.

15. Jeffrey M. Jones, "How Religious Are Americans?" Gallup, December 27, 2021, https://news.gallup.com/poll/358364/religious-americans.aspx.

16. Ibid.

17. "How Covid-19 Has Strengthened Religious Faith," Pew Research Center, Religion & Public Life Project, January 29, 2021, https://www.pewforum.org/2021/01/27/more-americans-than-people-in-other-advanced-economies-say-covid-19-has-strengthened-religious-faith/.

18. Ibid.

19. Ibid.

20. "The Socio-Economic Contributions of Religion to American Society: An Empirical Analysis," accessed March 11, 2022, https://religiousfreedomandbusiness.org/wp-content/uploads/2020/04/1.2-trillion-US-Religious-Economy-2-page-summary.pdf.

21. Ibid.

22. Ibid.

23. Ibid.

24. Ibid.

25. Ibid.

26. Ibid.

27. Ibid.

28. Ibid.

29. Richard Fry and Kim Parker, "Rising Share of U.S. Adults Are Living without a Spouse or Partner," Pew Research Center, Social & Demographic Trends Project, February 3, 2022, https://www.pewresearch.org/social-trends/2021/10/05/rising-share-of-u-s-adults-are-living-without-a-spouse-or-partner/.

30. Kimberly Howard and Richard V. Reeves, "The Marriage Effect: Money or Parenting," Brookings Institution, September 4, 2014, https://www.brookings.edu/research/the-marriage-effect-money-or-parenting/.

31. Richard Fry and Kim Parker, "Rising Share of U.S. Adults Are Living without a Spouse or Partner," Pew Research Center, Social & Demographic Trends Project, February 3, 2022, https://www.pewresearch.org/social-trends/2021/10/05/rising-share-of-u-s-adults-are-living-without-a-spouse-or-partner/.

32. Hugh Whelchel, "Why America's Freedom Depends on the Morality of America's People," Institute for Faith, Work & Economics, February 5, 2018, https://tifwe.org/america-freedom-morality-people/.

33. "What Is Civility?" Institute for Civility in Government, February 18, 2016, https://www.instituteforcivility.org/who-we-are/what-is-civility/.

34. "Policy," Centre for Independent Studies, accessed March 11, 2022, https://www.cis.org.au/app/uploads/2015/04/images/stories/policy-magazine/2002-spring/2002-18-3-nicole-billante-peter-saunders.pdf.

35. "The Rules of Civility," George Washington's Mount Vernon, accessed March 11, 2022, https://www.mountvernon.org/george-washington/rules-of-civility.

36. "Policy," Centre for Independent Studies, accessed March 11, 2022, https://www.cis.org.au/app/uploads/2015/04/images/stories/policy-magazine/2002-spring/2002-18-3-nicole-billante-peter-saunders.pdf.

37. Ibid.

38. Grace Panetta, "These 11 Political Friendships Proved Party Lines Don't Have to Divide Americans," Business Insider, February 3, 2021. https://www.businessinsider.com/nine-famous-political-friendships-transcend-party-lines-2018-11.

39. Ibid.

40. Daniel A. Cox, "The State of American Friendship: Change, Challenges, and Loss," Survey Center on American Life, July 20, 2021, https://www.americansurveycenter.org/research/the-state-of-american-friendship-change-challenges-and-loss/.

CONCLUSION: THE PATRIOTISM OF PERSISTENCE

1. Ronald Reagan, "Farewell Address to the Nation," accessed March 11, 2022, https://www.reaganlibrary.gov/archives/speech/farewell-address-nation.

ABOUT THE AUTHOR

NEWT GINGRICH is a former Speaker of the U.S. House of Representatives and 2012 presidential candidate. He is chairman of Gingrich 360, a multimedia production and consulting company based in Arlington, Virginia. He is also a Fox News contributor and author of forty-two books, including *Beyond Biden* and many *New York Times* best sellers. He lives in McLean, Virginia, with his wife, Callista L. Gingrich, former U.S. ambassador to the Holy See and CEO of Gingrich 360.